The Knights of Rhodes

The Knights of Rhodes

BO GIERTZ

Translated by Bror Erickson

RESOURCE *Publications* · Eugene, Oregon

THE KNIGHTS OF RHODES

Resource Publications
An Imprint of Wipf and Stock Publishers
199 W. 8th Ave., Suite 3
Eugene, OR 97401
www.wipfandstock.com

ISBN 13: 978-1-60899-333-8

Manufactured in the U.S.A.

Special Thanks to Birgitta and Martin Giertz
for allowing this translation to go forward.

And hear us, O world, you, who would commend or condemn,
So quick to throw flowers or stones,
We have never sought what you acclaim
Nor shunned what you are accustomed to defame,
You saw us fasting,
Each prepared to make the final sacrifice—
When we, the wanderers, lay down for the rest eternal,
Give others great names, call us the faithful.

Erik Axel Karlfeldt.

Contents

Translator's Preface

Bo Giertz, the late beloved Bishop of Gothenburg and author of The Hammer of God, wrote this novel in 1972 long before September eleventh (coincidentally a chapter title in this book). Yet the book is written with prescient genius, tackling all the hard questions and issues confronting Christians in the west since 9/11: Can a Christian be a soldier? What is Islam? How is it different than Christianity? What is the proper response to aggression, torture, etc.? In tackling these hard questions, he writes a superb novel exposing people for who they really are.

If The Hammer of God is a narrative exposition of the distinction between Law and Gospel, then The Knights of Rhodes is a narrative exposition of the theology of the cross. Almost nothing goes right for the Knights Hospitallers. As the Ottoman Turks under Suleiman's leadership lay siege to the Hospitallers' little island kingdom, you see two theologies of glory clash, and the Christians lose. In the process you see the Christian characters as sinful men, adulterers, connivers, ambitious, racist, and revilers. They aren't exactly Sunday school heroes, but they are real men, real Christians, and real heroes through whom Bo Giertz exposes the human condition raw and laid bare in the midst of war, ugly for all to see. Yet for all the ugliness, the story is sublime as Christ, the Cross, and the forgiveness of sins are brought to the fore.

Today it is common for western citizens to denounce the crusades and the crusaders as barbaric. Here you see another side. There is no hagiography here, but you see these men for all their faults as lovers of their countries and western civilization, defenders of their countrymen and faithful Christians. Perhaps you may develop a fondness for these men who gave their lives to defend, if not exactly the same values we cherish today, then the environment in which these values developed. One might say they lost. For sure they lost their city, their fame, wives, children, goods, and for many even their own lives in the face of defeat. Yet, as they fell back and retreated to Malta, these men halted or at least slowed the militant advance of Islam. Had they folded easily, the Renaissance, the Reformation, the scientific and cultural advances of the West may never have happened. Religious freedom and tolerance might not be known at all in the world, as they are still unknown in many places today. Peace and life might not be valued as much as we in the West think they ought to be.

It has been my joy to translate this book little by little over the last couple of years. I thank Birgitta and Martin Giertz for their permission to publish this translation. Thanks are also due to Laura, my wife, who has had to put up with my nose in a book for days on end. My uncle Per Olaf Eker, who tracked down the meaning of so many Swedish nautical terms and their English equivalents, deserves special thanks. The translation work would not have been done without his help. I must also thank Dr. Gene Edward Vieth, Jr. for his help in editing and revising this book. His work has made the book a much more enjoyable read. What a tedious chore it is to copy edit! I am humbled that he found this work worth the time and effort. It goes without saying that any error's that may remain, remain my own. My congregation, First Lutheran in Tooele, Utah, you might say has been a patron of this translation also. I never exactly asked for the time to translate, but they have provided it for me nonetheless. They are a wonderful congregation—patient, loving, and generous. I am indebted to them, and so are the readers of this book.

Monday the Eighteenth week after Pentecost 2009

List of Persons

THE KNIGHTS OF ST. John of Jerusalem had grown since the twelfth century in the Holy Land where the Knights Hospitallers began as a service for pilgrims and crusaders. They were responsible for a huge hospital in Jerusalem with two thousand beds, and they maintained shelters and small hospitals along southern European pilgrim paths. Soon thereafter, the brothers of the Order were also tasked with defense, and the combatant arm—the knights—became the dominant arm. When Palestine was lost in 1291, The Religion (as the order always called themselves) created a home for themselves on Rhodes, as well as some other islands southwest of Asia Minor [Eastern Turkey] (from 1309), and made it their own little island kingdom.

The brothers of the order consisted of knights, serving brothers, and chaplains. They were organized into eight *langues* according to their different nationalities. Three of the langues were what we would call French: Provence, Auvergne, and France. Two were Spanish: Aragon and Castile (with Portugal). Then there were those of Italy, Germany, and England.

Each langue had its *auberge* on Rhodes, something between a cloister and an officers' mess. The langue was led by a Pilier, who also possessed a high office in the order particular to his langue. The Pilier of France was the "Hospitaller" (overseer of the hospital). The Pilier of Auvergne was the "Marshal"; of Italy, was the "Admiral"; of England, was the "Turcopoler" (commander of the coast guard); while that of Castile was the "Chancellor."

All these—always distinguished from each other—were "Knights of the Grand Cross" and were simply called Grand Crosses. They had a seat in the council that served as the government of Rhodes.

The Grand Master was the order's chief and also the head of the state.

In the homelands, the order of St. John owned property and fields like other orders and cloisters. Property was under the "Commander," who managed the *commandery*, often a pensioned brother of the order, yet an active one. The commanderies took some of the revenue and delivered the rest to the order's purse. The commanderies were in their turn gathered to the "priory." A priory could encompass a whole land and was led by a Prior or a Grand Prior. The Grand Priors were the order's highest representatives in the homelands.

GRAND MASTERS:

Fabrizio del Carretto: about seventy years old, Italian, Grand Master since 1513. He successfully defended Saint Nicolas in 1480, the prominent fort in the Mandraki, against the superior force of the Turks. He died on the tenth of January 1521.

Phillip Villiers de I'sle Adam: Fifty-seven years old, entered the order of St. John already at ten years old, held a series of commissions, and was Grand Master from 1421–1434. Died on Malta.

The earlier Grand Masters, whose memories were still living in Rhodes:

Dieudonné de Gozon: 1346–1353

Philibert de Naillac: 1396–1421

Pierre d'Aubusson: 1476–1503

Emery d'Amboise: 1503–1512

GRAND CROSSES :

Andrea d' Amaral: around seventy years old, Portuguese, Chancellor.

Gabriel de Pomerolx: Frenchman, Grand Commander, Grand Master's deputy, Pilier for the Provençal langue

Paolo d' Acola: Italian, Admiral, died in 1521.

Bernardino d Airasca: Italian, Admiral 1521–1525.

John Burk: Englishman, Turcopoler, (commander of the Coast Guard).

Christopher von Waldener: German Pilier, given command of the German wall in addition to the castle; also responsible for order in the city.

Preian de Bidoulx: previously in French service, came to Rhodes in 1518, and became Prior of St. Gilles, the castle in Lango (Kos) m.m. One of the first to join the Provençal langue, died at the age of sixty from a small wound after a skirmish with the Turks just outside Marseille.

KNIGHTS:

Didier de Tholon: Provençal, Grand Master 1525–1526

Passim: (His real name was Antoine de Grolée) commander with a long service record behind him on Rhodes. Auvergnat. Entrusted with the order's standard.

Raymond Rogier: commander of the Auvergne wall.

Jean de Fournon: commander of the artillery in the same sector.

Jean Beaulouys: called *Le Loup*, "The Wolf," Auvergnat. One of the order's best seamen.

Pierre Dumont: Auvergnat,

* *Jean Chalat*: Thirty-seven years old, Auvergnat.

* *André Barel*: eighteen years old, Auvergnat, came to Rhodes in 1521 and was received as a novice.

Jacques de Bourbon: "the Bastard of Bourbon", Commander, later Grand Prior of France, was actually the son of Louis Bourbon, First Bishop of Liége (died in 1482). He wrote a detailed and vivid account of the siege: *La grande et merveilleuse et très cruelle oppugnation de la noble cité de Rhodes,* Paris 1526. Died in 1537.

* *Antoine de Golart*: twenty-one years old, a novice at seventeen, belonged to the French langue.

Lodovico de Moroso: Italian.

Gabriele Solerio: Italian,

Jacobo Palavisino: Italian,

Ramon de Marquet: Aragonian, commander of the reserves.

Juan de Barbaran: commander of the bastion of Aragon. (The so-called Spanish wall)

William Weston: Englishmen entrusted with the command of the English wall, was captain of Saint Anne, the world's largest ship, and Grand Prior of England, said to have died of a broken heart on Ascension Day 1540, when Henry the VIII disbanded the order of St. John in England.

Henry Mansell: Englishman, entrusted with the Grand Master's banner, was shot in the head during the fight on the English Boulevard on the ninth of September, lived on for one month, but died from the wound.

Thomas Pemberton: Englishman.

Serving Brothers;

Antonio Bosio: born in Lombardi, of Spanish descent. He had a brother, Tomaso, who became Bishop of Malta. The son of one of his other brothers was the Giacomo Bosio, who wrote a famous history of the order of St. John.

Bartholomeo Policiano: Italian, Vice Chancellor, the order's "chief of expeditions," responsible for the archives,

Brother François: called Shooter-Frans, about thirty-five years old, Provençal, born on Rhodes to a Greek mother.

Brother Gierolamo: around fifty years old, Italian, surgeon in the hospital.

Chaplains:

*Fra Giovanni: around thirty-eight years old, Italian, chaplain to the Grand Master.

*Father Dominique: around forty-five, Frenchman.

Remaining:

Gabriele Tadini da Martinengo: forty-one years old, born in northern Italy, officer and fortress engineer in Venetian service, became a knight of the order of St. John in 1522. He took part in many later campaigns, for example in service of the emperor in Pavia in 1525. He died in 1543 in Vienna.

Suleiman: called "the Magnificent" in western lands, in Turkey "The Law Maker" or "The Legislator." Twenty-six years old. Sultan 1520–1566

Amuratte: (Murad) Turkish usurper of the throne, Son of Zizimi (Djem), who fled to Rhodes in 1482 to escape his brother Bajazet (who was Suleiman's grandfather).

Jacob Fonteyn: (Jacobus Fontanus), lawyer from Brügge in Flanders, came to Rhodes in 1521 as a judge in the superior court. Later wrote a description of the siege, in Latin, *De Bello Rhodio libri tres*, Rome 1524.

(*) *Richard Craig*: Englishman, commander of the security troops.

Anasthasia: Fonteyn told her story without giving her name. Tradition says her name was Anasthasia.

Iaxi: supply master for the navy fleet.

(*) *Father Gennaios*: Greek Priest.

(*) *Jannis*: Greek from Rhodes, cook.

Leonardo Balestrini: Genoese, Archbishop of "Rhodes and Colossi" (for the Latin Church). There was also a Metropolitan for the Greeks of Rhodes (Klemens), unionate with Rome.

Gianantonio Bonaldi: Venetian. Merchant and ship captain, resident of Crete.

Apella Renato: Jewish doctor, convert, employed in the hospital.

Blas Diez: Spanish Jew, baptized, d'Amaral's butler.

(*) *Ibrahim*: Turkish prisoner of war, d'Amaral's gardener.

Roberto Peruzzi: Judge, belonged to one of the Italian families who resided in Rhodes.

The above people are all found in the sources of the time with exception of those who are preceded by an asterisk. The asterisk within parentheses means that the person is found in passing, but not given a name.

Prologue

THE YEAR 1521 BEGAN a new era in a new world, with new nations, new continents, new knowledge, new thought, and new rulers. Never before had so much power been gathered in such young hands.

In France, His Most Christian Majesty, the twenty-six year old King Francis I ruled when he cared to rule, and not hunt, dance, and write love letters in poor verse to Madame de Chateaubriand. Spoiled, admired, successful, and self-centered, he could already look back on great successes. Counted among the greatest of his successes were that he beat the invincible Swiss at Marignano, and his cousin Henry in wrestling when they met the summer before at Camp du Drap d'Or, the Camp of the Golden Cloth, the boasting camp, a most absurd gala and spectacle of luxury.

Henry VIII, the vanquished, was the oldest among the youngsters, already filling out twenty-nine years. He too had thrown himself with an insatiable appetite on all the possibilities that the monarchy and a full treasury offered. He was an impressive athlete with a lust for life. He hunted, reveled, loved, drank, rode, danced, and shot to his heart's desire. He left the detestable paper work to his Lord Chancellor. But he was also an educated man, a driven disputer and author, who just finished a polemical pamphlet against the heretic Luther. Over the last year he had begun to slowly pull in the reins. After all the magnificence of Camp du Drap d'Or and the spectacular fraternization with his cousin Francis, he had very calmly dealt with Emperor Carl in order to keep other opportunities open.

Emperor Carl was the youngest of the youngsters, still only twenty years old. That past October he had been crowned as Emperor of the Holy Roman Empire of the German nations. Commonly described as poorly gifted, a bungler when it came to foreign languages, ugly, serious, and reticent, he had inherited lands and crowns that his father and his grandfathers had brought together: the Burgundian and the Austrian land inheritances along with Spain and all its vassal lands in southern Italy, and beyond the sea where the empire continued to grow. Cortez completed the conquest of Mexico, and Magellan had rounded Cape Horn to cross the Pacific Ocean completing the first circumnavigation of the world. The foreign envoys that followed the youth cautiously watched the emperor during his trip through the Netherlands and Germany, reporting that he did not appear to be quite as incompetent as was thought.

In Germany, a man rode on winter roads to the diet in Worms. Curiosity had peaked before the meeting with the Emperor, and possibly even more at the prospect of seeing brother Martin from Wittenberg. He had received the Emperor's safe-conduct, and everyone knew that he was thinking about coming. But what would happen if he did was anyone's guess.

In Rome, Pope Leo X hurled the final condemnations against the rebellious monk on the third of January. At forty-five years old, Leo was already an old man, out of shape, fat, shortsighted, in debt up to his ears, and spoiled since his childhood when he began using church income for his own needs, made happy with an abbot's diocese at eight years old, a bishopric at eleven, and an appointment to cardinal at thirteen. He was soon well positioned in the Holy City, but tragically incapable of understanding men who treated the question of their salvation with deathly seriousness.

That same January three men skied through the snow covered Swedish border forests on the way to Mora. Two of them had fetched the third, a twenty-six year old of the Vasa dynasty. None of them thought that that name would one day have the same fame as Valois, Tudor, Habsburg, and Medici.

Beyond the borders of Christendom, yet another youngster took the lead. At the same time as Carl V was crowned in Aachen, the tenth Sultan of the Ottomans ascended to his father's throne. He too was twenty-six and was named Suleiman. Ruler of one of the world's most powerful kingdoms, he was also an unknown quantity. In Rome, in Paris, and Madrid, people breathed a sigh of relief. Selim, his father, had been the old threat from the east, towering over them with the dreaded crescent moon. Now everyone hoped for breathing space, to plan their festivities, engage in intrigue, and cultivate old mutual grudges.

On Rhodes

O<small>N</small> R<small>HODES</small>, <small>THE</small> G<small>RAND</small> Master, the old Frabrizio del Carretto, lay dying.

He breathed heavily behind the curtains in the great bed of carved Cypress wood. It was dark in the room and cold. The wood shutters in the window squeaked and creaked in the wind; one could hear the rain patter on the windy side.

On the second day of the year, the Grand Master began to have the shivers. It was now the seventh day, the fever only climbed, and he began to realize that he would never again go down the great stone stairway to the fortress garden. He had selected his successor as the rules prescribed, the Chancellor d' Amaral. And now he lay there feverish, coughing and wheezing, while memories passed by in the border between delirium and consciousness.

Where was he now, really? Certainly, he was on San Nicolò, the night of the great year 1480, when everything hung by a thread. There he lay now, among the stone blocks, commander of the little battered fort that could not be allowed to fall. Day and night the Turks' frightful bombards belched out their fire over the bay, out of mouths so great that one could crawl into them. They came dangerously, howling and roaring like hounds from the abyss, these stone balls so huge that a grown man could just barely get his arms around them. They crashed into the gathered piles of broken stone. Far away, on the other side, the impact felt like a punch in the chest. Everything lay in ruins, but in the middle of the ruins they gathered the splintered blocks with their chafed and broken hands making new walls. There they hid, just a handful of knights and about two hundred slaves, who would do the impossible. He would do it. He, Fabrizio del Carretto, had received the honor of leading the command in the hold that could not fall in this final trial of strength with the Grand Turk.

It was quiet in the night, for three days and three nights the stone balls had mercilessly plowed their furrows in the stacks of ruins. Now the cannons were quiet over there on the other side of the Mandraki's black water. He knew what this meant, and he waited. It was a July night, warm and humid with a wind from the sea that made everything wet and gave no relief. He had not been out of his armor for many days. The sweat ran in small rivulets down his legs. It burned and itched under the back plate. The stones under him were hot like an oven.

The Grand Master tossed and turned under his wet sheets, one leg burning the other . . . May they come soon.

And here they come! Long black bodies against the cape, rowing with cautiously dipped oars. One, two, four, six . . . There was no point counting: the whole surface of the sea was covered with galleys. They were spread evenly, gliding each in their own place into the Mandraki and across to the pier on the other side. They came in a great pincer maneuver, like a dragon opening his black mouth. His teeth were ships.

No alarm was needed, only a whisper that went from man to man among the heaps of stone. The matches were already glowing red behind the blocks. All orders were given. No shot would be fired before La Bella Batteria, the thick German cannon sitting here next to his side, opened fire.

Now the time had come. He only needed to give Master Gerhard a glance and lift his forefinger. Then flames would spew out of the cannon's wide mouth. Then all hell would break loose with fire out of every black hole in the blood-drenched piles of stone. The black smoke was colored red with new flashes. Salvo after salvo broke out from the French wall far behind them. The black water heaved with jetsam and flotsam. The boats lifted, rolled and sank. But they still came on, perpetual new rows of oars glittering in the cannon flash. As a powerful swell, the Janissaries rolled in over the block in the beach line, a crest that broke and sank only to come again.

And now it was hand-to-hand combat. Hacking and slashing with the heavy two-handed swords that cleaved the Turkish mail with the in sown metal plates as if they were cotton jackets. Hacking and slashing—always a hairsbreadth before their sweeping scimitars. The Frankish sword had the advantage. It had two edges. It bit back and forth. It could both slash and stab. But it was a heavy job. Hacking and slashing—and protecting the eyes. There was no protection under the helmet's visor. They tried to strike there. And it was there that the sweat ran down from the forehead. It ran into the eyes filling them and hindering their sight.

He groaned and tried to dry his eyelid. He was conscious of the fact that he might not be there in another minute. Time had come.

"Luigi."

"Your Eminence??"

A furrowed face looked in through the slit in the bed curtains.

"Tell the Prior that it is the time for him to come with the sacrament."

"Yes, Your Eminence."

Now he only had to wait. In a little bit, the great bell would ring in the campanile. All the knights would stream out from their auberges. The Prior of San Giovanni would hurry to put on his bishop's garb. They would come in procession through the loggia into the courtyard, in front of the great stairs, and there they would stand and wait, all eight of the langues, each one led by its Pilier, the aldermen and as many knights as could be found in the city with torches in their hands while their Grand Master was prepared for death.

He began to thank God. What a life he had led . . . exciting years in the galley ships, the blue sea, sun-drenched islands, quick raids in between service in the castle with the smell of the pine forests around them, and the deep blue sea on the horizon. The great year 1480 . . . "Thanks, Lord, we held out. The Grand Turk was forced to retrieve his hundred thousand, filled with shame and disgrace. We were suddenly known and honored throughout all of Christendom. And then, Lord, you gave me these seven years as the Grand Master."

They had been laborious and worrisome years. The Grand Turk had more than doubled his power and horrifying resources during these years. Now, he was not very far north, within sight of Rhodes, doing just as he had done over centuries. In a sweeping military expedition, he had taken all lands in the east and south, Syria, Damascus, Jerusalem, and all of Egypt. Rhodes was now in the middle of this world power, Christendom's last and most defiant outpost. But for how long?

He had done what he could to prepare for the storm. He had built and built and built ramparts, walls, and defenses of a thickness and strength never before seen on earth. When it came to fortification, Rhodes was number one in the world.

It was commonly known that the Grand Turk, Selim, he who was called "The Cruel," had prepped for an annihilating blow to this island where his grandfather's armies were so ingloriously defeated. Everyone knew this. The Pope had sent help. King Francis of France likewise. Their ships were still in the harbor, a flotilla of twenty sails.

But then Selim suddenly died. Then, in Syria, his governor raised the standard of rebellion. The Grand Master saw a chance to get out of the deadly entrapment from all sides. He sent Gazali all the help he asked for, lots of cannons and ammunition. He had overwhelmed the Pope and the princes of Christendom. Now or never, now was the time to unite and finally make a real effort. If Syria and Egypt could be helped, if they could gain their freedom once again, then the balance would be recovered. He saw a great hope shining through. He celebrated the happiest Christmas in a long time. He would depart this life in peace.

Now the great bell rang. Now, they too came—no, it was he who would come, old weary Carretto from all his planning and accounting, the parades, and council meetings. He would come home to his Lord. There he would meet the holy martyrs, even those who shed blood by his side in San Nicholas among the piles of stone in the glorious year of 1480.

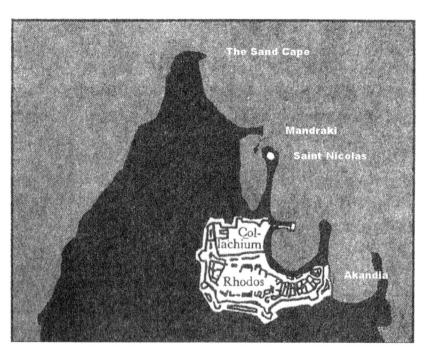

Shooter-Frans

BROTHER FRANÇOISE CAUTIOUSLY BRUSHED the only black cloak he owned. It was so threadbare in the stitches that he had to brush softly. He was happy today, happier than he had been in a long time.

Really, he wasn't ever called anything but Shooter-Frans. He didn't think anything of it. It was a stamp of inferiority that he bore through life as if he didn't have the strength to end it.

He belonged to the serving brothers of The Order of Saint John of Jerusalem—or "the Religion," as they were always called on Rhodes. He would never be a knight because he was a commoner. He almost wasn't allowed to become a frére servant, a serving brother. His mother was Greek, his father—whom he had never seen—was a French sailor on the Religion's ships. They married at the last minute and with great haste. Then the men of San Giovanni—the flagship—suddenly had to go out on caravan, and all furloughs were ended. Brother Françoise met with both annoyance and trouble when he tried to be taken on as a serving brother. Essentially, a man had to be of legitimate birth—if he didn't have a count or the like for a father. Luckily, the old priest Eusevio was still alive, and with his help he was able to prove that his mother was in a Christian marriage when he was born.

His father was always gone on caravan, and because of this his mom was among the poor, who ate in the hospital at the Religion's expense. He had gone in and out of the hospital, the splendid sick house directly across from the great Church of Mary, ever since he was a boy. It was there that he began to help the serving brothers as an assistant, taking buckets out, sweeping the yard, and then gradually making beds and taking food to the sick.

So he developed the desire to become a monk. He never had any luck with the girls. He had no business sense. Always browbeaten, he couldn't speak clearly. He always stammered and blushed. It wasn't hard for him to promise obedience.

In the order, he was considered a Provençal, though he was born on Rhodes. However, the only language he was at home with was Greek. When he spoke French, it was a blend of Provençal and Italian, many different Italian dialects mixed with Castilian, Catalan, and Portuguese. Many spoke with the same blend of languages here, not the least the merchants. But no one laughed at them.

Why should they always laugh at him? He couldn't help the fact that he walked with one foot out. That he was short and stout. That he easily blushed or that he lisped and sputtered when he talked.

He really wanted to prove that he was capable of doing something. So he tried to go from the hospital to military service. He was successful in that endeavor and it became his undoing. Had he stayed at the hospital at least he wouldn't be called Shooter-Frans.

They put him in the artillery. There it didn't matter that he was somewhat crippled: the pieces stayed right where they were. He slowly advanced in the common progression from the ammunition basket to the load pole and then to the match. It was a great day when he let loose his first shot. He had blundered, so it jammed and the huge twenty-four pounder hopped backwards. Then they laughed at him as usual.

Then he was commandeered to the Grand Carrack, the Religion's pride, the Mediterranean's biggest boat. And on the day of his misfortune, he stood a little proud, if still a little nervous, with the match at the culver furthest back on the starboard side. It was on the deck, in under the half deck. It was roofed and smelled of pitch, sweat, and dirty clothes. They had hunted a Turkish parandia, a wide freight ship, headed for Karpathos. They had gained on her, and now they were bearing down on her at full sail, hoping to board. It had been a little dot on the starboard tack. Now they were almost side-by-side. Yet the Turks didn't want to heave to, so they were going to give the ship a broadside. Brother François stood there with his smoking match. He meant to lay it to the touchhole just a moment before the muzzle pointed right at the Turks. The sea was heaving high and the carrack dived, rose, and dived again. Then the order came, and he fired the shot. But Brother François wasn't able to determine whether or not the moment was right. He shot after the others, and when the shot finally cracked, something inconceivable happened. A block as big as a horse's head came sweeping across the deck with a rope trailing after it. It hit the helmet of brother Preian de Bidoulx, who was standing at the ready to lead the boarding party. The rope took three rail pieces with it, knocking over a powder fourth and two artillerymen. Then it smashed into the pots in the cook's sandpit, spilling the afternoon's soup before it shot out with a report like a gigantic whiplash over the forward battlements with the great sail following it like a banner fluttering in the hard wind.

The carrack righted itself. The wind took in stern castle and, windward as she was, she laid herself across the wind so that the sails smacked and hit all corners, while the Turks laughed and thumbed their noses as they got away.

There was an investigation. It found that Shooter-Frans had done what one had one chance in a hundred to do: he had successfully hit the main sheet, which came from the flap of the sail far out before the gunwale to its little black hole in the planking above the stern.

After this master shot, he had been transferred back to shore again. Ever since that day he had been called Shooter-Frans, and it would stay with him for life.

But today was his great day, a day when no one could deny him his importance.

He would choose the Grand Master.

The tenth of January the Old Carretto had died. On the eleventh, he was placed in the black clothed council hall, in a high black catafalque with the knights on taborurets by the four horns and an honor guard clothed in black with halberds. The burial was on the twelfth, and Shooter-Frans had his special place in the procession, understandably behind the knights and the chaplains, but before all the civil lords, even the famous fortress architects, the papal galley captains, and all the rich merchants. It still meant something to belong to the order of Saint John of Jerusalem's Hospitallers and Knights.

And today, the twenty second, he would choose the Grand Master.

Ever since the burial, this choice had been discussed. It was discussed in all auberges by the whole knighthood, by Grand Crosses and commanders, by God's chosen and common knights. Up to now, even the novices had poked their noses into everything, though they had no right to vote.

But he had it, Brother Françoise, frére servant of the Provençal langue, and it was noticed. Every one spoke politely to him about the vote, both knights and chaplains.

There were three parties that quickly demarked themselves. As usual the Frenchmen kept together—and there he himself ought to have been counted. They wanted the Grand Prior of France, Phillippe Villiers de I'sle

Adam. He was a heavy name. Everyone knew it: He was a tested military man, a great fortress builder, an experienced diplomat, and was known to have a good hand with the people.

The Spanish, as usual, were not inclined to have a Frenchman, and as usual would get the Italians to support them. The Spanish had a heavy anchor too in Andrea d'Amaral, the Chancellor, but they weren't certain of his chances. No one said why, but everyone knew it. Amaral was a first class military man, a tough, disciplined man and completely fearless. In addition he was a cultured man who could recite the classics from memory just as well as the washed out black blotches in his writing cottage. But he had no hand with the people. He kept to himself and came off as arrogant. He had a way of sticking his aquiline nose in the air and lifting his grizzled eyebrows that annoyed people. He always looked down his nose to those he talked to. He had a surly smile on his face when he listened. That is, if he even bothered to listen. Occasionally, he appeared bored to death. No, no one would seriously put forth Amaral.

So some bright boy had hit upon a third possibility. Should they not consider an Englishman for once? There was, of course, Turcopilier Docwra, present Grand Prior of England, a smart guy, good military man, and above all an exceptional diplomat, well known and liked around the royal courts in Europe where he worked diligently as the Religion's ambassador. Couldn't they use just such a diplomat? Right now?

It was on this point brother François had been honored this day with the usual hints dropping in familiar small chats. He knew his importance and it had made him infinitely happy.

Now this was the situation. He could not directly choose the Grand Master. He could only be with and select three men from his langue, who together with three from each of the other langues would choose three great men. These three in turn would choose a fourth, who would be with them and choose a fifth—yes it was a little involved, but finally there would be sixteen, and they would go in a conclave and choose the Grand Master.

So in the end he didn't have much of a say in the matter. For the Provençal langue would vote French. That was clear. But that some considered him to play a small part in bringing about a conceivable wedge within the French block inspired him with an unusual yet pleasant feeling of meaningfulness.

The Chancellor

THE COMMANDER OF VERA CRUZ, Knight of the Grand Cross, Grand Prior of Castile, Don Andrea d' Amaral paced back and forth over the floor in the great hall unable to sit still. He looked out over the garden, turned back to the door and the far side, looked absentmindedly out through the arches in the stair hall, turned completely around, stood and slapped his sole against the stone floor, went back to the window and drummed on the marble slab.

Today, the twenty-second of January was the vote. As Carretto's successor, he would open the election. As the chief candidate he could have declined, but there was hardly any reason to do that. It was, of course, a purely formal tradition.

Chief candidate?

Was it such a sure thing? The matter ought to have been clear. He was the order's best naval officer. The fact was, he had been in charge this whole last year while the old Carretto slowly faded out. But there was also this Phillippe Villiers de l'Isle Adam, who had stood in his way as long he could remember. He couldn't stand this man. He fussed over people. He smiled to the right and left. He looked appreciative when people spoke rubbish. He worked in small words of praise where an honest chewing out would have been more suitable. No wonder he was popular. And it paid on a day like this.

In some miraculous way, appearances always worked against him when they were opposing each other. Like the day at Layazzo, a decade ago, the greatest day of victory they had experienced in a century—his great victory. But how many thought that it was his victory today?

The Chancellor remembered. He had led the galleys through the gray sea that slapped up through the oar beam and washed over the rowers to Cap Andreas on the far east side of Cyprus. There he met l'Isle Adam with the ships, all eighteen sails. Then they set out east with orders to seek and destroy the Sultan of Egypt's flotilla in the bay of Layazzo, the port of Alexandria. It was there to protect a convoy of at least fifty masts that would carry one of the greatest loads of logs ever seen in Alexandria's harbor. Now was the time to destroy it. It would be used to build an armada in the red sea that could crush the Portuguese and forever block the back way to India. The lumber was in Layazzo, or could it possibly be loaded already?

This meant they had to strike fast and hard. He gave orders to seek the enemy and attack wherever they were to be found even on the road. But l'Isle Adam was cautious as usual. He didn't want his ships to take fire from the shore (if there even were any cannons there, a very unlikely scenario). He was scared of finding bad wind and being driven ashore. He wanted to wait and ambush the enemy on the sea. If he now desired to do it . . .

This time they fell out in orderly fashion, quarreled, squared off, and had their swords half drawn when the chaplain got between them. Then l'Isle Adam yielded and said something to the effect that he would take the risk to sailing inland for the sake of unity. It sounded pious and noble. Naturally, it made an impression on the captains, who stood there embarrassed and taken aback.

And naturally they did what he, d'Amaral, had anticipated. They met the Egyptians on the open sea. There was a magnificent battle. He boarded the Sultan's flagship. He himself was the first over the gunwale. He still remembered the giant-like Mamluk that he knocked back so hard his head bounced against the deck. He remembered his duel with the young admiral, the Sultan's own nephew. Brave boy, but what help was that?

Then they burned the timber on the beach, stowed the cargo space full of prisoners and the decks with cannons. Then they manned the boarded vessels with skeleton crews and took the disabled ships in train. They came back almost twice as strong as they sailed out.

But how many remembered that today? If they remembered any of it, it was probably the legend of l'Isle Adam's nobleness.

The Chancellor looked out over his garden again, down where Ibrahim, the Turkish slave that had become head gardener worked. Ibrahim was a godsend. He had discovered him one summer day on the galley San Giovanni. They had been on caravan longer than expected. The rowers began to get sick from sitting in chains week after week. They had festering sores from sitting and cramps in their legs. They had become incapacitated with lumbago. Then he did something very unusual: He let them go on land in turns in a protected bay with a sandy beach and un-scalable mountains on all sides. Under the observation of expert shots circling with drawn crossbows, they were able to bathe in the warm clear salt water, wash their festering sores, stretch out in the sand, and gorge on grapes from a wild vineyard. When they came back on board, down in the hell after three hours in paradise, he happened to see a Turk who had stuck some small red flowers in his wet hair. This awakened his interest. Not everyone takes flowers with them to hell. He called to the man, who to his surprise spoke very good Greek. He was a gardener from the out-skirts of Constantinople, who was taken with a cargo ship of vegetables outside of Mytiline.

So he purchased Ibrahim from the Religion because at the present he needed a gardener. And he never regretted it. He did his job quietly and peacefully, slow but orderly. And if he ever opened his mouth, it was always worthwhile to listen.

Now the campanile's bell began to ring. The election would begin now. By evening he might possibly have given his first speech as Grand Master. How much would he dare to say? It was best to begin cautiously with the old phrases about sacred memories and an inherited obligation. But then maybe also about some of the victories that were won at the negotiation table by wise predecessors, who understood that it was best at times not to chase after the wind and not challenge fate, all for the goal that stood above all others: to not jeopardize this little kingdom built upon such great sacrifice. But now he had to go . . .

His Own Undoing

THE UNBEARABLY LONG PROCEDURE had finally ended. The conclave was finished. The langues were called into the church. The sixteen electors sat ceremoniously in the chancel. In the middle stood the admiral, old Paolo d'Acola, short and broad shouldered, the tip of his nose almost touching the powerful split chin reminding one of a parrot. He looked at his colleagues and asked who the Grand Master elect was:

"Signori, tenete per fatto qual che habbiamo fatto?

{"My Lords, Have you legitimately considered what we did?"}

Without a care for the others' confirmation, he looked straight out in front of him, conscious of the endless tension in the church.

"The forty-third Grand Master of this Holy Saint John of Jerusalem's Hospitallers—and Knights' Order has been chosen."

He enjoyed the endless silence for a second before he continued:

". . . brother Phillippe Villiers de l'Isle Adam, Priore di Francia." The rest was drowned out by the roaring assent that went through the church, the spontaneous standing ovation by the French and shows of loyal support from the election's losers also.

D'Amaral despised playing theater. He turned around and walked out, without looking to the right or the left, straight way through the crowd in the loggia and down the Grand Rue to his own house.

The faithful Blas Diez waited by the door. He immediately saw how it had gone. Without a word, he took the black cloak with the white eight pointed cross, folded it carefully, and took it to the closet under the arches. He was disappointed too. Even a valet in one of the city's finest houses can dream about moving up as a camarilla in the castle.

The Chancellor went upstairs to his little office on the right, the only one with a fireplace. It was very quiet.

Within the hour the door clapper knocked almost eerily in the dark stair hall, where the twilight already stood thick under the arches, and the first star looked down through the roof opening.

Blas Diez knocked two times before the Chancellor answered.

"What is it?"

"A visitor, Lord."

"Tell him I won't be receiving anyone today."

"Lord, it is Señor Commander Luis."

It was quiet for a moment. Then he came out, tall and straight, but ominously pale as his seamen feared to see him, il Terribile.

The Commander went up the stairs a little hesitantly.

"What do you want, Luis?"

"Only to bow and say that I revere my prior, my admirable chief from so many caravans, my Chancellor and my friend."

There was a warmth in his voice that coaxed d'Amaral into asking what he wanted to know most of all and yet wanted least of all to ask about.

"How did the votes fall?"

The Commander looked troubled.

"Nine to seven, if what they say is true."

The Chancellor took a breath between the discolored lips.

"Madre de Dios, it all hung on two votes. If two fools had a glimpse of reason, Rhodes could have been saved."

The other looked up curious.

"Yes, just saved," the Chancellor broke out. "From going under. Today they have elected their last Grand Master. They have chosen their own destruction."

"Señor Canciller, you can't say that."

"Yes, on my honor, I meant it. This will be the fall of Rhodes. It has come to be at last. And they do not deserve better. They are unthankful, dimwitted, clouded by great memories of the past, and helpless as soon as someone rubs them the right way promising that everything will be like the old days."

The Commander crossed himself. He looked pale in the lifeless winter twilight.

"Señor Canciller, may God preserve you from such thoughts. I will only say that we are many, who are not so unthankful. May I wish my Chancellor a good night under God's mercy? I ought to go to Compline now."

He bowed and vanished in the dark.

Compline? No, not tonight. The Chancellor shut himself in again. The fire that Blas Diez lit in the great open fireplace kept falling over into a red heap. He sat down in front of it and warmed his hands.

Yes, he meant it. He had understood this for a long time. Should this little island kingdom be able to remain in the midst of the great Turkish Empire then one had to be finished with peace. One had to take up that which the order of St. John promised to do. To always, everywhere, and by all means fight the unbelievers. And why not? Who believed any longer in the only way to heaven? Did not the Sultan have more faith than those in Rome?

Seven to nine. Besides their own six votes, the Frenchmen had also managed to gather three. He could only wonder which.

When Blas came in about an hour later with more sticks of wood, he asked as gently as he could:

"Blas, have you heard anything about how they voted?"

"Yes, Lord, there were nine for Señor Villiers and seven for Lord Turcopoler."

"What did you say?"

"Yes, for Lord Thomas Docwra, but as to who voted for whom, that is anyone's guess."

The Chancellor got up, walked over to his chamber servant and grabbed him by his coat with his strong hands on both sides of the neck lining where the shirt's lace flowed out.

"Docrwra! What do you mean—who said that?"

"They all say it. Tomaso with Pomerolx, Pierre and Andre' in the French house, and our own boy up there . . ."

It was the entire well-informed servant staff. Good to have them all together. He would not need to speak of the matter with some equal.

"Thank you, Blas. You can go."

Really, they had acted so shamelessly! Let him piece together some miserable compromise that ended in such a fiasco! And for such an order he had risked his life a thousand times, froze on the sea, slept in a coffin, ate moldy bread with rancid oil, vomited with disgust and fatigue, was wounded six times and had splinters in his legs on a heaving galley for three horrible days.

What had he done wrong? He was born during the sign of the lion, and he had let the day's best astrologers discern his fate. When God withdrew such luster, the planets still manifested it in heaven. And they said that he would do as well as he wanted if he only did the right thing at the right time.

Had he not acted boldly enough? Maybe it was a lesson for next time. The play would go on. Now he could act freely, unburdened from all sentimental consideration.

The Hospital

THERE WAS A LITTLE Greek from Simi looking up at the ceiling in one of the small rooms in the hospital, the Religion's great infirmary, "Our lords, the palace of the sick." He was barely twenty years old and newly enlisted in the fleet. No sooner had he checked into the grand barracks than he caught fever, and seemed to have nothing but water, mucus, and blood pouring out of him. Doctor Apella had just diagnosed him as non-contagious. He laid him down next to an unfortunate comrade within four stone walls with a little window to the street and an open fireplace on the inner wall. There were some pieces of wood burning in the fireplace, and it felt good against the cool atmosphere.

He lay there hoping that brother Frans—who was always called Shooter-Frans— would look in. He spoke Greek, and there weren't many who did here. Yes, Doctor Apella understood Greek, but not any of the priests, who normally came in during the morning rounds after the last mass in the grand hall. The little Greek longed to see a priest come, a true priest in a black coat and a high round coal black hat and a gold cross on his chest. A priest like Father Eusevio back home in Simi. He felt forlorn, depressed, and very, very worn out.

But Brother Frans never came. Today he was responsible for the cleaning in the grand hall. He stood there by a pillar at the far end of the long row that supported the high ceiling and gave a helpless look down the endless floor. The thirty-two beds with their canopies and drapes looked like a tent caravan camp along a street. Everything was strewn about the beautiful brick floor, the result of careless servants and thoughtless knights. It had been cold. The sick were coughing and had high fevers. Because it was winter, no boats went out and the knights had time to address their small ailments, rashes, boils, and colic troubles. The ward filled up fast. One could see what a struggle it had been to keep everything in order all fall. Every knight had the right to have an attendant with him. That was the worst. Their shirts and slippers, warm ruffles and nightcaps, prayer books and medicine bottles were all strewn about without the least respect for regulations. There in the middle of the hall the notice was posted that nothing should be found in the hall but that which the sick needed with them in bed. The rest was to be stowed neatly in the small storeroom made expressly for that purpose. These were found built into the wall behind every bed. This was how doctor Apella wanted to find it when we walked his rounds. He would begin those rounds in about half an hour.

Nothing suited Shooter-Frans worse than putting others to work. He gave his order as if he asked a favor. He looked sad when he had to tell someone that the chamber pot absolutely had to be emptied and that it was not good to put the food tray on it. It was taxing for him to get over his fears and go about stammering out his tactful reminders. As a rule he would promise to clean, fold, and wipe up so that it would all get done. Not until brother Bartolomeo came running and warned that the doctor was crossing the square would the work get into full swing. Yet, even when the doctor stood in the arched doorway at the far side of the colonnade, which ran around the garden, it still wasn't all quite perfect in the hall. But they still hoped to dodge a reprimand for neglecting their work.

 Doctor Apella now stood there on the cold blue winter day. He was short and stout with a round face, wide bent nose and protruding eyes, a little melancholic, sometimes anxious and most often observing as usual. He was a remarkable man, this Jewish doctor. He came here and opened a private practice like most of the others. He was efficient and received many thankful patients even among the knights. That was how he converted and was baptized. In baptism, he chose the name Giovanni Battista, a meaningful homage to the order of St. John and their patron saint.

The doctor had a complete escort with him as usual. There was the director, Dominus Infirmarius, and the surgeon, brother Gierolamo. Then there were two of the knights' own accountants, who oversaw everything day and night and would approve the expenses by drawing some unreadable doodle under them in the books. Shooter-Frans, who could read passably, but could not write, suspected—for good reason—that a good share of the knights were not very familiar with the art of writing.

Doctor Apella greeted the personnel with usual nods in all directions. He couldn't see the sick, because they were behind his heavy curtain. They needed this in the cold. The fireplace was only by the short wall and only the closest beds were glad for it. For the sake of the cold, all the window shutters were shut at the base of the ceiling. This made it dark, but not much warmer.

The doctor began his rounds at the southern end. There he had his own cause, the coughing and lung diseased, those who had kidney stones or rashes and those who only lost weight and faded away. He would stand with them all and let them talk, passing the time with them with his big friendly eyes. He would pry open all the bottles and jars and check to see how much they had consumed since his last visit. He altered prescriptions, checked their boils, and dressed their wounds. He was a remarkable healer, Doctor Apella, studied and book smart, even of the fine and cultured sort. He never touched a sore and apparently never picked up a knife. He left that to sawbones and surgeons, who worked with their hands and had come a long way if they ever came to be considered as hospital staff.

That is what Brother Gierolamo did. After many years as a simple blood letter, boil cutter, and leg healer, he got enough of a reputation to be a doctor when it came to treating wounds and bone fractures. So he came to the hospital and was enlisted as a serving brother. Soon he had a reputation that rivaled doctor Apella's, but the doctor wasn't at all jealous. He could stand and look on with great interest when Brother Gierolamo stuffed the bowels back in a belly that the Turks had made a hole in. Then he soothed them with warm oil, and made sure that there wasn't any hole in them. Doctor Apella used to give good advice on the matter of the plasters that one would set. They could have long discussions over whether one should stitch it together at once, or just put on another draw plaster that kept the edges of the wounds together.

So the round gradually reached the other end of the hall. There brother Gierolamo took the lead. Here were the broken legs, boils, and leg sores that he tended to with a knife and ointment as well as his own homemade medicine. In the bed furthest down lay Amery, who was brother Gierolamo's pride of the day. Brother Gierolamo had mastered an art that no one else here knew how to do. He could clear bowels so it went right through. Such happened often by pikes and scimitars in the waist or just a simple dagger during a fight in harbor. They were considered almost hopelessly lost. But one time Brother Gierolamo, who was from the Piedmont, had traveled north of the Alps. He swore that he would never do it again because while he was there he only encountered sour weather, sour cabbage, sour oil, and sour wines. But a good thing happened to him:

the art of repairing bowels. He had learned it from brother Henrik, an old wound healer, who served in the German Order. He had shown him how to cut away the damaged bit, force in a little silver tube approximately three quarters of an inch in through the cut, and with folded in edges, sew together both intestine ends over it and bind them fast. He first tried the art on a serving brother who was wounded in the abdomen when he tried to board a pirate ship. All were grieved for his sake, because he was an unusually capable man. All were just as glad when he was pieced back together. It was pretty hard, because he was a strong brother. It was hard to hold him even after giving him two doses of opium under the nose. He still lived in the greatest of good health and maintained that he could feel the silver ring if he fasted for a while and pressed his hands under his navel. Since then Brother Gierolamo kept a little store of such silver rings among his instruments and he had accomplished the same feat many times. Many suffered heartburn after eating, the wicked fever that nothing could stop, as a side effect. But some escaped.

The prospects looked good for Brother Amery. He felt cool and good today and said that he was hungry. The doctor and Brother Gierolamo were agreed, though, that he ought to continue to fast longer if he valued his life. When he persisted asking, the doctor became angry and said that he who presumed to give him so much as a breadcrumb would end up in the tower.

They finished up in the great hall and now came all the smaller halls, which were in a row on the upper floor around the great courtyard. Each of these smaller halls had doors opening up out onto the colonnade. The people in these halls were from the boats in the harbor, from the city, and the villages in the countryside. They were somewhat sorted out according to their ailments. There was a room for childbearing women and another for those who had scabies and rashes. The room furthest away in the corner was the dysentery room. The doctor went in there too, but he didn't let anyone but brother Frans come with him. He looked in on the little Greek and shook his head. Then he looked at the other one, and said that he could drink red wine diluted with two parts warm water. Then he ordered that the latrine bucket be filled with lime at least one hour before it was emptied.

Shooter-Frans stood and looked at the little Greek, who was not much more than a little boy. He lay there red from fever with a damp film over the eyes. Brother Frans had seen many dysentery patients before and could normally predict what would happen. This one had about eight hours left, maybe twelve. He would have gladly stayed with him, but the doctor went and he had to follow.

After the rounds were completed, there was inventory. They changed the bed linen often in the hospital. The Religion prided itself on keeping the hospital clean to the great amazement of many visitors. But this demanded constant supervision of the stores. Brother Frans counted, piled, folded, recorded the count, and started again. He could not stop thinking about the little Greek. Time passed, and now he had nothing left to do. All alone, he had come from the islands. Do you think they knew at all at home that he was sick?

Finally, he finished the first part of the inventory. He had counted through the quilts, sheets, mattresses, bed curtains, tin mugs, feather pillows, and delousing powder. It was almost dinnertime. Shooter-Frans passed by to look in on the dysentery room. It was as he expected. The little Greek was even worse. He walked over and stood by the furnace like bed.

"Can I help you drink something?"

The little guy nodded.

"Is there anything else you want?"

The little one looked up, helpless. He tried to wet his lips with his tongue.

"A father," he said.

"You want a priest? Didn't you receive the sacrament this morning?"

The little one shook his head. He wanted something else.

"A father," he said. "One who can speak Greek like you."

Shooter-Frans thought. It was difficult. Father Athanasius was gone away. The other chaplains were all Frenchmen and Italians. It used to not mean anything. They could still all give absolutions, the sacrament, and extreme unction.

He brooded. The little guy looked at him pleadingly.

"A father, a real one. Like home . . . "

Shooter-Frans nodded.

"I'll try."

He went out through the archway, down the wide stairs, out through the door and stood there perplexed. So he started down toward the city. Was this really important? What if the chaplains got mad? But then he remembered the boy had dysentery. That was enough evil. It was clear that they should go to those who had dysentery too just as they went to those who had pocks or the plague. But they would still be glad to escape having to do it.

He went at random to the Greek Cathedral; he could always meet someone there. But it was empty in there. There were only a few women praying before an icon of Hagios Fanurios. But just then a real priest came down the lateral isle. Shooter-Frans limped along and stammered some words, just as the priest would have disappeared behind the iconostasis. When he heard the Frank speak Greek like a native, he was friendly at last and listened a little longer. Yes—he would come. So he gathered up his things and followed. It turned out that he really should have been going to a baptism, but a dying man needed to come first. Shooter-Frans was starting to feel a little anxious. What if he had misdiagnosed the little Greek? Was it really so urgent?

But the Greek priest did not seem to be mad about anything. He had small shoulders and sad eyes. His name was Gennaios, he said and that he too was from the islands. He had heard of the sick boy. The little Shooter-Frans now began to speak and chat about himself.

When they got there, the priest went into the dysentery room right away and shut himself in. Shooter-Frans went away to the cafeteria, but it was already empty. He learned that the infirmary asked about him and was now looking for him. It was a very painful examination. Where had he been? What had he done in the city? Why didn't he go to dinner? Who was the priest he took into the Hospitallers' territory? Was it really one of the Catholic Greeks that recognized the Pope and not one of the schismatics? Shooter-Frans stammered, bowed, turned red, and stared helplessly before him, unhappy because he always did everything wrong. Then he finally got the order to fetch the Greek priest.

That troubled him too. He did not want to disturb the priest, but Father Gennaios stayed in there a long time. But when he finally came out, Shooter-Frans was comforted, knowing that the priest was thankful for being called. He had been needed in there, he said. Then he went to see the infirmary, and they spoke for an hour, at first very loudly then calmly. When the Greek went on his way, the infirmary looked very respectful. He didn't say anything else about the matter to Shooter-Frans.

In the evening, the little Greek died. In its own way, this comforted brother Frans too. At least, he hadn't called the priest unnecessarily.

The Unfathomable

CHANCELLOR D'AMARAL SAT ALONGSIDE a path in the garden and warmed his frozen bones under the beautiful February sun. It had been a cold morning in the cool council hall, and the negotiations certainly hadn't done anything to warm his heart or feet. Everything was going wrong, just as he had predicted. Naturally, they had immediately sent delegates to Rome and Marseille to inform them of the election results. Now, the new Grand Master found himself in France as an ambassador, visitor, and corrector with extraordinary powers to negotiate for more troops, more boats, and new cannons. He was also able to collect outstanding debts, outstanding leases, and regular responses from the order's property, extra war tributes and as much he could press out of advances and loans. That fit him.

Then they chose an acting deputy, and—naturally!—it was a Frenchman, this round stomached, pink-skinned, reddish-blond bearded, smiling and wasteful Gabriel de Pomerolx. It fit them.

The larger political picture also looked dark. Naturally, things had gone like he thought they would. The rebellious Gazali had been defeated. He was thrown out during the siege of Haleb. Then he was overcome by Suleiman's Janissaries, who fell upon him just outside of Damascus after an unbelievable day's march. Some said that he attempted to flee disguised as a dervish, but had been betrayed by his own men. In any case his severed head was now on the way to Constantinople in a courier's bag. And all the cannons that Old Carretto had so generously contributed were now in Turkish hands. The councilors and instructors he had sent with the cannons had escaped home by sea, mostly thanks to a strong January storm that made even the best Turkish captains seek peaceful harbors.

The Chancellor sat and looked at Ibrahim, the garden slave, who slowly and methodically stacked stones around a new terrace along the top of the garden. What was he really thinking about? Turks were the best people a person could want as rowers and assistants. They never caused a disturbance. They worked quietly and diligently.

"Ibrahim?"

"Yes, Lord?"

The Turk looked up a little bewildered.

"Come here a minute. Don't work. What are you really thinking about?"

Something came to life in the Turk as if he had made a decision. So he said:

"About paradise, Lord."

The Chancellor looked surprised at first, but it faded.

"And you believe that you will go there?"

"Naturally, Lord, because I have a better faith."

"Better? Better than what?"

Again something lit up behind his dark velvet-brown eyes.

"Than yours, Lord."

"You will have to explain what you mean by that."

The slave hesitated.

"May one speak from his heart?"

"You may, Ibrahim."

"God is one."

"True, Ibrahim."

"He is exalted, higher than the heavens, unimaginable, glorious beyond all understanding. It is impossible to conceptualize him."

More than one would want, the Chancellor thought, but he didn't say it.

"If we could conceptualize him, he would no longer be God."

"That is true, Ibrahim."

"Neither could he be God, if he were like we are."

The Chancellor remained quiet. He should have contradicted him here, but he wanted to hear more. He looked encouragingly at the Turk, who stood there and stretched the waistband of his pants, wondering how much he could say without landing on the rower's bench again.

"Lord, we would never venture to say that the infinitely exalted would have a son with a woman. That the glorious and divine, the blessed and unspeakable, whom we cannot find a word for—that he could be found in a wretched, sweaty human body that is susceptible to sores and colic, has to stuff itself with porridge and go to the bathroom like we do. Lord, it is blasphemy. Therefore God has given us victory. See for yourself, Lord: Egypt, Syria, Africa, Byzantium, and Bulgaria—all are liberated. God restores his glory everywhere again through us his unworthy servants. How would we have been able to do it, if God were not with us?"

That is the question the Chancellor thought, precisely the question. But he only said:

"In the end, it still comes down to how one lives."

"Yes, Lord, and it is just for that reason that we Turks do not steal. We give our alms, pray the prayers he prescribed, and are all prepared to die for him."

"And the wine you are not allowed to drink? There is said to be both taverns and drunkards in Constantinople."

"Some drink it, Lord. God comes to punish them. We are ashamed of them. But are the Christians not forbidden from whoring? Or lying? And they do these things openly and without shame."

"You can go now, Ibrahim."

"Are you angry with me, Lord?"

"No, Ibrahim, but we have more to do than talk the time away, both you and I."

He went to his desk. But it was tedious and slow writing to the property administrators of Barletta, Messina, and Capua with the usual nagging notes to hurry and send help to scrape up the last of the money and personnel. The Turk's word would not leave him alone.

If Christ was God's Son, why didn't He give them victory?

For three-hundred fifty years, He had only given defeat to his faithful: At Hattin's Horn, at Margat and Acre, at Nicopolis and Varna. Jerusalem, Ceasarea, Nicea, Constantinople, Smyrna, Ephesus and Corinth, all had fallen. All the holy, apostolic cities were now under the half moon, except for Rome—and it too would fall one day, if one wasn't ready to put an end to the peace.

At one time this question plagued him, almost insufferably. He would lie on the galley's quarterdeck in the warm humid nights, the stars blurred behind the haze and stench of the rowers, who snored and groaned in their chains and excrement while the Latin sail lifted its pointed top to the heavens. Black thorny shorelines shadowed the horizon, almost always enemy territory, islands that had already fallen or that could fall any day. He wondered: What is God doing? What are His holy mother and all His saints doing? Now he had stopped questioning. Life had taught him this hard lesson. If God cared about such things, then he always kept the best galleys, the most powerful artillery, and the hardest disciplined soldiers. In the end, that which decided the matter was money, weapons, cleverness and self-will. It was a game where the clearest brains and the hardest hand took home the victory. To bring God into the game only made it more complicated.

The Walls and Hands

IN THE TAVERN FIVE Florentines, brother Antonio Bosio flagged his old friend Gianantonio Bonaldi with a shout, fell upon him with greetings, kissed him on both cheeks, showered him with questions, and offered him the house's best wine, which by chance came from Crete where Bonaldi also called home, Venetian as he was.

Brother Antonio Bosio was a renaissance man, a real mover. He could get by with most of the languages spoken in these parts, was known by most of the merchants, knights, servants and spies who roamed about here, and was best friends with anyone who could give the Religion any help—the saints would not forget—a proven connoisseur of all the Mediterranean's wines, boats, and pirates, and trusted with many dangerous and delicate tasks by his Grand Master. Among the serving brothers of Saint John of Jerusalem's Order, he had held a unique position for many years that gave him a great deal of exemptions. In principle this was enough to arouse suspicion, but as far as anyone could tell, his childlike enchantment with serving his order and his Grand Master never waned.

He had met this Gianantonio Bonaldi one blistery evening on a dock in Chios. They had both been in the same straits, no ship heading home and at risk of being locked up by the Genovese Castellan, who at that moment was almost as irritated with the order of St. John as he had always been with the Venetians. Brother Antonio had convinced a Greek fisherman to take them with promises of a gratuity greater than a poor fisherman's income for half a year. They split for the sea in the midst of a storm and darkness, and that also helped. When they were seized by a Venetian force outside of Negroponte, they cleared themselves using Bonaldi's good name, and when they fell into the hands of the old pirate Santolino (who, aside from Turks, captured any and all Venetian vessels), Antonio Bosio took him in arms, thumped him on the back, and reminded him of all the fun they had had together that winter. Then Santolino took them to Rhodes, escaping the Turkish fleet, which set out to take him dead or alive. They continued to Lango, escaping all the Turks, and once more finding themselves in the galley benches (which, of course, was always a risk when sailing these waters). From Lango, Antonio helped his newly won friend continue to Crete despite the fact that the order's relationship with Venice had hit a new low point. The Venetians declared that members of St. John's, disguised as pirates, captured one of their ships while Rhodes indignantly replied that they completely fabricated this story in order to hide that they were playing under the covers with the unbelievers and put their good before their religion, always playing by the old maxim, Veneziani, poi Christiani. Venetians first, then Christians.

Now they sat there and drank their good wine. Gianontonio Bonaldi had come from Crete with a boatload of wheat, wine, oil, and gunpowder, all marketable wares in Rhodes, particularly after winter when the shipping had slowed down. Stores were lacking and prices climbed. It was his first time in Rhodes and Brother Antonio invited him to see the city in all its glory.

"You must see the Grand Master's garden. When I was a boy, there were real ostriches there. The Grand Turk had given them to the blessed Grand Master d'Aubusson. They would eat scrap iron, you know, and laid eggs as big as your head in the sand. They never brooded over them. They only stirred them. They hatched by themselves. And there was a rare dog that also came from the Sultan. It was as big as a greyhound and gray as a rat without a hair on its body except for the nose, and so fastidious that it never ate meat that hadn't been slaughtered the same day. Man, it could jump too! As high as you are tall."

"Is it still there?" Bonaldi asked a little skeptically.

"No, it died of offence when Carretto became Grand Master. It could not suffer the Piedmonts."

Brother Antonio paid generously. He kept his vow of apostolic poverty, at least in such a way that he insisted on paying if he had any money.

"Then we will go to the walls," he decided. "You have to see Carretto's new tower."

They went through the city district that had been the Jewish ghetto and brother Antonio narrated.

"This is where Misac Pascha broke through in 1480. They successfully shot the Italian wall to pieces, came through the breach, and made it here. But d'Aubusson had allowed them to destroy the houses from here to the wall and stack up the stones as an emergency wall. There were as many Turks in the breach and on the walls as there are bees in a beehive. You couldn't see any space between them. The Grand Master stood in the midst of the worst crowding. He swept and hacked as if he were harvesting grain until he took a pike in the side. It went straight into the lung and he came close to dying. Afterwards, he was sick for a long time. But we saved ourselves, thanks to Signor San Giovanni Battista and God's Holy Mother. They revealed themselves, you know, here up in the heavens."

He looked straight up.

"You really saw them?"

"Not our people. They stood right under them, and they had other things to do just then. But from the bottom of the moat and the crest on the other side they saw them clearly. The prisoners and deserters told us afterwards. That is why they gave up and fled."

Bonaldi nodded thoughtfully; he did not belong to the gullible.

They went up the long ladder to the wall's crown, thirty-two rungs high. There the Venetian stood, surprised and overwhelmed.

"But this is a city square!" he said.

He was right. On both sides of the wall expanded *strada di rondo* connecting the walkways to the crest, broader than the city's broadest street. Fifty men could easily walk there, shoulder to shoulder. They were still working higher up, and the path was cluttered with stone blocks, tools, slaves, and stoneworkers, whose chisels clinked against the stones like a final extended bird trill of steel clangs and hammer hits. Through the windows you could see the dark blue sea. It was wide open, shining white and completely level. Only the breastwork along the outer edge cast a blue shadow. The cannons stuck out their round tails with even space. A patrol of guards went on their usual rounds with shiny pikes and their metal hats nodding.

"This is our wall," brother Antonio said with pride. "Posta d'Italia, the portion that the Italian langue defends. Carretto allowed all this to be done. See, just twelve steps behind the old wall they have built up a new one and the whole space is filled with stone, mortar splinters, and clay stamped and packed hard so that it is as hard as solid ground. This time it won't break open so easily."

"Are you so sure they are coming?"

"Sooner or later. But come now, you should see the best. He went to the crest and looked through one of the cannon ports."

"All French embrasure of the latest model, twelve feet thick and beveled on the outside so that their damned stone balls will come to naught and bounce away."

"There aren't any shield shutters to let down," said Bonaldi competently.

"We have done away with those. They are only in the way. Do you see? All the holes are slanted. They are so long and narrow that it is almost as easy to get a shot through them as to stand two feet from a door and look through the keyhole. And yet they still cover the whole terrain out there. So finely calculated, they are."

Brother Antonio had climbed up on the guard wall and dragged his friend after him. The Venetian stood speechless again. He had never even imagined a moat like this. It was like a river between perpendicular paths crossing through a mountain massif. And in this valley the new tower jutted out, a massive center tower surrounded by something just as giant-like circling around to the east, not quite as high and completely polished, but a single vast edge. Only at the crest did you catch a glimpse of any oblique-angled embrasures.

"Isn't it elegant?" asked brother Antonio.

"In its way," answered Bonaldi cautiously. While he thought that former fortress builders would turn in their graves if they knew that such peasant-like work would replace their proud tower.

"We also have the world's best fortress builders. Because Carretto called Basilio della Scuolo here, but the Emperor will certainly want him back now. And our own Zuenio is no hack either. You should see his map, which Luigi d'Andugar brought with him to the Pope when he left three weeks ago. Made of plaster, you know. So that one can take in the towers and the boulevard with the curtains, defenses, and barbicans and everything modeled to scale precisely as it is. Currently, we are the foremost in the world.

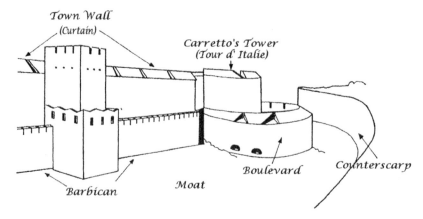

"I wonder," said the Venetian. "We have a man in Crete who can outdo whoever he wants."

"Who would that be?"

"His name is Martinengo Gabriele Tadini da Martinengo. He was sent by the signor in order to look over our fortresses. He looks at fortresses the way we others look at women. It is immediately clear to him what a person needs to do to conquer them or to stop those who will try it. He sees exactly where the balls will hit and what needs to be done for protection. You can ask him to calculate with twenty pieces or a hundred. He knows at once where to place them and what they can do."

"We need that man here."

"But I don't believe you can have him. The Duke of Crete is very firm that no one may take service above him. He does not want to upset the Turks."

They stepped down from the walls again, and went across through the city a short ten-minute walk to the opposite wall that separated the convent, the order's city, from the business district. The Venetian was surprised by all the new houses.

"Did the Turks do such great damage?"

"Only in one district. Worse was the earthquake that hit it the following year."

Bonaldi remembered. There had been a frightening earthquake in 1481, unusually devastating even more so in this sector.

"It is very strange," he said, "that it should have happened the year just after the great siege."

"Strange! It was the very same day the Grand Turk died, Mohammed, the arch tyrant. He took Constantinople, and then tried to take us. It is not so strange that the earth buckles a little when great people like that go down to hell."

Bonaldi looked a little askance at his friend, from the side. It was amazing, what some knew to reply to everything. Brother Antonio had already decided to change the subject.

"Up there in the church, you know, there is John the Baptist's right hand. The one he baptized the Savior with."

"How did you get that?"

"From the same Grand Turk that stole it in Constantinople. It was Bajazid who gave it to us so that we would keep his brother Zizimi under the order's protection. He fled here, as you know. His son Amuratte lived out the remainder of his life in the castle at Ferakles. That was a day, you can be sure, when the Holy Hand came here. The old people still talk about it. There was a procession that went from Porta San Antonio all the way down to the square. There were Flemish tapestries and Turkish rugs hanging from all the windows, and there were garlands between the houses and awnings over the square. They were needed because it was warm. And the Augustinian who preached kept going a long time with all the skill of a rhetorician in three parts, and yet he was still unable to say everything. I have seen it myself, as close to it as I am to you now. It is true what they say, that one can see the teeth marks."

"The teeth marks?"

"Yes, you don't know about that? When the hand was in Antioch there was a dragon that plagued the whole district. He mostly ate animals, but to make sure that he would leave the people in peace, they sacrificed one of the citizens every year according to a lottery. One time the lot fell on a poor little girl. Her father was a pious man, and a true worshiper of the Holy Hand, and so he went to it and prayed for help. Then he kissed the hand as was his custom. But this time he took the opportunity and bit the thumb, and a little piece broke off. He baked it in a piece of bread and when the dragon came to devour the girl, he threw the bread in his mouth. The monster choked on the spot. Then he just wheezed and died . . . "

"I wonder if there are any dragons," the Venetian said doubtfully. Now he was beginning to speak with caution.

"If there are? Come I will show you!"

Brother Antonio shined triumphantly and dragged his friend with him down behind the church and out through the Anthony's Gate. They continued along the newly built defenses between the walls and out through the brand new Gate D'Amboise. He took the time during the walk to catch his friend up on all the remaining treasures of the church: a thorn from Christ's crown of thorns ("It blooms every Good Friday, they say, but I have never seen it"), one of the crosses that Saint Helena allowed to be made from the bronze basin the Savior used when He washed the Disciples' feet, one of the thirty silver pieces that Judas received ("I have seen it, you can get a wax imprint. It is supposed to help with both childbirth and seasickness"). A great piece of the Holy Cross, an arm of Saint Blasio, one of Saint Stephan, one of Saint George, one of the Apostle Thomas, the head of Saint Eufemia, one of the eleven thousand virgins in Cologne, one of Saint Filomene Vergine, one of the Holy Saint Polycarp . . . "

But now they had come out on to the drawbridge and brother Antonio looked triumphantly at the dragonhead sitting very prominently, nailed up above the city's gate. It was old and dried out, but all together terrifying, bigger than a horse's head with a sneering jaws that went behind the ears showing their malevolent teeth.

"I think that looks like a crocodile," the Venetian said.

"What is that?"

"A type of great monster that is found in Egypt, in the Nile."

"There are dragons in Egypt? Among the unbelievers? It serves them right. Precisely what one would have thought."

"But how did it get here?"

"You don't know? I thought the whole world knew."

And while they wandered back through the city, Brother Antonio told the story.

The Dragon in the Marsh

Back when Hélion de Villeneuve was the Grand Master here, there was a dragon that lived in the swamp on the other side of Mt. St. Stefan, only a half hour from here. He harried that area for many years. First only goats vanished and maybe a donkey or two. But then he began to take children. Then someone complained to the Grand Master, who offered a reward to anyone who would take him dead or alive. But he shouldn't have done that. Some returned, bloody and muddy, and with leg skins torn down to their calves as if they had been tortured. Others were never heard of again. Those who got away would describe it. There was no doubt that it was a dragon, twenty feet long with a tail that could break a horse in pieces when it struck. A manslayer, he ate men like sausage. One man tried to shoot him with the strongest crossbow he could find. It just ricocheted off the horrid knots on his back. It didn't bother him anymore than if one were to scratch him behind the ears. So everyone knew that he was hexed.

This story annoyed the Grand Master. On the whole, the dragon made it unsafe to take any path to the city. He lay and lured far away from his swamp in the mornings when people would go to market. It was next to impossible to see him because he could disguise himself as an old fallen tree trunk. Then when someone came within reach, he scampered out like a lizard, sinking his jaws into a steer or a servant boy.

The Grand Master, though, didn't want to lose anymore of the brothers. So he gave an order that no one should go out to slay the dragon. The most vexing part of this was that the Greek priests spread a rumor that it was God's punishment for us having come to the island and introducing the true faith. They went around muttering that we were excommunicated by the Patriarch of Jerusalem so it was not so incomprehensible that such an abomination would rummage about here.

But now there was this Gozon, who later became Grand Master. He was a tall man, a lean Auvergnat. When he was a boy back home, he would ride through moors and dry out in the sun so that he was only skin and sinews. But he was strong. There was no one better to send out for a corsair that got away with a galley. He didn't take the Grand Master's order seriously, thinking that he could, at least, take a look at the monster. And he did many times. Then he got permission to go home to Auvergne. He couldn't stop thinking about this dragon and how he might go about slaying it. He was so obsessed with hunting it that he went to his yard and drew a picture of the monster. The smith was a clever fellow, and after a few days he had bent together some bars of iron to act as a skeleton for the mockup. He had put hinges on it so skillfully that the dragon could strike with his tail and open his teeth if you pulled on some straps. Then all they had to do was secure tree limbs to the bars and the dragon was finished.

Gozon had two squires who were always willing to have a little fun. He taught them to pull the straps so that the wood dragon squirmed as if it were living. Later they tied a long rope to the straps and sat safely while Gozon charged it with his field lance. They pulled as much as they could so that the dragon threw himself at Gozon, jumping and clubbing him with his tail while he tried to stick it with the lance. But it wasn't just him; he also trained two bulldogs he had not to be afraid of the monster. He taught them to bite on the underside of the body where he saw that the armor was thinner and to hold on fast no matter how much the dragon thrashed about.

When he thought they trained enough, he gained permission and took the two squires, the horse, and the dogs with him back to Rhodes. Then he gained permission to come and go as he pleased. By the second day, he smuggled his armor out of the capital and over to the mountain. In the evening the two squires came with the horse and the dogs. Then he started to get anxious, so he took a good hour in the church praying before the altar to get as much protection as possible from the dragon and his hellish art.

Then he set out to hunt. The squires had their orders. He wanted to attack it by himself, alone. If he died, they should carry him back and buy three masses for his soul. Then they were to take the first boat home to Marseille without saying anything to anyone. But if he was successful in piercing the dragon, they should come and help.

It wasn't long before they found tracks in the grass, almost as if a tree trunk had been dragged through the forest. They were following the tracks when Gozon suddenly spurred his horse and began to gallop.

There wasn't much time for him to gain speed. The dragon was lying right there in front of him, waiting. At the last second, the horse turned to the side and he missed his mark with the lance. Gozon turned around and tried again. This time, the lance hit its mark just like in a tournament. But the horse was so completely terror stricken that he made a turn, throwing Gozon out of the saddle. The horse bolted and screamed as only frightened horses can do. It ran past the squires, who were scared to death, and climbed up some rocks, thinking that their lord had been eaten. But he got up on his legs and hacked at the dragon with his sword. But the beast was, as I said, hexed. He may as well have been hacking at a Turkish cannonball. The beast tried to bite him. Gozon would jump to get out of the way. He began sweating hard. The hounds tried to help him, holding fast to the underbelly as they had been taught, but the monster simply flung them off. They flew through the air with huge pieces of skin hanging from their teeth. The tail hit Gozon so that he saw stars and fell down. Then the dragon chased after him wildly. But just as he lifted his head, Gozon ran his sword through the underside of the dragon's neck. The sword broke through the enchanted skin. The dragon shook, and thrashed, but Gozon held firm with both hands. He must have cut the monster's carotid artery as they were rolling around. Blood spurted and oozed out of his throat like water from a gargoyle in a thunderstorm. The dragon ended up on top of Gozon because he wouldn't let go of the sword. When the dragon finally had had enough, he sank down on top of Gozon, who had also had enough and fainted in the mud. He might have drowned there if the hounds hadn't barked and got the squires down from the rocks. When they ventured forth and saw what was up, they put the lance handle and tree branches under the dragon and turned him over. When they had broken Gozon free and lifted up his visor, they saw that he was still alive. They scraped the worst of the mud off of him and put him on his feet. He was fine after he rested a bit. But because it was forbidden to fight with the dragon, he did not want to announce to the watch to be admitted to the city without first going to a farmhouse that belonged to a Genoese. When the Genoese learned what he had been up to, he broke out his best wine and laid the table with cheese, olives, and bread. Then brother Gozon ate with a fresh appetite.

The next morning a servant came with the horse, loamy, sweaty, and still saddled. Gozon was so annoyed with the cowardly wretch that he took his saddle and gave the Genoese the horse as thanks for the hospitality—

on the condition that he could only be used as a work horse and would regularly be thrashed if he thought himself too good for it.

But then the real story you should hear began. Brother Gozon returned to the auberge with his chain mail full of dried mud, dents in his armor, a black eye, and a whole swarm of sailors and servants behind him whooping and cheering. The rumor had already spread. The brothers clapped for him, and the Auvergnats wanted to have a victory feast. But then came one of the Piliers, the Prior of Aups, and simply asked him if it was true that brother Gozon had fought the dragon alone.

"True enough," he said. "Though the hounds helped me."

"Then Brother Gozon has disobeyed a given order. I may herewith request Brother Gozon to leave his weapons and follow me. Provost, show the way."

The provost showed the way to the prison tower. Down in the cellar, brother Gozon sat in steel vices with ten pounds of iron on his feet. There was a tremendous disturbance on the street, but the prior sent out the guard and drove the people away. Patrols saw to it that no one was able to gather together and stand or talk around the tower. What an ordeal that must have been.

So what were they to do with Brother Gozon? He could have been shot on the spot. He had broken an order that demanded his life. The very least one could do was to take his knighthood from him and send him home without spurs or sword. But no one really wanted to do that. When the people and the seamen could not gather at the tower, they went to the church and ordered a mass, and that could not be denied them. First they ordered a mass of thanksgiving and then three masses of petition. They kept this up in all the churches for the entire morning. There was an unbelievable crowd. The people burned masses of light all calling out to Saint Paul, Saint Michele, and Saint Stefan. When they went home, they knew that the saints were staying with Brother Gozon and helping him.

This dragged on until Friday when the issue was brought before the capital assembly. The Grand Master did not want to have an extra assembly and appealed to the Piliers only to give a sentence. A prisoner could be judged just as well on Friday as he could on Tuesday. Some ordeal that must have been. So they had a trial on Friday, and on Saturday it had leaked out that the Grand Master had demanded capital punishment. Gozon had promised to keep the order, and it would cost him his life. He figured he would be disarmed, and that he was. The Piliers put forward all that Brother Gozon had done, and how he killed at least one hundred Turks and now a dragon in the bargain. So he received the lightest sentence that could be given. Everyone went to the chapel. Brother Gozon was called up to the hall. He was stripped of his red surcoat with the white cross and his spurs. Then he was sent to his private quarters. There he would stay under house arrest while waiting for the next ship home.

No one in the city was pleased with this decision. For that matter, neither were any of the remaining knights in the convent. It had leaked out that the prisoner would rather be executed than sent home in disgrace. But the Grand Master simply said no to this.

So some brothers made up a letter of petition for Brother Gozon, which every commander signed. The Grand Master received it, but was like a wall.

Then the day of St. John the Baptist arrived. After the fast, when all had confessed their sins and taken the sacrament, there would be the general assembly in the grand hall. The Grand Master sat there on his throne, just as unaffected, with all the Piliers, Commanders, and land-owners around him while the knights, chaplains, and troop commanders took their places. The Grand Master decided that the meeting would be open and allowed the doors to be opened. The people who had been crowding around outside now rushed in, crowding and howling until the guard established order. Then dead silence fell in the room as the Pilier of Provençe rang his bell and read the letter of petition for Gozon.

Now the Grand Master received it where he wanted to. He called Gozon in and said that he had seriously offended. No one should turn a blind eye to his orders. But wrath has its time, and forgiveness has its own time too, as Ecclesiastes teaches. So he asked if the former knight, Dieudonné de Gozon would once again take up the Religion. If he would, he may bow his knee here and now, confess his sins, renew his oath, and receive his surcoat and sword back. The whole hall shouted with joy and rang bells. There has never been a feast like it on the day of St. John the Baptist since. Later Brother Gozon became a Commander, then a Pilier, and finally Grand Master. But when he killed the dragon they promised to throw him in irons and remove him. What an ordeal that must have been.

The Test

"MAYBE THIS?"

The treasurer held up a heavy gold chain, rattled it, and let it shine in the little bit of sun that made it through the half open wood doors. They—him, the Grand Master's deputy, and the Chancellor—had gone up to the top floor in a gate tower where the Grand Master kept the treasures that could be used as gifts of respect to visiting potentates.

"Too valuable . . . and too common," said Pomerolx, the deputy. "He would only weigh the gold and then tax us as if we were one of his provinces."

It was an issue concerning Sofi, the Shah of Persia. He had sent his envoy to Carretto. Disappointed and perplexed, they had heard that he was dead and buried. They had deliberated in their incomprehensible language whether to get horses and ride to Ferakles where the pretender to the throne, Amuratte, a cousin to Suleiman's father, lived under the Religion's protection as their guest and hostage. They had probably promised him help and eternal friendship if he could organize a rebellion against Suleiman. Right now they could use that. The shah feared that the Janissaries would cross the border any day. That the Grand Turk also wanted to conquer Persia was no secret.

Because Sofi was a thankful ally, one ought to send him fitting gifts of friendship, but they had to be kept within certain parameters because no one knew what political course the new Grand Master was planning.

The treasurer looked around in the rubbish perplexed. They may as well have been with a pawnbroker who had noble clients. There were rings and chains, gold plated spurs, bags of golden cloth, Turkish armor, and scimitars with scabbards inlaid with precious stones, and hunting helmets lying all over. Most of it was war booty, though some of it had been royal gifts that were deemed useless and stowed away. Just to be on the safe side, these had been furnished with notations of origin. Then there were inherited things that had belonged to dead brothers of the order.

Pomerolx, the deputy, moved some Venetian dishes and pulled out a large chest finished with gold borders, precious stones, and enameled plates. He lifted the lid and pulled out a chessboard of different colored squares.

"You have to press them in a certain order. Nothing opens the secret lock without the code. We give it to him with a sealed letter so he alone can know the secret and keep his shady agreements and bottles of poison safe and undisturbed. He puts value in that. That and a bundle of the green Florentine silk, some hunting guns, and one of the fine Nuremberg pistols with wheel locks—and two falcons. That will be sufficient."

The falcons were standard gifts. The Hospitallers had perfected this way of hunting. You could not find better falcons anywhere in the world. And they had plenty of them.

The Chancellor nodded unwillingly. It would be politically shrewder and wiser to send gifts to Suleiman than to maintain friendship with his enemies.

"We should also consider the Frenchmen," he said. "And the Pope's galley captain. They should have a royal gratuity when they return home."

"Who said they are going home?"

Pomerolx sounded irritated.

"Common sense and the report from Constantinople."

Pomerolx was silent. They had just read the secret reports from Constantinople, prepared by agents who neither Pomerolx nor the Chancellor could name ,written with invisible ink according to a jealously guarded secret recipe. They were written between lines in shipping documents and catalogues of goods and smuggled out by merchants whose names were just as carefully guarded. All the reports were unanimous. They spoke about energetic armament. There was work around the clock in the cannon foundries. Grain was stored up as high as mountains. At least a thousand transport camels were on their way to Constantinople, and all Sipahis in Anatolia and the Balkans were on alert. On the other hand, it was almost normal in the shipyards. There was no doubt that this year there would be an overland campaign, probably in Hungary. It was a much higher probability there now, as the Hungarians in their madness had shamelessly abused and murdered Suleiman's ambassador, sending home his severed ears and nose.

The Chancellor said dryly and a little scornfully what the others thought.

"As soon as it is known, requests are made by our allies to sail home. And what can we do, but give them some gold chains and let them go?"

"Are we agreed then?" Pomerolx asked. "And the Lord Chancellor can set up a protocol?" D'Amaral nodded reservedly. Fifty years as a knight of St. John had taught him not only to receive an order without blinking, but also to know the bitterness of receiving it from one who ranked far below him in seniority.

Somberly and quietly, he crossed the castle courtyard preoccupied. The salutes of the watches and uncovered heads bowing while sweeping their berets that he encountered on his way out irritated him.

Arriving home, he pulled out the secret reports. He wanted to go through them again and make a statement before the council meeting. A good hour had passed, when there was a knock on the door. It was the Turk Ibrahim.

"What do you want?"

The Chancellor furled his gray bushy eyebrows and looked at the slave irritated. To come un-summoned, he was still taking his forbidden freedoms.

"Make it short."

"Lord, I want to buy my freedom."

"You? What can you pay?"

"Whatever you demand, Lord. I have become rich."

"You? How?"

"My uncle has died. God has taken his soul. He did not ask for me or anyone else either."

The Chancellor gave his slave an inquiring look. Really—he would have been free, if only a stingy old uncle had come out with the money.

"I heard it from the mate on the fuste they took to Lango last week. He is from Galata like me. He is not strong so he was sold and Don Esteban bought him. We met when I went there with the clementines.

The Chancellor smiled sternly.

"Really, you go and chat in the kitchen. That virtual little spy center? You know that that is forbidden."

"Yes, Lord. And that you would have done the same in my shoes."

"You say more than is wise. And precisely what I am thinking. What will you give for your freedom?"

"Lord, the common usually pay a thousand aspri."

"For simple people, yes. But you are rich."

"Then I will give double."

The Chancellor gave him a quick glance. This was not the normal bargain. Just as well—he was short on time, as always.

"And then I ask. When can you pay?"

"Lord that is the problem. Only you can free it to me. I have to travel to Constantinople."

"Impossible. Why?"

"They think that I am dead. If I don't emerge now, then one of my half cousins and his half brother will come and collect the inheritance. Kadin will take most of it. But if I come home, the matter is clear and I will come back with the money myself. I swear it on the prophet."

The Chancellor sat unsettled and looked out the window. What was this? A very unusual request. An unusually transparent swindle, so transparent that it just might be the truth.

What should he do? Ask Don Esteban to interrogate his new cook? Try to control what he says? If he still says anything.

He looked at the Turk. Calm as always, superior and secure in his paradise and his better religion.

Better? That could be tested. This was the occasion.

"Ibrahim, I accept your offer and I trust you. You give me your oath on the prophet that you will come back in four months and have the money with you. And if you do not have the money together, then you come back without it and stay in my service until it is paid off. Clear?"

The Chancellor sat quiet for a while. The slave had gone, maybe with just a hint of new vigor in his long stride.

Better religion? We will see. It is worth the risk.

August 1521

JANNIS, THE COOK ON the Grand Carrack stood and prepared lunch in the burning heat of August. The powerful ship, the Queen of the Mediterranean, headed with a fresh west wind to Nice, accompanied by three small caravels like puppies behind a St. Bernard. Yesterday, she left Marseille heavy laden with cannonballs instead of stone for ballast, splendid bronze cannons stored in the cargo hold, and every conceivable nook and cranny stuffed with lead shot and sacks of saltpeter, metal helmets, harquebuses, barrels of sulfur, and vats of wine—and to top it all off there was the new Grand Master's personal property. His Eminence, brother Phillippe de l'Isle Adam himself was onboard.

So Jannis wanted to make his very best lunch. It was Friday, a day of fasting, and the crew's bean soup boiled in huge kettles. But Jannis wanted to give his new Grand Master something better. He thought about preparing marides, small deep fried fish to delight his Grand Master and earn himself some well-deserved recognition.

Jannis stood dipping the fingerling fish with a ladle into the oil that simmered and bubbled in a three-foot pot of burning coals in the huge sandbox on the deck right where the forecastle stood like a tower with its two cannon decks shaded by a large wood bow directly over Janis's sandbox—that was the only place open fire was allowed on board.

The oil hissed and sputtered, and the intensive smell enticed a circle of spectators, sailors from Rhodes and Lango, the enlisted people from Zaragoza and Flanders, and then the perpetually hungry and omnipresent little hired hands, who kept the ship's cabin tidy, but most of the time had to keep out so that the lords would be able to deliberate undisturbed.

Naturally, they spoke about the Grand Master. What kind he was. "An unlucky one," said one of the Spaniards. "Decent but scrupulous," said the cabin boy, who after these two days knew that he had an envied expert knowledge.

"There is no one I would rather have next to me if the Turks board," said one of the sailors. "But he is an unlucky man," the Spaniard persisted. "Just look at the caravel we should have had with us. Just finished and just off the land in the midst of the Rhone. And immediately it leaked and sank to the bottom like a stone."

He shook his head.

"Muy malo. He who has commanded should have his turn. It is almost the most important."

Some of the Italians nodded: cartivo augurio, spiteful warning.

The talk continued while the Grand Carrack heaved in the sea as it began to get rough. The long projecting forecastle raised its nose like a swordfish to the sky only to dive under the white caps the next second. One needed good sea legs to keep his balance. The cook did not have good sea legs. He lurched forward. He tried to stand with the ladle in the pot. It turned over and the boiling oil spread out over the coal fire, continuing like a flood of hissing flames out over the deck. This set sticks of wood on fire along with ropes and rags, which unaccustomed feet stumbled over and dragged with them, and oakum that the artillery had left after their last salute. A short ell hung above the cook's laundry, dry and fine, just ready to be taken down and right above a flagstaff. In a second it was all swept up in crackling flames. The wind blew the flames over and up into the castle. There was new oakum there, ready for next time it was needed. There was also a little barrel of gunpowder, only enough for two shots but still sufficient to make a fireworks show of spurting fire brooms, circling splinters, and sooty rags of old sail cloth.

The whole fore cabin was now swept up in belching sulfuric smoke. The fire climbed up the starboard's shroud to the foresail's top. The shroud had just received new cranks, clean, dry, and newly tarred with no salt crust. Flames hopped playfully between them and climbed quickly up the mast.

Screaming men were forced into the cabin's forebill. They threw their arms up, shielding their faces from the heat. One soldier who could swim jumped overboard on the portside where one of the following boats was already closing in to help. Two others threw off their gear to follow.

"Stop there!"

The men looked up. It was a voice that demanded immediate obedience. All obeyed.

"No one leaves the boat without my order. If anyone jumps in the ocean he will stay there."

The screaming and running men were still. It was the Grand Master himself who stood there with one foot on the portside rail and the other on the deck so that he hung out over the planking, visible to all. He waved.

"All men here! With all the buckets and pails you have. Get the cannon sponges too and all the water and sand bags. Start going already! Haven't you seen worse fires?"

They had, all who had been around a few years. They had seen clay pots with naphtha come sailing through the air and slam down on the cabin deck like hissing volcanoes of flames and smoke. They had put them out with water and sand, with shovels and wet sails, or threw them over board. Most of them they managed to put out.

So it was this time. The Grand Master got five men up in the mast. After them followed cloth pails and wood buckets fastened in the flag halyards, and water soon flooded down the sail. There it boiled and sputtered and put out the flames. The deck was washed, burning rubbish was pushed overboard, gunpowder firkins were secured, and cannon sponges were hung heavy and soaking wet over glowing wood and burning ropes.

When the fire was extinguished, there was an immediate investigation. Jannis sat there weeping with a handful of prepared fish in a tattered wood plate, and the rest strewn about in the sandbox and on the deck, sooty and burnt black. He confessed without excuse. After a little circumlocution the truth about the oakum on the deck came out too. The Grand Master looked around.

"Who is the Master Bombardier in the cabin?"

"I am, Your Eminence."

"Ah, you, Sangallo. It has been you for quite some time. Weren't you the first shot before?"

"Yes, Your Eminence."

"Well, now you are the first shot again. Francesco Fontano is Maestro. We'll see if he can keep better order around the men."

The Grand Master had already put his foot on the steps to go up into the cabin when he remembered Jannis.

"Let me taste your fish . . . Not bad. But God has created this kind of fish for dry land. And this he has done for you also, Jannis, maybe for one of the auberges. We'll see when we get to Rhodes. From now on, give me bean soup like the others."

They all cleaned, scrubbed, spliced, and prepared, and started talking again.

"He has no equal," said one of the old men.

"But he is an unlucky man," said the Spaniard. "And, what's more, we began this trip on an unlucky day. You should know what it says in the stars."

"You speak like the heathen. Why do we have the saints?"

"I will light a candle to Saint Nicolo in Nice; you will see that it helps."

But it didn't seem to help. They passed Corsica and put Sardinia safely behind them. But then it began. Over toward Sicily storm clouds began to tower above the sea, higher and blacker the closer they came. The wind allowed no escape from the bad weather. It loomed a wide bank on the horizon and the winds pulled everything to it. By the fourth hour, it was as dark as a winter-twilight.

It had been thundering on the horizon for an hour now, and the lightning lit up the bank of clouds in front of them. Now the sea began to crash against them. The clouds drew closer, a curtain of white smoke against the background of a bluish-black wall of clouds. They slowly pushed their way forward. La Gran Carracca looked as if it would poke the clouds with its high masts.

The captain gave the order to take in the sails in good time. It was a heavy job. The great sail was three times as long as the deck was wide mid-ship, and thick as a mast. It needed two winches to lower it. There were only a few ells remaining on deck when the lightning fell. How much, no one knew. It only hissed, blinded, and burned so that men beat with unconscious convulsion. The brown hands around the winches let go of their grip. The pole fell breaking down across the deck. The men lay around knocked over and angry. It was worse in the stern castle. It had three stories there: the half deck, cabin deck, and poop deck; at the very top, like a crown on a leaning tower, was the Grand Master's cabin. Smoke seemed to engulf it. It looked like certain death for anyone inside.

But the door opened and the Grand Master came out. He ran across the poop deck to the stairs, reaching for his sword belt and sword that he always wore in service. He gripped the handle firmly and stopped, stunned. Lifting the sling, he stared at the mutilated blade. It was broken about a hand's width down the from the hand guard. He ran ahead with the stump sheathed, swinging again down the steps to the next deck, continuing over to where the injured lay without thinking about it.

But there were many who came to know what he was holding in his hand. The men whispered about it while they carried away their dead in the pouring rain. The lightning had broken the Grand Master's sword to pieces, just as they do when they deprive a man of his knighthood. This was now the third and worst warning.

"Brother Giovanni . . . What do you think of this?"

The Grand Master had called his chaplain. The danger was over. The storm went north, La Gran Carracca was still seaworthy, the eight dead men lay shrouded between the rows of cannon on the baggage deck, and there on the table lay the sword split in three places next to the undamaged sheath. You could still see the family l'Isle Adams shield whose motto read: Pour la Foy.

The Grand Master looked at the priest with his clear light blue eyes and asked again:

"What should I make of this, Brother Giovanni?"

The chaplain looked at the sword. When words came, it seemed as if he was stalling for time.

"First, you ought to give thanks as always."

"I have done that. Thanked God that the ship didn't catch fire, that the gunpowder didn't explode, that the lightning cracked around me and not at me . . . but then?"

Ships of the Mediterranean around 1520

"Then you should ask yourself if you needed a warning."

"I have been thinking about that too, just that. Do you believe He is telling me something in particular here?"

"What do you think, brother Grand Master?"

With some trouble the Grand Master had finally persuaded the Chaplain not to say, "Your Eminence" when they were together in private. Now he said Fra Gran Maestro instead, or Frater Magne Magister when they spoke in Latin.

Now it was the Grand Master who stalled before he answered.

"First, I don't think this will end well. Most on board believe the same. But if it is so—should we turn around? Should I abdicate myself?"

"Stop!" the chaplain said. "You can't question that. He who has received an office such as brother Grand Master's has received it from God. He cannot abdicate himself from such an office."

"But then why did He let the caravel sink by the bridge in Vienne? Why did He let fire break out on the ship? Why did He cast lightning on us today? God certainly has something to do with that? Or did the devil do it?"

"Possibly both."

"But isn't that impossible?"

"On the contrary, that is what most often happens in the world. God and the devil play chess. We are the pieces. But we are neither completely white nor black. In every heart there is a chessboard where God and the devil play."

"There are many pieces to keep them busy."

"And precisely for that reason, it is so hard for us to follow the game. Occasionally, God makes a move that we can't understand. In order to check something only He sees coming. Or to get into a position only He can exploit. Up until the end, all the small pieces stand together trying to discern what is happening in the big scheme of things."

"Do you mean that the devil had something to do with the play today? Though God took it home in the end?"

"Something like that."

"But you said it could be a warning. For what?"

"That you will have to find out yourself, Brother Grand Master, possibly to believe that everything is in line and clear if only we stay on God's side. Though we just then found ourselves in middle of the worst crossfire."

"Do you mean by that that I should continue calmly?"

"Calmly isn't quite the right word, but so as one travels in God's hand with fear and trembling and yet confident like the disciples in Jerusalem. Without really knowing what would happen. *Praecedabat Jesus et sequentes temebant*, it is written. Jesus went ahead and the disciples followed after trembling. It is a miracle that they followed when He went ahead."

There was a knock at the door. The Grand Master nodded to his chaplain to go, only saying:

"Thank you, Brother Giovanni. I think I will follow Him."

Kort-Oglu

"**S**TILL NOTHING . . ."

Young André Barel said what everyone else was thinking. He was only eighteen, gangly but strong, sun-tanned and even leaner since he started on this long voyage over three weeks ago—the first long voyage of his young life. After three weeks he had finally overcome his seasickness. He came aboard the Grand Carrack in Marseille in the company of a knight named Jean Chalant to whom his father entrusted him. Now he was traveling to Rhodes to ask for admission into the celebrated Order of St. John of Jerusalem. His family tree was in the chest that he sat on, cautiously rolled up in a piece of blue silk with all the fine genealogy and all the coat of arms neatly illuminated in court colors and with all the forefathers' and mothers' high-sounding names and titles printed under the coat of arms. This was the first thing he would do in Rhodes, bow his angular teenage nose to the stone floor, kiss the Chancellor's hand, and humbly ask to have his pure noble birth tested and confirmed.

He had rested up a few days on land in Siracusa where the little flotilla went to repair its damages after the bad weather and storm. The first days on the ground his legs continued to heave and sink under his feat. Now he was sitting again on this seesawing ship deck. Like the others, he had made himself a place to sleep here on the half deck in front of the cabin on top of some chests with a knocked over barrel at the head and a cannon carriage to brace his feet against when the boat rolled. He was tired and beaten black and blue, but he hadn't puked once yet. He was proud of that. He wasn't the only one who found it hard to sleep either. But it was more concern about Kort-Oglu than the seafaring that kept most of them awake.

Even before they left Siracusa, it was rumored that Kort-Oglu was waiting in ambush with all his complete flotilla of pirates somewhere between Morea and Crete. Kort-Oglu worked with the Sultan, just as there were the privateers that worked with The Order of St. John and therefore had a free city in Rhodes. There was a perpetual sea war in these waters—and the remaining waters from Syria to Algiers—a war Kort-Oglu controlled masterfully. With his quick galleys, most of them small light fustes with possibly twenty pairs of oars, he would wait in ambush behind points and sweep forward in white lines of whipped up foam, like a flock of flying seagulls, with seasoned artillery manning the cannon and enlisted men shaking with eagerness like a pair of hunting dogs.

"Still nothing . . . "

He was suddenly quiet, and looked troubled. They sat here on the half deck, where one could just barely peek under the great sail and follow the horizon over in the east. Maybe he shouldn't have betrayed himself. But none of the others smiled. There sat Antoine de Golart, who was only a few years older than he was, but was already completing his three years in the caravan. He had been kind and friendly from the beginning. You could ask him about anything, even those things you were ashamed of not knowing. He had attained a lot of useful information from him. Now he knew that a "Grand Cross" was a high official and not some sort of decoration. He knew how the eight langues were connected and what caravan meant—that a caravan was really a year of combat duty at sea, but that in everyday talk any time spent on a warship was called a caravan. Chevalier Chalant sat next to Golart. Chevalier Chalant was the middle-aged Auvergnat, who would serve as his patron. He was broad shouldered, stocky, and swarthy with dark penetrating eyes. His forehead had two deeply crossed wrinkles at the root of the nose. He commanded immediate respect and a person feared to betray his ignorance around him.

None of them had changed their expression. The third man in the group, the lawyer Fonteyn, who also came on board in Marseille, made no secret of the fact that he was ready. He was Flemish, a learned man with double chin, pale face, and well dressed.

It was the lawyer who took up the thread, as usual, with a Latin cliché. He liked to speak Latin, highly ornate humanist Latin.

"*Quam mutabilis fortuna!* Who could believe it? In Bruges they said that La Gran Carracca was the biggest, and best equipped of all the world's warships . . . "

"Not the biggest anymore," said Chevalier Chalant expertly. "She was when we took her, but since then the Portuguese have built Santa Catarina do Monte Sinai, and the English their Henry Grace à Dieu. They are the biggest now. At least until we have Saint Anne finished."

"Let's go for number three then," the Lawyer said irritated. "And yet we are still sitting here afraid of some small Turkish pirates."

There was something about his nearsighted eyes that made it hard for others to tell who he was talking to. He looked smug as if he had just caught a lying evildoer contradicting himself. The Auvergnat looked at him amused.

"One shouldn't be afraid, Lord Doctor. But war is a risky business. We are heavy-laden, a little too heavy. We only have sails and are dependent on the wind. They have both sails and oars. If the wind stops, they have every advantage on their side. They can take us from the front and then we have nothing to answer them with. If we are able to successfully turn broadside, they only have to row out of range of our cannon and turn back. Then we will have them right in front of us again. Just like dogs grabbing hold of a wild boar that can no longer run."

"But the wind is blowing briskly now. Straight west, right?"

"Fortunately, Lord Doctor. But it is the sixth of September and the winds can no longer be trusted."

A fifth came over and joined the group, Sir Thomas Pemberton, an Englishman, an old and experienced galley captain. He had overheard what they were talking about.

"What way do you think he is going?"

"With the course we are now on I'd have to say we are taking the outer route. South around Cerigo—which you see," said the Auvergnat, holding one hand out to the sinking sun and the other in the boat's longitudinal direction, looking in the angle between them.

Pemberton nodded.

"So he too thinks that the Turks are waiting in the sound."

The sound was the passage by Kap Maleas north of Cerigo. It was the shortest way between Italy and Rhodes.

"But an old fox like Kort-Oglu certainly hasn't taken it for granted that we will take the shortest route. If I know him, he is already addressing the matter."

"I have had a lot of dealings with Turks," the Englishman continued thoughtfully. "You can't find better people to have at the oars. They toil and work quietly. Syrians and Egyptians are hopeless. They will always talk, discuss, and object. It doesn't matter how much you beat them . . .

And we won't talk about blacks. If they sit in cold water just one afternoon, they will catch a cold and die. No, give me Turks any day."

The Frenchmen looked amused.

"It almost sounds as if brother would rather be on the other side with
the Sultan, the way he is so infatuated with Turks."

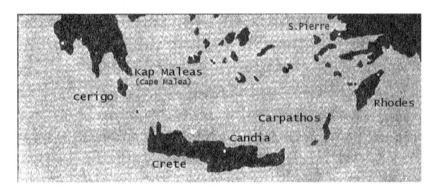

"I said as slaves. If I were there, I couldn't have any Turks rowing for
me."

"Are you sure?" Asked the Frenchman. "It is rumored that Kort-
Oglu mans his galleys with nothing but Turks, free willing people who
fight when there is battle and collect their share of the booty."

The Englishman looked almost indignant.

"If that is true, then it is really bad. In that way they could carry twice
as many soldiers in a galley as we can. And we can't demand real soldiers
to sit next to rowers. That would be like demanding them to cut and carry
stones!"

It looked as if the Frenchman was thinking hard about something,
but he was interrupted.

"Sails over there, off the portside!"

The lookout's loud voice bellowed from the top of the great mast.
The Captain's rough base voice was heard from the cabin.

"How many?"

"Five or Six."

At the same time, the Grand Master's gray grizzled beard stuck out
over the rail. He glanced over the half deck.

"Chevalier Pemberton," he yelled. "Do me the service of going up to
take a look. Then report back to me."

He didn't say: don't yell so that the whole boat hears it. But Pemberton knew immediately what he meant. He sprang up on the sail and climbed passed the topsail continuing up along the rope steps to the eagle's nest. In a second he stood with both elbows over the sail's upper edge. They could see his head swing back and forth like a black spot against the light evening clouds with a touch of red around the edges. Then he came back down and ran past them up the steps to the half deck. It was a good hour before he came back.

"Well?"

"Maybe two fustes and a brigantine. You could barely see their tops. They were not merchant vessels."

"Where were they going?"

"Turning. Northwards."

He didn't say anything else. It was enough information for the older men. The younger men were able to guess. Only the lawyer asked.

"Did they see us?"

"Hope so," Pemberton said dryly. Both the lawyer and the young ones looked at him amazed, but they didn't want to ask any more. The Englishman smiled contentedly and rubbed his long wiry hands slowly.

Chalant nodded.

"Of course they saw us, like the finest engraving in the evening sky long before we saw them, just as they planned."

André Barel looked at his friend Golart perplexed. But he couldn't see what they were apparently so happy about either. The lawyer muttered something in Latin like *gladiatores isti sanguinem semper sitientes*— gladiators are always thirsting for blood. Pemberton still looked content.

The little flotilla continued on the same course, southeast to east. The sails were set for the starboard tack. The last orange red daylight glowed in the west.

Someone struck the bell outside the cabin three times. It was a call to gather for Compline up on the cabin deck where the little travel altar was ready. All the knights and the serving brothers climbed the steps like monks. The daily hours were obligatory and a matter of routine for them. Young André Barel followed and so did the lawyer. The chaplain turned around with the stole over his shoulders. The Grand Master was already standing in his place to the right of the altar. It was very quiet on board while they read their confessions and received absolution. Many of the men down on the deck bowed their knees amidst all the clutter and crossed themselves. They knew that they stirred in dangerous waters.

It was almost dark. The small oil lamps on the altar were screened so that they could not be seen on the sea. No one was able to read anything in their light. It wasn't needed. As so often before on this trip, André Barel was amazed that these weather-beaten knights could remember so much Latin by heart. They managed psalms and responses with the same ease and comfort as formation and morning reveille. This was a side of knighthood that he didn't think much about. He was inclined to leave the liturgy entirely up to priests.

After the blessing, the Grand Master gave the orders for the night. Everyone would sleep at their post with weapons and battle gear within reach. Cannons and harquebusiers would be kept loaded. Sailors would await further orders. He wished all a good night and asked them to try to sleep now in the evening.

Everyone went to their places. It squeaked and creaked when heavy chests were moved on the deck. Buckets dipped into the splashing waves and were hauled up again. The deck was cleaned up behind the cannons to give them free room to recoil, and the artillery went to sleep on the exposed deck planks.

The lords slept on their baggage where they spread out their cloaks. The young Barel couldn't get the question off his mind:

"Did he plan to battle when we rounded Cerigo? Or did he figure we would get ahead of Kort-Oglu?"

Chevalier Chalant answered a little curtly.

"You will see. He knows what he is doing. Keep your eyes open so you can learn a thing or two."

The young one was quiet and tried to sleep. But just when he was about to fall asleep, he was awakened by an order and padded steps. Then the blocks creaked and screeched in the racks and rigging high above his head. Against the starry sky, he could see how the heavy yard swung around the mast. The wind that had come in from the starboard quarter—he had learned that one never said "askew from behind"—now came from the portside. They must have changed course from southeast to northeast, provided that there wasn't any wind coming from the northwest.

He looked at the stars. That wasn't it. Polaris stood there where it should. Something he had learned on his first sea trip.

The day dawned mother of pearl pale with a little hint of red. The wind blew fresh. When he searched the horizon, the sea lay open forever, but off the stern he could see land on both sides with a wide sound in between. Chevalier Chalant was already awake. He looked at the closest land to the north.

"Kap Maleas," was the only thing he said.

The young André Barel understood. They had taken the shortest route, through the sound where Kort-Oglu ought to have waited. He looked around again, long and hard. There wasn't a sail to be seen. Where was Kort-Oglu?

There was only one explanation. He was somewhere outside the south point off Cerigo with a cordon of patrols sent down to Crete so as not to let anyone get by them. He must have gotten a report of the Grand Carrack's course yesterday evening, which the Grand Master had since changed!

"Was that why we waited so long to change course? Until it was dark?"

Chalant looked at him smiling.

"Precisely. You have to be careful you don't have evening skies off the stern, you see. All you need is just a little pale streak down on the horizon to be seen. You can be sure they had a little fuste out there that kept a lookout on us from as far away as possible. Had we changed course a minute too soon, Kort-Oglu would have been warned. Now he is looking for us near Crete."

"Tricky calculation," said the young man.

"Yet it seems so simple. But do you know what the best part is? That we were just at the right point, right when it got dark, so that we could change course. Remember that we took in the topsail and bonnett at one o'clock yesterday?

"I thought that was because it was blowing so hard."

"Not at all. We had cleared the wind. It was only that we had traveled too well. We would have come so close to land that we had to promise to stay on course before it was dark enough. These are things a person has to know how to do if he wants to give Kort-Oglu the slip."

"But what if we hadn't passed by their reconnaissance boats and not waited to be seen?"

"Then you have to have a sixth sense. Those who have it become the best commanding officers, and Philippe Villiers has it."

La Mogharbine

SPIRITS RAN HIGH ONBOARD. It was already afternoon. The wind blew just as hard and favorably. There wasn't a trace of Kort-Oglu to be seen and with every hour they came closer to Rhodes. With this wind, one ought to be home in less than two days.

"Monseigneur Saint Jean kept his hand over us, it shows."

"He has always done that well. Look only . . . "

Chevalier Chalant made a gesture to the north.

"Turkish the whole way ever since Modon fell. It was the last the Venetians had left on the mainland. Not one cat escaped with his life. Now all is Turkish all the way to Hungary and the corners of Venice. Cerigo and some other poor small islands are all they have left, and mostly thanks to us."

"But, of course, the Venetians have Cyprus," objected the lawyer.

"Which they have to pay tribute for. True to my word. They try to keep it secret, but they do it already and negotiate. The Grand Turk is likely to demand fifty thousand ducats a year. He already counts it as halfway his, and that they will learn soon enough."

"And look at the other places," he continued. "They have Crete left, the only one that they really can control in these waters. But then it is nothing but Turkish lands all about. Syria, Egypt, and Cyrenaica, and Algeria since Barbarossa has made himself secure there. We alone are left. Only we have a foot in Asia's ground in Saint Pierre. We alone still do what we want. Still there—two days trip from here with good wind."

He looked as he thought at the horizon in the east where the sea spread itself out dark blue and endless.

"Certainly the Baptist has his hand over us."

There they had turned one of the chests on the half deck around and chewed their evening ration. Young André Barel felt accepted and ventured forward with the question that he had held onto for long time.

"Say, Chevalier, how did the Religion really manage to take this boat from the Turks?"

"It came from the Sudan of Egypt, boy. There weren't any Turks on board and it might have been just as well. The Sudanese built her in a shipyard in Tunis. This is how she came to be called Mogharbine. It means "Daughter of the Evening Land." or something along those lines. At that time she was the world's biggest boat, a little clumsy, to tell the truth, with seven decks. It was too high in the poop and bad for tacking. But well built: nothing but oak, teak, and copper rivets. She was to carry spices from Alexandria. Most of the time, she went either to Tunis or Venice only a couple trips a year. D'Aubusson already had his eye out for her when we were feuding with Egypt, but he wasn't able to get in sight of her. Then d'Aubusson became Grand Master and he gave Jacques Gastineau command of la gran nave. At the time, our carrack really wasn't much to brag about. Then Gastineau picked up the scent. When he was home-bound south of Crete, he learned that there was something to retrieve closer to Africa and set the course for there. Everyone onboard was upset because we wanted to go home."

"Were you yourself on board, Chevalier?"

"Yes, of course, it was my second caravan year. We had been out so long that the water began to seem endless, and we all yearned for fresh meat and fresh baked bread. Our Greek pilots also thought that it was pointless to hunt after something down by Africa's coast at that time of year when all the big boats have to try move up to Karamia in order to take advantage of the northeast wind. So it was better to set out for home to Rhodes and stay there and wait. But Gastineau wouldn't listen at all."

"The next morning we heard mass as usual. Afterwards, Gastineau prayed his own prayer of thanks as always and no one was to disturb him during that time. But I did. I had the watch, and what did I see if not a whole mountain of sails climbing up out of the sea, almost like Stromboli or Etna. When I finally made the report the whole crew hung over the rails and stared at the monster."

Gastineau stepped calmly up from the deck, looked and said: "Yes, there we have her. So he called attention and gave a speech in his own way. 'It is with such great carracks as it is with heaven,' he said. 'They are troublesome to capture, but it is worth the trouble. But we need to hurry. This is why I have driven you so hard.'"

"And he really had. For the whole trip, we had to constantly set the sails and go over to another tack. And if it didn't go far enough, then we had at least gone over the maneuvers."

"'And now we will show them what we can do,' he said."

"The wind blew south and La Mogharbine beat as near as she could to the wind, apparently on her way to Tunis. She was pretty slow. We laid ourselves in on the windward side, and waited. Gastineau put out the ship's boat, and sent his best man—d'Ecluzeaux was his name—to speak with the Egyptians. I had the honor of going along. It was completely exhilarating to climb up on this cargo-boat for the first time. None of us had seen anything like it. We thought we stood on the great tower in Rhodes when we came up on deck, and we felt very small. All around us stood Mamluks and artillery with drawn sabers, and none bid us welcome. Then we finally saw that they had at least three times the people we had. We passed through between the curved blades and came up to the cabin deck. Right where we have the altar now, the captain waited with the first mate, the Mamluks' Aga, the commander of the artillery, and all the other cultured people they had on board. The sun reflected off their turbans, scabbards, and silver braids, and the gold work shined in their heavy tunics. But they were ill equipped to fight. D'Ecluzeaux bowed politely and gave them greetings from his chief saying that we had orders to bring La Mogharbine to Rhodes, and that it would all be much easier if they cooperated by not giving him any trouble so that he didn't have to take any drastic actions. The unbelievers were almost taken aback, but the captain, who was a fine old gentleman, gave a long speech that was interpreted for us. He had served his Lord of the Sudan for all of his reign, which Allah measured to continue for a hundred years, and although unfathomably unworthy to remain in the service of such a brilliant lord, he had been entrusted with command of the most impressive vessel that ever sailed on a sea. He would rather be dressed in women's clothes and take orders from a eunuch than abdicate such an honor. And that he was not at all intimidated by an infidel pirate's tub, which compared to his Mogharbine was no more than a rusted and tattered tin bucket beside the marble well in front of the Sultan's Palace. Yes—it is only some of what he said. We bowed, thanked him, and said that we would carry his beautiful words with us as long as we could keep them in memory, that we wished that his beard would grow and his shadow not diminish and other such platitudes. All this took a very long time and that was the purpose. For now, Gastineau had come as close as he wanted. When we climbed down to our boat, we gave the agreed upon signal with a red cloth that meant that the Egyptians wanted to fight. At the same moment all the sails took in wind again and then I saw the most beautiful maneuver I have ever seen anyone do with a boat. She came down on the Egyptians with full speed from the windward side opposite their bow, luffed a little to the starboard side and fired a broadside from the portside. This broadside beat to pieces the planking along their deck and demolished the battery that had the best chance of reaching us. The Egyptians, it seems, had expected that Gastineau would pick us up first, or, for whatever reason, they waited—in any case they were not clear to fire and then they were completely engulfed in the black smoke that came down on them. Within the cloud, Gastineau now made a cross turn to port just as swiftly and surely as we had trained, and, when the smoke began to disperse, he came along side the Grand Carrack. Now he was only a few fathoms from her with the whole starboard's broadside directed at the sundered cannon deck. We had come so close that the Egyptians could not train their cannons in the castle on us because they were much too high and our boat was so much lower. It continued to go that way, and they were so astounded that they gave up, and it was good for them that we did not have to shoot a broadside through the tattered planking straight into the crowded throng on deck. But though they capitulated, we did not board until they handed over all their commanders to us. They still had three times as many as us. Then we boarded her, disarmed the Mamluks, and took command of the sailors. I am one of the first in Christendom to have walked this deck because I went to the leaders when we first went to negotiate with them."

"And then?"

"Yes, it wasn't bad returning to Rhodes. No one on board whined any longer to Gastineau because he drove us so hard. She was worth approximately a whole year's income from out of our order's property. The captain was himself joint owner. He had bound himself to deliver these wares within a certain time, and so that he would not wind up in disrepute, he tried to buy them back from us. He didn't get them for the going price. He grieved himself sick over that."

"But those were really fortunate times, when we had one Sultan in Cairo and another in Constantinople. Now we have Grand Turks in both places, and it is not for the better. We got along pretty good with the small row we had with the old Camsoun-Gauri and his Mamluks."

"And then we renovated her. It was good that we took her with the rigging unscathed. She had bowlines, gigantic ropes, and tack that we had never seen before. If it had been piled all together in one big heap on deck, I wonder if we ever would have sorted it out. Now we have lowered the poop and strengthened the forward castle. We also took away one of the decks under the water line so that one can go straight down in there. Then we placed Monseigneur Saint Jean and the other saints on the back wall in the place of their tortuous heathen doodling. She has now served us faithfully for fifteen years, smelled a lot of gunpowder, and taken a few hits."

Chevalier Jean Chalant was quiet and looked thoughtfully to the east where a new night prepared to climb up out of the sea.

So he said:

"This will be her last trip for a year. I wonder just where she will sail next."

September 11

PISKOPI, KHALKI, ATAVIROS, SIMI . . .

The whole morning they had hung on the railing while Antoine de Golart pointed out islands and mountains as they all emerged. Now they followed the coast of Rhodes. It felt wonderfully calm to be within Christendom again, just like home waters.

Young André Barel examined the beach and landscape with watchful eyes: white villages, yellow gray castles, lots of forest, remarkably green. It was the eleventh of September.

As they followed the coast, a new mountain chain emerged from the sea in the north, away from the island Simi, closer to Rhodes than any other land.

"And there, what is that?"

"Turkish land," answered Golart. "It is the outer most point of Crimea. Behind the furthest point you see is the bay of Marmaris. They have a fine harbor there. It's called Fisco. That is where they came from in 1480."

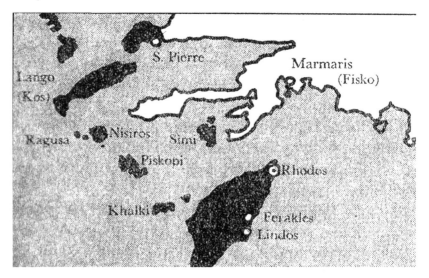

"How long does it take to get from there to here?"

"Four hours with good wind. From when they round Cape Marmaris so that we see them."

Doctor Fonteyn, the lawyer, appeared hesitant.

"Do you mean, my young friend, that the Turks can get to us within four hours warning?"

"Precisely, Lord Doctor. Here on Rhodes we never know if we have more than four hours of peace. A great invasion force cannot be gathered without us knowing it, but small raids on our coast are always possible. So we always have the people prepared and the watchtowers manned. But see—the capitan is coming!"

His experienced eyes had just discovered her behind the point. Far off by the north point, a sandbank peeked out, and some red standards with white crosses could be seen moving behind it. Just in front of its black nose was the fearful ram capped with a wolf head of bronze. The colorful cannon brigade followed the arrumbada, then the thirty-one pairs of oars that sank in the water and lifted again with absolute precision. Over the oar beam fluttered a row of banners all red with white crosses, and finally came the poop deck with its red silk tent and snapping streamer. She was a grand bird who pranced with surging plumage and floating magnificent feathers. Red banners, golden-bordered standards, and long two-tongued streamers spread out in the wind from the yardarm, the top of the mast, and the flagpole.

After the flagship, the other galleys came. Cannons on the ramparts shot salutes, and The Grand Carrack with its small followers responded by flying all flags going to the top. Rhodes received her Grand Master.

They rounded the huge sandbar at the point and turned down to the harbor on the other side. In a moment Antoine Golart had more to explain and to point out to the lawyer and young André Barel than he could keep up with. They had heard enough spoken about this remarkable city, Christendom's strongest hold within the Turkish sea, but even so they had not yet experienced it. It was a very modern city, newly built with walls of lion yellow limestone shimmering in the sun. The towers and courts, moats and outer works all shined of good health and good maintenance. Defense works climbed powerfully and commandingly up from the slope to the crest where the Grand Master's palace lifted her crenellated tower.

The harbor was like a round lake flanked by forts and watchtowers, surrounded by a high wall, and closed off by an immense chain that crept up like a black snake out of the deep and disappeared in through the dark hall at the foot of a slender tower that lifted itself high over the city.

And what a colorful display! All the wall crests, all the jetties, all the wharfs were crammed with people in their most joyous and colorful Sunday clothes. They waved and screamed *Eviva!* and swung their hats. The women trilled high joyous trills like they were at a wedding reception. The trumpets clattered, the church bells rang, and the cannons thundered from the walls.

Outside Fort Saint Nicolas, which rested alone out in the blue sea standing authoritatively and sunlit and bulging with cannons, La Gran Carrack let her anchor go. The capitan backed up to her. A ladder was let down and the Grand Master stepped down and came onboard. He was received by his acting deputy, brother Gabriel de Pomerolx. The gong sounded and the rowers rowed again in perfect time against the water while the slender galley glided into the harbor.

The Grand Master sat and looked out before him. They had laid out a long wood bridge over the shallow water in front of Porta Marina and decorated it with cloth of various colors as was customary for the landing of high lords. The Grand Master followed it with his eyes. Was it not a pair of ells longer than normal, longer than it had been in former years?

"Say, Pomerolx, has the harbor silted in again even more?"

"Yes, Your Eminence, that is a fact."

The acting deputy looked unhappy, almost guilty as if it were his fault.

"Tell the harbor Marshall that I want a report. Let me see . . . Tuesday morning."

Yes so it was. In years past he had only announced whether or not La Gran Carrack had scraped bottom when it came in heavy-laden. Then he found others to take responsibility for the matter. Now it was he himself who had to do it. He was the Grand Master.

They stepped down on the bridge. The noise was now deafening. The salute cannons sprayed out new fire brooms. Hats, handkerchiefs, and Spanish cloaks waved from the tops of all the walls. The noise even drowned out the drums and trumpets.

They went through Porta Marina entering the sunshine on the other side. The council waited under the high walls, the Piliers and Grand

Crosses, the Priors of San Giovanni, the Greek Metropolitan, all the clerics, both Greeks and Latins, all the knights and representatives of the city's citizens—the merchants, bankers, artisans—Venetians, Genoese, Florentines, French and Greeks, Catalonians and Portuguese.

Bodyguards in red liveries stood in their positions along the long straight street that led up to the upper city along the convent's wall between the barracks. The Grand Master slowly made his way up, greeted at every step by old friends and new faces. Walking through the two towers within the walls, they entered the knights' city amidst new salutes and ovations. Pressing forward through the street, they reached Grand rue right in front of the French auberge, turned to the left and continued up to the castle. But they didn't go in, not yet—first they would celebrate a High mass in San Giovanni.

The Grand Master sat himself in the seat below the throne. Before he took his place there, he would take an oath to govern the Religion's establishment only with the advice of the council to God's glory and in the best interest of the Religion. That would be after the mass, in the grand hall of the palace.

He listened. The Prior, who also was the order's Bishop, celebrated by himself today. It was the Holy Martyrs Prothus and Iacinctus day. Now the Prior chanted the epistle about He who is the Father of Mercy and the God of Comfort, He who comforts us in all our trials so that we can comfort others . . .

"Amen," the Grand Master mumbled. "May it be so, also with me, and through me."

" . . . *Sicut abundat passiones Christi in nobis*," sang the Prior. So that Christ's superabundant suffering comes over us . . . "

Interesting that it was just so that could be felt on a day like this. Most would consider this day the high point of a man's life, the fulfillment of all he could desire. But what he needed most of all today was comfort, strength, and something to keep his hand steady. Up till now, he had always had someone over him, someone to give him orders. Now he would give orders. They stood there and waited. They would do as he said—and hold him responsible if anything went wrong. He felt it piling up on himself like a mountain behind all the grandeur, incense, choir singing, crowds of people, and the curious watchers. A mountain that would fall over him as soon as he sat down on the Grand Master's throne in the palace feast hall. They would all come forward and kiss his hand. Then it would all break loose even today. The fortification work, the economic worries, secret reports, inventory reports, lawsuits, roll calls, powers of attorney, letters of safe conduct, death sentences, and appeals for mercy. Pomerolx had already suggested that they had let all the really important business pile up waiting for his return. And in the midst of all this, he would move all his belongings and get his house in order, his huge house. Alone, always alone. He needed Him badly, the Father of Mercy and the God of Comfort.

Hospitaller

CHEVALIER CHALANT CLIMBED UP the wide stairs to the loggia that ran along the upper floor of the Auvergnat auberge. He came from the long ceremony in the palace still gripped by the seriousness of the hour. Even he had kissed his Grand Master's hand as a sign of obedience as he was bound by his oath to his order. They all stood there, possibly three hundred knights in their long black capes with the white eight pointed cross on the left shoulder, and the same right in front on the black jacket. It was a great contrast to the splendor of the prelates and the magnificent attire of the various citizens. They felt as if they were monks and no longer knights.

He opened the door. He had a room here in the auberge. He had tucked his young protégé there, the young André Barel. He could not be part of the festivities in the castle, yet neither could he wander around the city by himself if he wanted to be found suitable for the position of novice. The boy had appeared a little surprised by the strict court of an order of knights. Well—he would learn soon enough.

Chevalier Chalant soon found that the boy had done the wisest thing he could have done while he waited. He stretched himself out and went to sleep. He woke him up and gave him a piece of bread, which he covetously chewed. They had not eaten lunch onboard, and dinner was not served before sometime after the sun went down, right before Compline.

Someone knocked on the outer door. They heard Antoine Golart ask for them.

"I asked him to come," said Chalant explaining.

"I thought you could go out and see the city."

André bowed thankfully, smoothed his jacket out, tightened his belt to stifle his hunger, and followed his friends out to the loggia's terrace down the wide stairway and out into the little square. They were both tall, André Barel still lanky in his teens, angular and jerky in his movements. Golart was fuller with a round, bright, and good-natured face. He already moved with the certainty that came with the experience of leading command. He bore the all black uniform of the Order, and his friend's garb clashed against it with his red jacket and tight fitting blue trousers.

It was beginning to get dark, and a gold colored sky burned above them absent of clouds. They turned to the left, passed by the cathedral, and came out in another little square with a huge tree to the left where sparrows held an evening concert. The stone paving ended down by the seaside so that the square seemed to run out through the borders to the harbor. To the right was a magnificent house with heavy arches over barred black doors. In the middle of the façade, an apse bent out with three windows that looked like they belonged in a chapel. Otherwise, the wall stood shut, windowless and silent.

"What is that?"

"The hospital. Our sick house."

"It looks like a palace."

"Yes, it is also called the Palais des Malades. There we have our lords, the sick. There you will begin at once, if you are accepted."

"There? I thought I would learn to handle bombards and boats."

"With time. With time. But first you must show that you are suitable for it."

"In there?"

The eighteen year old sounded so indignant that his friend began to laugh—a good-natured chuckle that got his light-complexioned face to light up. He tried to sound serious.

"Yes, there. Those who do not learn to obey can never learn to command. He who does not want to serve the sick is not trusted with any other service either. And we are, of course, Hospitallers, you know, servants of Christ's poor."

Young Barel was silent.

"What does one do in there?"

"All sorts of chores. Whatever one is ordered, and if you are asked to do something unpleasant, remember that they watch how you take it. Are you ready to clean vomit, whatever might be coughed up, and filth?"

"I don't know. I have never tried."

He let a thought dampen his spirit.

"How long does one serve there?"

"His whole life. I work there on Tuesday. We all have our turns, the Grand Crosses and the Piliers too. But now let's go down to the city."

He led him through two dark arches among a mess of fortifying walls. Suddenly they stood before the collachium on a lighted street full of shops and people. Above them they could see the two round crested towers of Porta Marina. It looked as if it were a great feast day. All the shops were open. Everything was lighted, not only under the icons but also in all the windows and all counters and tables. In the flickering light, he glimpsed colorfully dressed residents and various jackets with open slit sleeves. The taverns were packed. It smelled of roasted mutton and garlic. Everyone was murmuring, laughing and shouting. They played flutes and fiddles. It was like a great market day.

They made it through the crowd on the great square to the huge building in the back, a dark cube with a wide exterior staircase up to the second floor and a magnificent pillared hall under it.

"Courthouse," declared Antoine. "The maritime court sits in there, those who make judgments concerning things like shipwrecked and captured goods. Above, you have the appeals court. It is there that our friend Fonteyn will serve. And down here is the city's finest meeting place . . . "

He didn't need to say it. Under the arch hung hammered iron chandeliers with a shimmering swarm of small oil lamps. On the stone benches lining the way sat well-dressed lords in a wide array of Italian patterns and with wine, playing cards, and chess pieces in front of them.

Behind the courthouse the street was wider and followed the harbor wall. It was completely lined with shops and taverns. You could hear people singing.

"Spaniards, lively people," Antoine said competently.

They went closer and listened. "Dale, si le das, Mozuela de Carasa . . ."

A drum beat the measure. The voices were rough and hoarse. Suddenly, the drum stopped and a shrill falsetto sang solo, a quickly recited chorus that finished just as suddenly with a long drawn out o-o-o and then continued just as quickly amidst thundering bursts of laughter.

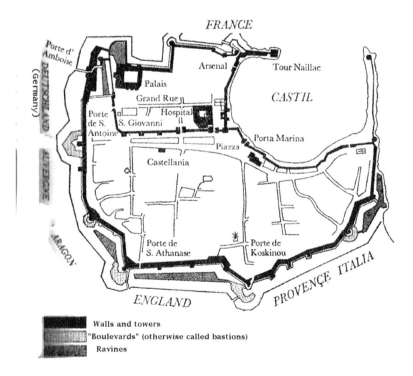

Walls and towers
"Boulevards" (otherwise called bastions)
Ravines

"It is a shameful show. Soon they will only have the indecent half left. Then they will jump over to something else. And so they laugh until the beards loosen up."

Young Barel looked at them. He had heard talk of these Spanish soldiers, King Francis' most colorful opponents.

"Those guys have the reputation of being the world's worst rabble. And yet at the same time the world's best infantry."

"No, we have the best infantry here on the island and on Crete. If I had to hold a castle, I would rather have them than these Spaniards."

They continued on, passing open stands with piles of grapes, watermelons, pomegranates, and eggplants. They went to new taverns with new shows.

"Listen," said Antoine, "There you have our Greeks."

The song came out of an open cellar vault with some coarse wood tables packed full of men in knee length pants and open shirts.

"Seamen from the galleys and our brigantines." Antoine said. "Shall we have a listen?"

They sang in their oriental manner, pensive, in peculiar progressions, with half shut eyes.

"What are they singing?" asked André.

"I don't know . . . But wait!"

He had seen someone in the crowd, a little round man who walked with one foot bent out with an embarrassed look on his face.

"Brother François, good evening!"

"Good evening, Lord Antoine."

He looked a little perplexed. What could they want with him? Didn't he have a right to be here?

"Can I help you with something?"

"Yes you can, brother Françoise, you who are so good at Greek. Can you tell us what they are singing about? Translate it a little for us?"

Shooter-Frans listened a moment, blushed a little and said:

"Lord Antoine, it is a love song."

"Excellent, let us hear what the Greeks sing as a love song. We have just heard the Spaniards."

Shooter-Frans listened again and began to translate right away. Because the song drifted slowly forward with long interludes, he could tolerably keep up.

> O mother . . . do not ask me
> How my beloved looks.
> Who can describe him?
> The women of Venice
> Turn around on the square . . .
> In Genoa they say:
> Where does this man come from?
> When the bell tower toll rings
> From monolithic heights
> He is the most gallant
> Among the Turcopolers.

"What does Turcopoler mean?" asked André Barel soberly.

"Our coast guard, you should know, people from the islands that we train and drill. Thanks, Brother François. It was good to see you again. We meet on Tuesday with our lords, the sick."

He winked at the little man, who gave an embarrassed smile and bowed. Then he started back for the auberge.

"In the beginning the Turcopolers were taught to be our little light cavalry when we fought the Saracens in the Holy Land. They are enlisted. Now it is the Greeks who man the watchtowers and sound the alarm when the Turks make shore raids. The Turcopoler is in charge of them. He is one of the Piliers, always an Englishman. The current one is John Buck. He doesn't think the Turks are coming."

"Aren't coming? Who thinks they are coming?"

"Most of us . . . There you have the current Auberge d'Angleterre where Buck is the Pilier. You can be sure that it is being discussed in there as among all the leaders."

They had come back to the little square by the hospital. The English auberge was directly across from it on the other side.

"And there lives our Grand Hospitaller right in front of the hospital. He is Pilier for our French Langue."

He pointed to the nearest house directly over the lane.

"Is it his weapon that sits up there on the way?" André wondered.

"Oh, you saw that? No, it was a Lord de Melay. He was Hospitaller during d'Aubusson's time but was relieved of duty because he did not appear right away when the Grand Master called in our reserves. It was 1479, when we expected the Turks. Melay didn't take it seriously. He did not believe they would come. But then he also ignited the spark of disobedience. Some Grand Cross he was."

They had come back to Auberge d' Auvergne, where André Barel was registered. The clock in Sainte Marie du Chateau rang seven times above their heads.

"That means it's time for dinner and Compline. Everyone to their barracks, a septaine for those who come late."

"A septaine, what is that?"

"That you will find out. I have done it, and have no desire to do it again. So good night to you."

He disappeared in the dark. Young Barel went up the stone stairs with pensive steps to encounter a new life.

The Alarm

THE TWELFTH OF SEPTEMBER dawned like the rest of the summer days on Rhodes. Long before sunrise, Chevalier Chalant shook life into his protégé and took him to morning mass in San Giovanni. He saw the boy, heavy with sleep and helpless, stagger up Grand rue and stumble up the stairs. Consoling, he said:

"Such is the knight's life, you see. Awake when you want to sleep, go to bed when you would like to be awake, just as they say when we are dubbed knights. But you get accustomed to it."

After the mass they went directly over to the Chancellor's office in the palace. They only met with the vice Chancellor, Policiano, but he received both a hand kiss and papers and promised that the reply would not be long. The Religion needed people, and there was no risk of unnecessary troubles if the papers were in order.

After a breakfast of water, bread, and olives in the auberge, Chevalier Chalant had work in the arsenal and got Antoine Golart to take care of the newcomer again. They saw the Chevalier cross the square and disappear into the arsenal through the ports where no one was let in or out except to work. They themselves got up on the wall that ran all the way around the barracks in order to get a look at the harbor. Today it was almost deserted in Chemin de Ronde around the top of the wall's crest, and one could see the thick breastwork with its embrasures better than yesterday. The city wall was in a half circle around the water. The line of defense continued with a breakwater crowned by a row of mills. Nearest to the window rested a domineering tower with four hanging corner towers up by the foot of the ceiling. That was where the great chain went in.

"That is the Tour de Naillac, named for the Grand Master," Antoine explained.

The harbor was full of ships, all moored along the pier where it was deepest. Antoine began to describe them: "a Genovese, a Portuguese caravel, a galiot from Naples . . . "

He stopped.

"What is this? The two Venetians are still in front of the others, those carracks with blue striped awning and long red streamers on the Bonaventur. They sailed away yesterday afternoon. I saw it myself from the palace. Something must have happened."

They went forward to the long battery that encompassed Tour Naillac with the encircling wall. A compatriot of Antoine's was on watch and they started in. They could see both into the harbor and northwards to the sea and the Turkish lands from there.

The Frenchman confirmed that the Venetians, who carried pilgrims from Jerusalem, had turned back in the morning. But it was only because of the headwind. The captains had sworn unchristian oaths because of their bad luck and provoked both God and Saint Nicholas. Such cargo demanded better treatment.

"At times it is good traveling with a head wind," Antoine said. "Have you seen anything of Kort-Oglu?"

The Frenchman had hardly begun to shake his head before the watch up in Tour Naillac waved his white flag. All was quiet.

The watch did not need to yell what it meant. They all heard. The cannon thunder was weak, but very clear somewhere in the northwest.

In the next second the watchman ran to his bell, and the alarm went. The toll echoed between the walls, and the alarm was taken up by another bell within the arsenal and a third down on the Piazza.

"It is a little alarm," Antoine said. "It is only for the galleys."

They went on to the wall's crest on the inside, to the harbor. There down below lay the galleys side by side unmanned and with the oars drawn up. They came just in time to see the door that led from the harbor directly to the arsenal open. Out came a division of seamen in double time, then artillery, knights, and soldiers, possibly a hundred. They quickly took their places on the nearest galley.

"They are the ones who lay at the ready," Antoine said. "Now la chiourme comes."

And then they came, a brown stream of naked bodies gushing out along the wall, stumbling, scampering, and swearing. They streamed on board and drew up the dark runners between the red banks. One could see the polished back plates shine on the slaves, who bowed down to lock fast the foot shackles. A sour stench of unwashed bodies wafted up the wall.

"Good and ugly still," said André.

"The law of war," said Antoine. "We risk all to go there, high and low. There is no distinction."

"The law ought to be changed."

"That is true of many laws . . . "

The first galley had already pushed off from land. The second began to be filled by its crew, who came in small groups called there by the alarm from their auberges, barracks, taverns, and rented hovels.

Now all that remained was to wait and see what would happen. André tried to ask, but Antoine only shook his head.

"Anything can happen here. You only make it worse by fantasizing. Now we will go down to the city. You have not seen the walls."

They took the way along the long street with businesses that went west out from the great square where they had been yesterday. In daylight the city looked just as impressive. New houses well built, all of the same gold limestone. Rows of businesses, all well supplied with all that could be found between India and the Azores.

"There is the Castellan."

Antoine pointed to a new house to the left with wide exterior stairs and sculpted stone arches around the vast windows. He did not need to explain what it would be used for. Two soldiers with open helmets and long halberds came down from the harbor carrying a Turk between them. It was a real Turk with a turban, a lively jacket, and wide pants, to judge by material and embroidery a wealthy fellow. The Turk protested. Antoine heard him say something in Greek, but the guard did not understand him. A little crowd began to gather around them.

"What is he saying?" asked one of the servants in Italian.

"He had been seeing an innkeeper whom he knows."

"He asked to be brought to the Chancellor. He says that he has an errand for him."

The soldier scratched behind his ear and then he looked at the other.

"The Castellan will clear it up."

They continued up the steps.

"A lot to witness," said Antoine. "It was the oddest thing I've heard. A well dressed Turk who asks for d'Amaral. We'll wait and see."

They didn't need to wait long. There they sat under the old holly in front of Kastrofilika's tavern. After only a few minutes, an orderly split by on his way up the collachium.

After fifteen minutes he returned in the company of Blas Diez, a baptized Spanish Jew who was the Chancellor's butler. And then, running to the other hall again, Blas Diez, the Turk, and the two guards. Antoine stared at them.

"This is the strangest thing I have ever seen."

The Chancellor looked up from his papers.

"So, Ibrahim, there you are."

"Yes, Lord Chancellor." He did not say "master" the same way he had always said it before.

D'Amaral understood and nodded.

"You have the money with you?"

"Yes, Lord Chancellor."

He searched in his wide pants, and fished up a little leather purse. He held it out politely, but not humbly.

"Then you are a free man from now on. I wish you the best of luck."

It sounded as if he announced that the audience was finished.

"Will the Lord Chancellor not count the money?"

"It is not needed, Ibrahim. I know that you won't cheat me. How did you get here?"

"On a fishing boat from Fisco. They arrested me when I came on land open and peacefully. And I trusted that the city watch stood close by and waited."

"What did you say?"

The Chancellor rang his bell. Blas Diez looked in. He just stood there.

"Send the idiots away and tell the Castellan that I take responsibility for this man. He is my guest."

The Chancellor had finished. He calmed himself.

"You are my guest, Ibrahim, as long as you stay here on Rhodes. You may live in the guest room, not in the old hovel, and you eat at my table."

They sat in the evening.

"Ibrahim?"

"Yes, Lord Chancellor."

"There is one thing I would like to know."

"What is it, Lord Chancellor?"

"Why didn't you stay home with your four thousand aspri? You could have spared them."

"That would have been a poor affair, Lord Chancellor. I would have lost my god."

The Chancellor looked down at his wood plate with the rest of the evening's paella. He was quiet and thought, of the infidel shall one hear it.

He looked up.

"How do you know that there is a god?"

The Turk looked at him amazed.

"But isn't that well known by all, Lord Chancellor?"

"But if one doesn't know it now? And wants to know it?"

"I have never thought about it, Lord Chancellor."

So it was. This Turk was honest for his god's sake. But whether or not god exists was something he had never asked himself. That did not hold.

In the Auvergnat auberge they were also sitting around a bare wood table and talking. News had come, big news. One of the galleys had turned back to escort a badly damaged carrack from Crete. It had sailed straight into battle with Kort-Oglu, who lay in wait for the two Venetian pilgrim ships.

One could only think of how the old pirate must have vexed himself that the Grand Master had slipped through his net without him even catching a glimpse of him. Since that evening on the ninth, he had once even received confirmation that the flotilla at full sail stirred in the channel off of Cerigo—and then it seemed the whole squadron had been blown out of the water. In his anger, he had hurried to Rhodes. And it would not have been a bad consolation to get the two fully packed pilgrim carracks. But they had been driven back into the harbor by the headwind.

"And they could well have cussed and blasphemed a little less about the good gift of God," said one of the serving brothers with a little sidelong glance at a brother chevalier, who could have quite a coarse mouth.

There was much more to tell. It had gone bad for the Cretan. He sailed well, but the Turks were quicker. The ships were smart enough to start shooting a long way off in hopes that it would be heard in Rhodes. Before the galleys made it, the Turks had already come alongside and thrown out their grappling hooks. And the Cretans prepared to buy their lives for as much as possible. They did not want to be slaves. But when the galleys began to come within shooting range, the Turks finally gave up, cast loose, and got away in their fast boats. The Cretans thanked God and steered towards Rhodes under escort while two galleys remained to patrol the sea at night and follow the Venetians part of the way in the morning if they found serviceable wind.

It was almost all that was talked about at the evening meal on this action-packed day. They talked about the other actions in more hushed tones. Rumor had gone out through the city. A distinguished Turk had come to visit the Chancellor from Constantinople. One who used to be a slave and who would now simply go back again.

Chevalier Chalant shook his head.

"An inconceivable story. Someone should ask d'Amaral."

But that was something no one wanted to do. That was a given.

Belgrade

SEPTEMBER CAME TO AN end. The morning sun was lightly veiled, and the air was cool in the day. In Auberge d'Auvergne the usual water, bread, and olives were set on the coarse wood table. The brothers who came back from mass tugged their slices of bread and stuck their fingers in clay dishes with oiled olives. There was hardly any talk. They had a long day before them and each one sat in his place thinking. Young André Barel thought about the endless piles of sheets, shirts, and pillowcases that had to be ironed and counted in the sick house. Some of the brothers would take over the next watch on the walls and had already put on the leather vests they wore under their armor. They had hurried, prayed their table prayers silently, and were ready to go when the door opened and a Spanish knight in full armor stamped in directly from the high watch. He wore his helmet, showing that he was on duty.

Everyone looked up puzzled. He looked upset.

"His Eminence calls the Lord Marshal to the palace immediately."

And then he said:

"Belgrade has fallen."

All was still. A quiet calm full of evil foreboding fell on the room. Only the Marshal moved. All wondered what this meant. Belgrade was Christendom's firm lock on land just as Rhodes was here on the sea. Up till now it had successfully defended itself against all attacks. Mohammed the Conqueror himself had been forced to turn likewise against the walls of Rhodes. If the new sultan wanted to be treated to Christendom, he had to break both these locks. Now it was done. One lock had been crushed. What would the future be?

The brothers were silent and went to work.

The watch presented arms. The doors opened and soon quick steps echoed in the wide stair hall. The high lords continued through the grand hall into the room where the Grand Master customarily received guests and seated themselves around the walls.

The Grand Master entered in the company of Preian de Bidoulx, the Castellan of Lango, who had come during the night on his fastest brigantine. Without much ceremony, he gave the word. He looked up with his one eye—the other had been lost off the coast of England when he served the French King—and began his report.

The news had come from Constantinople through one of the normal channels. One could figure that the contents were the chief facts that man knew in well-informed halls and channels of the seraglio.

"As we knew, Sabacz fell already in early July. The garrison was not strong, the walls of average measure, approximately the same as Ferakles and built with much the same material. Suleiman himself led the siege. They filled the water moat with bundles of wood. The Hungarians made a brave stand, but the enemy's artillery quickly made two great breaches. They could have retreated over Sava, but instead they stood, took the storm, and fell to the last man. Sixty heads on pikes made latticework when Suleiman entered. They say that that is approximately how many were left in the final stand. The Turks likely lost about six hundred."

Everyone listened intently. The Castellan continued.

"Afterwards, Suleiman threw bridges over the Sava. It was a hard job that they continued with great resolution day and night. Suleiman sat elevated under his canopy. He kept his eye on everything. In ten days it was done. Then a flood came and they had to start all over again. Then the main body continued over and marched eastward. They came to Belgrade the first of August. Pir Pascha had them legated there one month. Because of deserters, they knew that the walls were weakest in the corner where the Sava joins the Danube. So they set up heavy batteries on an island directly across from there. The Hungarians made a determined opposition, but they had too few cannons and they couldn't trust the Serbs. They were not able to keep the city when the people did not do their best. It fell in the first storm. The garrison drew back to the castle. There they were able to hold out well and beat back one attack after another. The walls were blown asunder, but they held fast in the ruins and behind their relief walls. Then the Turks began to tunnel under the walls, apparently on a large scale with the help of slaves and miners. They also made a net of approaches and earth embankments around the fortress that protected them from fire. Little by little, they worked their way closer and in the last week in

August they blew up a great powder charge under the one of the greatest towers, making a hole in the defense work that no one could patch. The Hungarians still had almost four hundred men left. They would have held out to the last man if not for the Serbian threat of mutiny. So they bargained on the twenty-ninth of August with the promise of free departure. But when they opened the gates, they were cut down. As far as anyone knows, none of them survived. Yes, that was the most important."

They all looked at the Grand Master. He crossed himself slowly, saying under his breath: "*Requiem aeternam dona eis, Domine.* Give them, O Lord, the eternal peace— and the reward of faithful martyrs."

Then he looked up.

"And now, my brothers, what can we learn from this?"

He looked at his old friend John Buck, the Turcopoler, almost appealing. Everyone knew that the Englishman had bet his best greyhound against Pomerolx's old kitchen cat that the Turks would never show themselves before the walls of Rhodes in his lifetime. He answered respectfully:

"I think that he who breaks a lock also goes in through the door. Suleiman will continue his campaign against the Hungarians next summer, possibly going all the way to Vienna. He will leave us in peace."

"And Lord Chancellor?"

The Grand Master looked at d'Amaral. His powerful face looked chiseled in stone. He looked straight at him and not a second lapsed before he answered.

"The Lord Turcopoler has my thoughts right. There is no reason to panic. Summoning many people now means emptying our assets. We may need them more in the future."

The Grand Master looked around.

"Who here agrees with what these brothers have said?"

A pair of silent hands were raised.

"I thank you, brothers, and in my heart I hope to God that you are right. But with the responsibility I have, I can only do one thing. I have to figure in the possibility that Rhodes stands next in turn. If for nothing else than that Suleiman can hardly carry out a great war with the Hungarians, Poles, or Germans without the full support of his provinces behind the sea. And he does not have that as long as we sit here. It is our task to see to it that he does not have it, and he knows that. Also—let us count on that possibility that we will meet with Suleiman. In such a case, when?"

All were in one accord on that matter. The soonest is next summer.

"And what have we learned today?"

Here a few different chief thoughts clarified themselves among the many assertions. First, Suleiman is not what the instigator of rebellion Gazali had counted on and the Old Carreto hoped for. He was not an inexperienced easy-going chap, who would need many years to become firm in the saddle and learn to be in charge of his world's very fruitful re-sources. On the contrary, he had shown himself to be what Christendom feared most of all: a Sultan of the old type, a soldier's commander with lofty plans, energetic, determined and hardy.

"And concerning the military side . . . "

The Grand Master nodded to the reporter, then the one eyed Preian de Bidoulx summarized.

Concerning the artillery: Nothing new. We may possibly need some twenty pieces, first of the long range, but most important of all, sufficient ammunition. The new thing here is their mining work and sapping. If they dig in out of range, then we cannot reach them with our artillery.

"What do we do then?"

The Grand Master looked at him questioningly.

"The matter is so new, Your Eminence. We have to think through it."

"Also, the usual measures: three commissioners who investigate and report? Whom will you have?"

So they came again to the old rut. The lords, their tension let out, began to look at each other and whisper with one another. But behind the assembly routine and the habitual procedures, there remained a weight, almost an iron grip that would not let go.

Belgrade had fallen. Only Rhodes was left.

War?

"ANGELOS, ANGEL CHILD, ENGLISHMAN, royal, rascal . . . Gregoris, God's gift, golden crowned, good pig . . . "

Anasthasia crowed over her twins. She had brought them out into the sun. The shining October sun felt warm and good here in the corner of the back yard under the withered grapevines.

Angelos was simply the least angel like, but the name still passed well. His father was an Englishman, from Anglia, the land of Anglos. And he was an angel, Papa Richard, hair of fire like the icon Michael the Archangel in church with the same glittering eyes, just as sinewy and bearded. Though pious as an angel was something no one could say about him, the wild brain.

"Angelos, Angelos, do you think the same way? You laugh, you scamp. Dangerous, you are, just as dangerous as your dad. Look at Gregoris. He could be a priest."

She tickled them both under the chin. Angelos laughed, and Gregoris looked at her with big wide and wise eyes. Angelos was red and downy with laughing eyes; Gregoris worthy, pale and wide-eyed.

"One thing I tell you boys. If there is not better order with you than there is with your father, then I will go home. Home, you understand. Home to your grandmother in Piskopi. And so you can pick up your socks, playing cards, clasp knives, armor, and chest keys all yourself. A-l-l yourself. Do you hear?"

Anasthasia was soon convinced that her boys understood her. She had been convinced of this already when they were a week old. She talked with them day after day, and it was not just a monolog. They gurgled and smiled and sneezed and she knew precisely what they meant.

"Papa wants there to be war, do you understand, Angelos? Then Papa can be a fine captain. Then papa can stay here. And if papa stays here and marries mom then there should well be war, but it must be over before you are big."

This was Anasthasia's problem in life. Her Richard had come with the enlisted English soldiers whom Sir John had with him. In any case, he was under their command, and as long as the Turkish threat lasted, he could stay. He had been here many years now and spoke passable Greek. He had nothing to stay for—except now he had her. At least he said so. But he had nothing secure to live off of. If there were calmer times, then all the servants would be sent home. He had tried to find some firm employment, but Sir John only shrugged his shoulders. There were not many firm places to choose from for those who didn't belong to the brotherhood. And those places were all occupied with young people. Sir John would have liked to help his compatriot, but . . . and so he shrugged his shoulders.

But today, Richard had come storming in completely unexpected, kissed her, lifted her up, swung her around and rejoiced: "There will be war! There will be war, war, WAR!"

And so he told her. There had come a fast Turkish galley with an envoy from the Grand Turk himself. One such silk-rustling Pascha with a turban as big as a mill stone, and he glittered as if he had stood in a shower of jewels. The Grand Turk only sent such out when he wanted to make an impression. And he only wants to impress when he wants to make demands. And he would receive a no to all demands here on Rhodes. That was a given. So now all signs indicated that there would be war, a glorious war with great gaps in the cadre and every possibility of promotion.

"Do you understand Anasthasia, you seductress? You may as you will! The Turk shoots the head off three or four captains and I am sure to get their place! Thanks to our Sultan, fatherly caregiver of all poor mercenaries."

An atrocious man! But one had to take him as he was. And she gladly took him.

In the secretary's office, one toiled as best he could to hastily put together a worthy program for such an honored guest. The Grand Master had already ordered that the Sultan's envoy should be cared for with all conceivable honor. He himself received the ambassador in a grand audience, already on the second day. In the evening he happily placed the ambassador in the city's best accommodations so that the council could gather in full force. During this time the Sultan's letter had been translated from Greek to French. It could also immediately be read. It happened in dead silence.

Suleiman Schab, with God's grace King of Kings, Sovereign of Sovereigns, all-powerful Caesar of Byzantium and Trapezium, absolute ruler of Persia, Arabia, Syria, Egypt, highest sovereign of Europe and Asia, protector of Mecca, prince of Aleppo, Lord of Jerusalem, ruler of the seas, to Brother Phillippe Villiers de lIsle Adam, Grand Master of Rhodes, greetings.

I congratulate you in your new worthiness. May your reign be fortunate, held with still greater fame than your predecessors of whose majority sought my father's friendship. Even I ask for your friendship and therefore ask you to rejoice with me over the victories I have won in Hungary where I conquered the well-fortified city of Belgrade, and many other strong places and prospering cities. I let all who were bold enough to oppose my will to run over the blades.

I myself now send my victory rich army to winter quarters so that in triumph I return again to my court in Constantinople.

Given in my camp in Belgrade, the tenth of September 1521.

The Grand Master looked around.

"What say the brothers?"

"A fethname," Pomerolx said. "The same sort of victory bulletin that the Sultan sends to other sovereigns."

"Made as an offer of peace," said the Turcopoler.

"But with the purpose of a threat," said d'Airasca, the new Admiral: "Listen to the words: Belgrade, which was so strong has fallen. Those who stood in opposition are all dead. My victory rich army is now going into winter quarters. In the spring they march again. Watch yourself Rhodes!"

The Grand Master nodded.

"And how does one answer such a thing?"

There was a long deliberation. The Chancellor wanted a soft answer, fitting gifts and diplomatic representation. Others thought there wasn't anything more dangerous than to yield. Kort-Oglu had been sent out to take the Grand Master prisoner and take him back to Constantinople. It was sufficient evidence to show Suleiman's aim. If one began to negotiate, the Sultan would sharpen his demands little by little while Rhodes was brought to ruin by her armament. It was better to give a restrained reply. If one ruffled the Turk, one was not corrupted. One only took him down a peg. He was civil or showed, at least, that he continued in the shadows.

They united on a short and tight reply. The secretary took note of the chief points according to the Grand Master's dictation.

"And who should we send?"

Then the thoughts completely went their own ways. The Chancellor thought of his task as a representative ambassador. Others thought that it was dangerous to send anyone of importance. If the Turks want to compel information out of him, they were masters at torturing people. And for the ambassador's immunity, the unbelievers had no respect.

"On the contrary, neither do the Christians," the Chancellor said. "What did the Hungarians do to Suleiman's envoy? You have them to thank if you don't dare go to Suleiman."

One shot at the matter. One would still gather and adjust the answer.

The question of the envoy resolved itself. The Turkish ambassador showed a highly improper interest in the defense work. One kept him surrounded by attentive knights day and night, but it was hard to control his company. All wanted to see the city with a manifest partiality for the quarters along the wall. And one evening a man passed by two of their seamen onboard after they swam out to the wave breaks and during a swim reached the harbor on the beach in the midst of the newly built outer works before the Italian wall, which they climbed up with great competence.

After that experience, one ordered a worthy farewell feast, packed the magnificent gifts in bales and loaded boxes, and left the reply letter in the hands of a simple merchant, who had a certain weakness for titles and fine acquaintances but knew absolutely nothing about defenses and artillery. The next morning the Turkish boat sailed away.

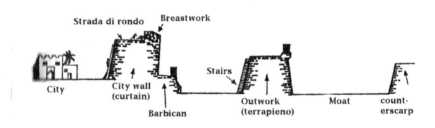

War!

THE YEAR 1522 CAME with pouring rain, an icy northeast wind, and evil thoughts. Up on Ataviros, Mt. Elias was snow-peaked through the clouds. All the window shutters were kept closed, but the wind whistled through the gaps and swept across the floor. Wherever there was an open fireplace in the knights' auberge, in the sick halls, and the fine merchant houses, men gathered together around the fire and thawed their frozen fingers. Commoners huddled together in their damp hovels, wrapped themselves in what they had, set their feet on a chest, and stood back to back. Anastasia took her coughing twins to bed with her to keep them warm, wipe their noses, and prattle with them.

Then the sun came back again. People fled outdoors and sat along the south side of the roads to thaw out their frozen joints and talk about the Turks as often as something new leaked out from the Grand Master's palace. The leak would make it to the knights' auberges first, then to the kitchens, the hospital, the arsenal, and the barracks, and then out into the city to the taverns and shops. They talked of how God punished the Tyrant, he who made so many fatherless, by giving his children the pox, and then taking one after the other from him. Everyone knew that the Tyrant worked day and night, that people hurried to council in the seraglio even in the final hours of an evening, that the Russians had gone there and kissed his hand and the council in Ragusa likewise. They also knew the shameless Venetians meant to make a treaty with him.

What one did not know was that there was a secret correspondence back and forth between the Grand Master and Pir Pascha, the grand vizier. The Pascha wanted badly to get one of the foremost knights to Constantinople. It was simply not acceptable to present an envoy of such low family to the court. The Grand Master requested a hostage or at least a letter of safe conduct with the Sultan's great seal. He sent another envoy that could not be of any real worth to the Turks. He crossed the sea together with Pir Pascha's envoy. On the other side, a saddled horse waited, only one, and the Turk galloped off. The Grand Master's envoy was left on the beach alone and afraid with no safety. Baffled, he went back on the same boat. In the council, one drew his own conclusions.

No one greeted the sun with more joy than the galley slaves. Over the winter they were forced to work on the walls breaking stones, making mortar, and pulling heavy sleds of block that the stone cutters prepared. Badly clothed as they were, they were more tired of the cold than anything else. Their prison cells in the mountain under the Grand Master's palace were certainly more tolerable in the winter than many unheated stone houses, but the work in the moat and on the walls never ceased no matter how poor the weather might be. It was noticed that people worked as if they were running out of time. The moats were cleaned and made deeper. Then one day the order came to make strange zigzag paths and deep well-like shafts with level spaces down at the bottom of the moat—that it would be used for now. On the grand boulevard outside the old St. George gate—long since boarded up—they took down the whole crenellation and began to raise the wall ell after ell. Then they filled the whole of the immense territory before it. This work alone could occupy hundreds of men for months. Really, it was the prisoner's joy to do so. When the sun began to warm again, one had it far better than on the galleys, in particular as the food rations were more abundant when the work was forced. There was a particular reason for this: the new Grand Master trusted more in soup kettles than in whips when it came to getting people to work. But it justified nothing for them.

Meanwhile the writers toiled up in the palace. Accountants summarized and checked, judgments and rolls were written out and ratified with a seal, the council assembled and the great protocol book was filled with conclusions up one side and down the other. Many diligent hands with many ways to cut a quill formed their letters in many different ways. During all this writing, one could hardly think that war stood before the door. Here the great paper mill revolved, which after centuries of experience had given shape to a clear administration of one of the world's greatest undertakings with goods and mills and rents to administer from Cyprus in the east to Ireland's westernmost harbor. For centuries people had given gifts, first to the pious monks, who took care of God's poor in Jerusalem and all God's pilgrims, and then to the good knights, who protected them from being killed by the Saracens. It had begun with small widow mites: one hen a year or a lamb for Easter, some marsh wood or income from a field. It had grown to pieces of land and vineyards, mills and forges. They had put these together into farms, and the farms into properties, and properties to commanderies—a knight, chaplain or serving brother who had completed their years on the other side of the sea and were now rewarded with a safe old age in the homeland. For these one-armed, limping, gout suffering veterans, it was unfamiliar work to receive kids, bundles of wood, wax clumps, bridge money, fractions of ten days work, and performance in kind, often according to simple customary law and hopelessly old contracts. One third would be recorded to the Prior and sent to Rhodes. They toiled and wrote, counted and stroked, examined and questioned, bargained and bickered, and finally they sent the final revision to the Grand Master in hope that his audit would declare that they now were "*visti, chalculati verificati et summati*", and thereby be approved and registered for all time. There were over five hundred such commanders from Messina in the south, to the unknown land of Mäleren in the North. Each one had a little kingdom for himself with a church, hospital, mill and bakery, court and prison, and often also a small fortress behind which people could flee from pirates, rogue knights, and prowling soldiers. And all appeals for better justice and conflicts concerning borders and priority of transport would be decided in the convent on Rhodes in the end. So there was enough to do.

One day in February—it was the eighteenth—there was a sudden interruption in the routine. The council had been called together and there was a long conference. The lords came out serious and resolute, as if they all received something particular to do. The Grand Master had had much to say.

In the new year, the usual flood of news had begun to dry up. In order to gain knowledge of the matter, the Grand Master had sent away a small dealer from the island of Ragosa, a clever fellow who spoke Turkish like a native. He had gone to Constantinople, spoke, dealt, and looked around. He was fortunate enough to smuggle out a cipher, and now they knew the answer. There was work day and night in the shipyards. They put up enormous stores of large cannon balls, beams, planks, pick axes, and everything that was needed for a siege. The whole city knew that the year's campaign would be somewhere over the sea. Some said to Cyprus, others Corfu, and others Cattaro in Dalmatien. The rumors were all suspiciously applied to Venetian possessions. Venice had, of course, just entered a new treaty and would pay a huge tribute for Cyprus. The rumors might have been planted in order to hide the real destination.

So the decisive news came. All seafaring to Rhodes was stopped. No ship with this destination was able to leave the harbor, and all traffic was controlled. It was not at all strange that the news had dried up. It was not hard for the council to decide. The Turcopoler was silent; only d'Amaral maintained that one should not be rash. One had gotten caught up in false alarms many times before and threw away lots of money on needless armament. But a massive majority thought that you could now hear the clock ticking. The Grand Master needed only propose what would likely be decided. He had the list clear in his head. In a sweep he appointed commissioners and work groups for the walls, for the provisions, for the ammunition, for the refugees, for the mills, for the bakeries, sick wards, slaves, and artisans. All would be controlled and set for war preparations.

That evening Brother Gierolamo went through his instruments and counted the distressed stores of opium sponges, those that would be held under the nose of people when one cut an arrow out or sawed off a leg. Doctor Apella stood and looked at the evening sky, sighing heavily. Zealous novices asked in the auberges, and scared brothers gave short answers. But at home with Anasthasia, Richard held up the city's best wine. He purchased it on credit and drank to their fortune.

Cures What Ails You

THE GRAND MASTER MADE his usual morning round on the walls together with the acting deputy, Grand Commandeur de Pomerolx, and the usual entourage of bodyguards and orderlies following him. They went along the crown of the old curtain directly from the palace out to the German wall, and then straightway to Boulevard d'Auvergne. The great defense work was as busy as an anthill with huge piles of loose stone block where sunburnt and sweaty people crawled around, strained their backs, lifted, pried, pounded, and loosed. The foreman, Protomaestro Mantoni, came to them with cap in hand.

"Your Eminence, today we must have the answer. Shall we put up the old merlon or will it be French embrasure?"

"Have you come so far already?" The Grand Master asked. "There seems to be a good piece left."

"Yes, Your Eminence, but if we are not going to put up the old crenellation then ought we to turn the stones in the wall or in the filling? It would spare a lot of time."

The Grand Master thought for a minute.

"You will have your answer in two hours."

"Naturally, they ought to be French embrasure," Pomerolx said when they had gone a little further. "Those old merlons don't hold after a direct hit."

"There is a lot one ought to do, but cannot, Brother Gabriel. These slanting embrasures take much more time than I thought. It is a question of whether or not we are finished with the Provençal and the English walls."

"But they started already in the fall. Thirty holes cannot take a half a year!"

"Thirty six," reminded the Grand Master. "We will hear from Master Ruffini."

They hurried through the intervening sectors, Auvergnats and Aragonians, were greeted from the right and the left, received information and winked to people to continue. Here there were only small repair jobs being done. At the English wall they were doing a great reconstruction. The first half was finished. The new breastwork towered almost as tall as a man. Embrasures carved down like small grooves in their particular angles. If you looked through them you could see how deep and massive the new breastwork had been. Within that sector they met Maestro Ruffini among a gang of stone hewers, who let their chisels dance over the stone block to the clang of hammering.

"Well, Maestro, how is your count today?"

"Nine finished, Your Eminence, five clear this week, sixteen underway. We can start the remaining five within the next week."

"And the sixteen underway? When will they be finished?"

"Three to eight weeks, Your Eminence."

Pomerolx ventured to come with a proposal.

"Could we not give Maestro a few more people?"

The Italian lighted up.

"From the boulevard d'Auvergne?" He asked.

"Impossible. On the contrary they need reinforcing. But if you could have a slave to assist each man, would that help?"

"Impossible, Signor Gran Comendatore, this is precise work. Each stone has to fit precisely. Not one is like the other and each is slanted in its own way. I may have to stand over these friendly fellows the whole day. One cannot use inexperienced people."

"Look here," he said, "for this embrasure I need eighty seven stones just to cover the outer plane. Only fifteen are the same as any of the others. And this is one of the simpler ones."

Pomerolx looked downhearted. There was not much to say. The design had not seemed so involved.

The Grand Master waved at one of the orderlies.

"Go to the Boulevard d' Auvergne and tell the Protomaestro that the old merlon will be saved and put up again on the new wall."

The orderly went, and Pomerolx scratched thoughtfully between his bushy eyebrows.

The March sun was already high in the sky when they came back to the palace. Spring was beginning in earnest.

Three commissioners were already waiting in the foyer. The Grand Master began with the commissioners' "sopra forni." They were responsible for the ovens. The reports were satisfactory. They could bake double the amount of bread they did now in the existing ovens feeding more refugees than was possible to receive.

"And fuel?"

"It is the normal amount for three or four months."

"But we need enough for a year, at least."

"It is on its way, Your Eminence. If we can pay cash, then we will buy however much you want. Could we possibly get an advance from the common purse?"

The Grand Master made a note.

"Go to the treasurer in the morning with a precise arrangement. Where can we store it?"

"The bakers all have sufficient space. One can of course pile it up. The rest we thought we could put in the arsenal."

"That won't do. Think if some of the slaves set fire to it. But there is a cavity behind Saint Panthaleon where we break stone for the wall. See if it is suitable."

He thanked the lords and let them go. Then came four merchants with Pietro Lomellino in the lead. They were commissioners for the mills and had many problems. Two thirds of the windmills were on the pier, the rest in high and fixed places, all with the risk of being shot up by long range bombadiers. If the mills were destroyed, the immense grain storage in the arches under the fortress yard would be next to useless. Therefore the commission had already made a great order of hand and horse mills from the isle of Nisiro that could be stored in reserve. Could they ask for some cash?

They got their money with some bargaining, said goodbye, and left.

Then the commissioners for the refugee accommodations followed. They were not optimistic. The worst was with the animals the refugees were sure to have with them. Where would one find fodder? They went over their plan to direct most of them to the castles in the countryside. That the Turks would spare gunpowder and people to storm them was a consideration they excluded. The enemy could not have enough people to watch them. One could let the goats pasture around the walls. They would return thin and worn.

Next there was a report from the commission for the work force, who were responsible for a fourth of the city's slaves not required for common work. The Grand Master dismissed them and was just about to gather his papers together to go when he caught a glimpse of his chaplain Fra Giovanni out in the hall. He let him come in.

"And in your line, Brother Giovanni, how is it there? Anything lacking?"

"Yes, Your Eminence, unfortunately."

"What then?"

"Repentance. Yours, Your Eminence."

The Grand Master sat up straight as he usually did when he took issue with something.

"That you have to explain."

"Don't misunderstand me, not by our Grand Master."

"Of course," said l'Isle Adam sharply. "Just there. When it would be real repentance, as it were?"

"Because Brother Grand Master, you know what the issues are in the order. And that is enough for many here . . . but it ought to be for many more. If we can we stand against the Sultan then it is God's miracle."

"I know that, Brother Giovanni, but we must of course also do what comes to us. That is why I run all day long around the walls and try to get the people to hurry up."

"We thank God for that, Brother Grand Master. But in the end it all depends on God, and he loves a contrite and sorrowful heart. We all ought to have one, but many of the brothers do not. They bicker over precepts and commands. They lie in wait for each other so that no one comes forward. They envy the lazy and fat brothers at home who sit around and have it good."

"We are calling them in now," said the Grand Master.

"Yes, I know and am afraid of that. What will come of that? Servants under your Grand Master's discipline?" The Grand Master was silent without betraying that he thought the same thing.

Fra Giovanni continued.

"And now they have here Spanish slaves and all the privateers and pirates, who are now called home. They are worse than the heathens and the Turks. They destroy the decent people we have left. What should God do with such a city?"

The Grand Master was still quiet.

"Brother Grand Master, we have just read the prophet Jeremiah in Matins. What is it God says? 'I will judge the city for this evil,' he says. 'It is you yourself who wanted this, when you betrayed your God, who would lead you on the right path. Who planted you as a noble vine, how have you turned into a wild vine? Should I not attack them for this? Storm her walls, and destroy them! Rip out her wild roots, they are not the Lord's!'"

The Grand Master looked up.

"I heard it and thought about this when you read it. What do you want me to do? Think that it is hopeless and bargain? For the sake of our sins?"

"It is never hopeless, Brother Grand Master. We should of course work as if all depended on us and pray as if it all depended on Him. The Brother Grand Master must take this war on. But I would be happier if more righteousness was found in the city. If only among us in the Religion, with all of our hearts."

It seemed as if the Grand Master was finished.

"Good," he said. "You may have ten minutes every evening at Vespers to explain Jeremiah to us, and I shall talk with the Archbishop about what we can do about all the robbers and evildoers, who will not fight for Christ. And yet possibly die for his sake," he said as an afterthought.

The Deserters

SERPENTINES, TWENTY-FOUR POUNDS; CULVERINS twenty-two; half culverins, twelve or ten; sacres, five; and falconets, three or four . . .

André Barel sat in the shade of the loggia outside the Grand Master's palace and studied. He read out loud from a stretched sheet of paper, which kept falling apart along the fold in the middle. It was cluttered with badly written notes from some years past.

Right after the eighteenth of February, all the novices had moved up from the hospital to the Artillery School. None of them had any idea that they would need to have so much book knowledge to fire a cannon. They had to be acquainted with all the different types, and there were plenty of them. At times it seemed as if the cannon foundries believed that they were casting statues, all of which had to be different. Though the Marshal tried to get rid of all odd pieces, they still had to keep at least twenty types of balls in storage. And every knight should know what fit in the different pieces, and in the blink of an eye be able to see if a stray ball—or one that came flying from the other side—could be used or not.

Today was a big day. They would be able to watch the sharp shooting from Saint Nicolas over the water at the deserted sandbar to the north, where they went yesterday to build something resembling a Turkish cannon platform—stable wood chests filled with sand with an inner room covered by a sheet of canvas and a thick wooden plank for protection from cannons, which were marked with a tree trunk on two bows.

But the excitement died away when they had to stand out in the heat endlessly practicing loading and reloading. They had to scoop the gunpowder with long shovels and pack it—not too hard!—and get the priming powder to stay in the wind. Then came instruction with a long study of how high one must aim over the target and why and how one should have had the canvas stand either twice as far or half as far.

Then they were finally ready to shoot. But then the lookout up in the basket shouted that a boat came in on the other side, and the match withdrew again. Everyone looked over the breastworks and someone yelled: "It is the Wolf, with Galliga!"

And true enough, it was. The Wolf, le Loup was an Auvergnat, a compatriot of André and a clever and rash seaman. One month ago he had gone out in the bitter weather to get grain from Italy.

"She is heavy laden," someone said.

The Wolf had obviously been successful and in short time!

As soon as she came out of the line of fire, the cannons fired a kind of welcome salute. The planks smoked in the air on the sandbar and the sand flew up. The Wolf stood at the helm by the stern and waved his hat.

"Are the Turks already here?" he screamed.

"No, but we prepare to feast," someone yelled back.

The Wolf sat at the lunch table in Auberge d'Auvergne and reported. They had been very foolish during the winter. His Catholic Majesty, Emperor Karl, was at loggerheads with his Catholic Majesty King Francis. Their troops fought with each other in Lombardy. The French had laid siege to Milan. Colonna and Pescara had come to the rescue. There could be a great conflict at any time. The Emperor had let Belgrade fall and the Hungarians go to the brink of destruction without seeing that his own Austrian estate was now in danger. The Wolf looked grim at the possibility that the Grand Master would get anything from the princes of Christendom more than the usual promises. And the new Pope, Hadrianus, whom they rejoiced over because he was a brother of the Order, had been a great disappointment. He had laid siege to all available commanderies in Italy and obviously planned to parcel them out to the people he wanted help from.

The brothers around the table bowed, distressed. They could tell even worse stories. The knights in the Italian langue were completely outraged on account of this. Here they worked like dogs, drilled on the walls, and took the risk of being galley slaves every time they went to sea and now their very fortunate place of retreat would be parceled out to home sitters with their noses turned up toward them. They requested to send a powerful delegation to the Pope to protest but got a blank "no" from the Grand Master. And then the worst came: about two weeks ago, the council gave public notification that three Italian brothers had disappeared. It looked as if they deserted to Crete in order to try and get home from there and avoid the unthankful service on the boat. It was the worst scandal anyone had witnessed in a long time.

But there was a comfort in misery. Antonio Bosio, the Jack, found himself on Crete in lawful and unlawful errands. If anyone could make this right, it was him.

Already the next week there came a greeting from the Jack in Crete. It came in the form of his best friend Gianantonio Bonaldi. They fell in each other's arms on the wharf by Porto Castello where Bonaldi was busy loading his ship with wine casks. Normally, men sold their wine in Rhodes, but this year no one was willing to sail there because one could land straight into the arms of the Turkish invasion fleet. Bonaldi had not yet determined where he would go, but after a great deal of intimate deliberation with his friend Antonio and a lot of secretive whispering and messaging, he let it be understood that the wine was going to Constantinople. Simultaneously, he increased his crew and took onboard a number of passengers, all young men, and set out to sea. At the summit of Karpathos, he changed course and here he was now with seven hundred casks of good wine and some first rate archers. None of them had any objections to enlisting, least of all to fight against the Turks. He also had a greeting from Antonio saying that he would come soon thereafter.

That same evening Brother Antonio stole out the back way from a noble house in Candia, looked around cautiously, and went out into the empty street. He took a detour between the gardens, a long detour, and came upon the square from the opposite side from the alley with the brothels so that no one would wonder what he was up to if anyone should even think twice about the matter. He grabbed a seat in the tavern San Marco, ordered some wine, and waited.

It had been a glorious time. He had poked around in all the villages here on the north side, hunting up all the dissatisfied wine merchants who were having trouble getting rid of their inventory and offered them a good price. He made inquiries about shippers with questionable business—and there were plenty of them that year—and chartered their boats. He organized the loading, always in different places and with well-varied hints of days of departure and destinations. And then he had prepared the little joke, which he and Bonaldi put together. Wherever the wine was loaded, there were people, young people, lots of people, people who were needed to set sail (they were, of course, old and impractical) for keeping the barrels under control (they could attempt), and for the unloading (one stood there helpless and incapable of turning). And everywhere they went, they asked if anyone needed passage to Chios, Cerigo, Smyrna, or Constantinople, and there were always quite a few, who wanted to travel right now. In good time they boarded with their baggage.

It was quite amazing that he was able to keep it up so long. The Signori on Crete had strictly forbidden all traffic to Rhodes. No one was to get caught up in the showdown that Suleiman now had with the knights. Venice would keep out at any price. The new Duke in Crete had, of course, attended the negotiations with the Sultan and signed the treaty with his own hands.

Now the man he waited for came. A middle-aged man in a black cap, suntanned like a seaman, short hair like a servant, straight like a lord.

"Good evening, Lord Lodovico. How are you?"

"Good evening brother Antonio."

The other inspected him suspiciously. He was one of the three knights who absconded from Rhodes.

"What are you doing here?"

"Only bearing greetings from home."

"Thank you, how goes it with you?"

"Like three days before the wedding. We clean and brew and organize fireworks so that it stretches the party out for many weeks."

The other could not break a smile.

"What are you brewing for the party?"

"Black soup, very hot, fiery love potions that sparkle and sputter. It works with some small draughts. We have the house full of goodies now. The only thing we lack is people. Guests we have enough of, but the hosts are spread thin. It is not good for great doors, if the guests shall be regularly entertained."

Lodovico de Moroso was quiet again.

"But I am not the one to judge. We all want to save the lives we are fond of. And if someone or other says no to the wedding, I can understand. For it can get pretty hot."

"What are you saying, man?"

"I am not saying anything, Lord Lodovico, I am only telling you what they say at home in Rhodes, in the auberges and in the squares. Of course, we have all received invitations in these days. And many of us have thought quite a bit about how we might excuse ourselves and defect. But I have also thought about the great wedding feast invitation that our Lord sent out. It was pretty stupid to excuse oneself from it and not a little shameful. Therefore, I think I will make way back to Rhodes in the morning."

The knight sat and stirred in front of him for a moment.

"Well then, do they really believe we are afraid?"

"Not I, Lord Lodovico, but many of them. There with the commissioners came likewise too opportune. And people believe so much the worse . . ."

That is true. The knight went his way without much ceremony. Brother Antonio drank his wine in peace and quiet, strolled along the street and was suddenly engulfed by the darkness.

Then one morning the watch on Saint Nicolas came to distrust their eyes. On the sea behind the sandbar there was a whole flotilla turning toward Rhodes, but it was not the Turks. It was nothing but small boats, sixteen of them, freight boats and fishing vessels heavily laden and full of people, who curiously scrutinized the fortifications as the harbor opened before them. In front was one of the Religion's own brigantines with the Red Cross flag cracking from the mast top. It was Bosio.

There were also reports to the watch's commanding officer of couriers running in double time to the palace interrupting the proceedings and a great gathering at the wharf. Antonio Bosio stepped on land in triumph, bringing with him four hundred men and sixteen boat loads of wine and weapons. He immediately called on the Grand Master. There he reported on his trip, even about his contact with the deserters—and Martinengo.

"Really? How did it go?"

"He is not unwilling, Your Eminence. On the contrary, I believe he would like to be part of such a great history. But he is unwilling to break with the Duke. He is, of course, still a Venetian. He has built almost all of their fortresses and has a reputation to consider and possibly a great future. So he prays that His Eminence might write the signore and request that he loan out Signor Martinengo for a year or so for fortification work on Rhodes. If he receives permission, he is more than willing to come."

The Grand Master looked thoughtfully.

"But if he does not get it?"

"Then he still would like to, and one can always arrange for it one way or another."

"Possibly, if one is called Antonio Bosio. Well, you are cleared for travel again. But rest a couple days first."

"Or a couple weeks, Your Eminence. Not for my sake," he explained. "But those on Crete need to rest a couple of weeks before they see me again."

The Grand Master laughed.

"Three weeks then. We can't wait any longer."

Always Ready

THE APPEAL JUDGE FONTEYN—*REVERENDUS Dominus Jacobus Fontanus*, doctor of law *utriusque*, as he was called according to protocol, was in the Sunday promenade. His round face with the small near-sighted eyes were just as pale as when he left Brügge. He worked hard, but always inside the house and often long into the night.

It was the first day in June, the Sunday of Exaudi, and there would be another grand parade. They had been doing this for fourteen days, and it began to be a little too much for a cultured man. But the people were apparently just as enchanted. They cheered when the crew of the Grand Carrack marched through the city one Sunday morning fourteen days ago with harquebuses, pikes, and standards. They clapped hands respectfully when a hundred Spanish knights made the streets into a dark red poppy field with one hundred white crosses on the same evening. They warbled and rejoiced on Tuesday when their own seamen from Marrietta and la Galliga had their grand parade with the Wolf among them. On Thursday, Seigneur Dinteville came with knights from many langues, a stately show with rustling standards and a great many horses, more horses than ever seen in this city. And now it was the merchants' day, the last Sunday, when the Genoese Fornarri was sworn in with all his people as citizens. He had really earned it. He had come with his carrack from Alexandria and a full cargo of gunpowder and many people on board. He had lain outside Rhodes to get news of the Turkish flotilla. The Grand Master had sent out galleys, and by hook and crook, great promises and polite coercion, persuaded him to put into harbor and enter him and his men into the Grand Master's service. Now he too seemed to be seized by the all too prevalent war craze and was met with ovations. He proceeded in his magnificent garb made of half reddish gold material that glistened and half violet velvet. He had fifteen merchants behind him. They all wore the same bisected garb and long sleeves in the same colors. However, the pinnacle had been the Cretans, the unshaved skippers of the fifteen small coast vessels that came with Antonio Bosio. When they came on Thursday with their four hundred men carrying bows, guns, and long two-handed swords, the people almost tore down heaven. Not all mercenaries were greeted in this manner, but they fought here just like at home and not just for the money.

The appeals judge arrived in front of the Collachi and was satisfied to see the watch present arms. They were beginning to recognize him. Soon he would be one of the city's most important persons. The Grand Master called upon him the week before and let him know that if the city were besieged, all processes were to be suspended, and all courts were to cease their activity. Fonteyn had been appalled. Then the world would be altogether ruined. But the Grand Master comforted him. He would appoint three war judges with extraordinary powers to answer to the order and judge all urgent cases with the power of life and death. The Grand Master, of course, would still be free to pardon in matters of life. The occupants would now call the lord appeals judge, hoping that he will place his eminent expert knowledge at the Grand Master's disposal—*scientiam praeclaram peritiamque singularem*. The Grand Master had actually spoken in Latin, a skill that Jacobus Fontanus particularly appreciated. He thanked him in the same ringing speech with beautiful sentences so long that he was finally unable to remember the subject anymore and feared that the verb came in the singular when it ought to have been in the plural. But it wasn't anything noticeable.

He met doctor Appella, who had also come out to see the splendor outside the hospital. He looked distressed. Fonteyn wanted to look polite and interested, so he asked how well the pharmacy was stocked, seeing as they would now be cut off from the outside world for some weeks because of the events. The doctor replied that they were well stocked with most things: Mandragora, Alun and Indian Poppy, silk thread and cotton dressings, and oil of roses, but that he would like to have a little more Bolus Armenicus.

"Armenica," corrected Fonteyn. "Bolus is *genus feminimum*, Doctor."

But then the little Jew grew irate, replying that all genus could hang on the gallows for all he cared, if he only had enough Bolus Armenicus to make enough salve to dress all the wounds he would see in the coming months. And so they left each other in the crowd.

But it was not hard to find company today. There stood Antoine de Golart and Chevalier Chalant, whom he had been with on the boat.

"Hello, Chevalier. What is new?"

"A good deal. Dr. Galliga and Mariette have come home with people from the outposts. We are concentrating ourselves. In the morning we will begin demolishing the bridges to all the gates. Then the doctor will only go out through the north gate by the commercial port."

The appeals judge looked grave.

"Are they so close?"

"It is better to demolish bridges sooner than later, Doctor. We figure that they will sail from Constantinople within the week, if they haven't already begun."

He was interrupted by the trumpet blasts and revelry down by the vaulted gate opening to the city. There they came. Gianantonio Bonaldi, the Venetian captain, was in front. He had come with his boat and his people to fight on the right side even when his hometown wouldn't do it. The approval there was stormy and without end. Soon there were only fifty men when there could have been fifty thousand . . .

On Monday, the Grand Master received the final reports concerning the uneven odds. Inspections had begun a month ago. First the knights, langue after langue, then the citizenry, ship crews, mobilized Greeks, and various Cretans. So as to be on the safe side, they had been split up into small groups so that the foreign agents could not get an easy overview.

The information was also secret. They indicated that the knights and the serving brothers together were 612. Of turcopolers, seamen, and other people in firm service there were 918. The city militia and citizenry had been strengthened with people summoned from the islands, and were now approximately 2,400. Then there were the ship crews and newly secured mercenaries together, 1,100.

The total amount came to 5,030.

"And the Turks?" said the Grand Master thoughtfully. "Certainly they were 80,000, or possibly 120,000. This time it was likely more rather than less. At best it will be one against fifteen, probably one against twenty."

He thought for a moment.

"So long as the walls stand, we can manage that."

On Thursday there was a signal fire from Fisco on the other side. It was a sign that the Turks wanted something. A galley was sent out.

On the arrumbada, between the cannons, squeezed between the artillery troops and harquebusiers, sat André Barel with his friend Antoine. They had been able to follow with some occasional reinforcements.

They watched Saint Nicolas glide past and the city shrink, at first only into a walled city, then to a little knotty knob on the beach no different than a clenched fist. Before them Asia's Mountains rose out of the sea. After a couple of hours, they could see the shoreline with the light edge marked by the waves' furthermost reach on stormy days. There were other things hidden beyond the horizon.

They had a good wind, so the rowers rested. Their stench was not as strong as usual. The boat had just been in the harbor. The excrement had been scooped up out of the pools between the bottom blocks down by the keel. Otherwise one would rather sit on the windward side of the rowing benches, but today it was even tolerable on the leeward side.

What do the Turks want? They sat and talked with Iaxi, the Greek supply master, who came along as an interpreter. He knew the Turks well. He always traded on the sea, freely and openly or in secret. A great patron like the galley fleet's purchaser had friends in every corner.

It showed too when they finally reached their destination. The stony beach was unoccupied and deserted below the cliffs. But within a shallow bay, a little camp gathered around a fire. There was a man waving them in, so they rowed closer to the beach. Turkish merchants with bales of cloth and rugs in piles had struck camp there in a glade of brush.

Iaxi called out to them from the arrumbada in Turkish, and soon there was a conversation. No one onboard—except for the slaves—could understand what they were saying.

André watched the Turks with interest. Bearded, overgrown men with hard girdles weaved around their stately bellies. He tried to imagine them twenty years younger, as soldiers. They would not have been easy to fight.

After an hour, Iaxi called up to the Commander on the poop deck:

"They can send an envoy to the Aga who lit the signal last night, but it takes an hour. They invited me ashore."

"Not without a hostage," the Commander bellowed back. "Tell them that one of them must first come on board."

Iaxi talked to the merchants again. Now they came down to the shore. He had a good-natured way of saying sensitive things, and they appeared to understand completely. They pointed out one of the most well-dressed men in the company, and Iaxi nodded. The ship's boat set out. The Turk stood down among the stones and stepped on board as Iaxi hopped on land. The boat turned back.

André cast only a fleeting glimpse at the Turk. He looked rich, but not very bright. He looked with interest at the shore. The Turks greeted Iaxi courteously and heartily. Iaxi was in command of the whole ceremony. It took an hour before they transported him up to the fire and the wares that lay a good piece in from the shore. They continued a bit in between the bushes. It was as if they were having a lot of fun.

But in the same moment, the laughter died and André heard Iaxi scream. The small forest in the back had grown to double its height in a second. About fifty men with Turkish banners, pikes, and swords threw themselves around Iaxi. They snatched him and disappeared, accompanied by the well-dressed merchants.

André turned to his friend Antoine.

"What do we do? Shoot? Go ashore?"

Antoine bit his lip.

"It's useless. There is nothing we can do. We have been duped. Perhaps we can take some of that merchandise as a little reminder of our friend Iaxi."

However, Chevalier Meneton, who was in command, would not allow that either. There could still be an ambush set. He ordered that they head back out to sea and begin interrogating the Turk, who came as a hostage. They found him to be a wretched small farmer, half Greek, dressed up and scared to death.

They had been utterly duped.

The supply master, Iaxi, bumped along on horseback in a sharp trot with his hands tied in front of him so that he could just hold himself in the saddle. Sipahis trotted beside him on good horses with long pistols and daggers in their belts, axes or clubs in their saddles, shields and bows on their backs.

He had collected himself from the first knockout and began to look around him, practiced as he was at putting everything into memory. They had ridden past Marmaris. The city was barely recognizable. The fortress was rebuilt and expanded, the whole environs covered in canvas, barracks, sheds, and storehouses. It swarmed with soldiers. Cannon balls as big as watermelons lay stacked in long ridges with almost uncanny precision. Stores of beams, rafters, boards, and planks covered the sandy beach. There were guards everywhere, and it was quiet as quiet as only the Turkish regiments could be in camp.

To his surprise, they did not go around Marmaris but continued along the back up through the tall forest. This was the way to Skutari and Constantinople. He was beginning to be a little scared, but still continued to look around. All along the way, the forest was filled with tents and horse camps, of steeds with sheep and goats, fires and boiling kettles, cannons and camels, and people, people, people, without end.

He wondered how they could have forgotten to blindfold him. It was a mistake to let him see all this.

Suddenly, his blood ran ice cold. They knew that it made no difference! He would never see Rhodes again. Never again talk with a Christian man. The only people he would ever talk to now were the interrogators and torture masters.

How long? Possibly three weeks, maybe six. They were masters at torturing people to death over a long time. How much would they get out of him? He prayed beforehand for forgiveness to Christ, the Holy Baptist, and all the saints. The most important thing now was to stand fast. Rather three weeks' hellish torture among the Turks now than an eternity with them on the other side. They could not take his faith from him.

The night before the next Sunday, Pentecost Sunday, the fire signal from Fisco was lit again. A galley went out again—with a little flickering hope that one could still get Iaxi back. This time there were soldiers on the other side. They said that they brought a letter from the Sultan. The Christians should come get it after they determined where best to cast anchor. But the Commander let the soldiers understand that this time they would not fall for their tricks. He asked what they had done with Iaxi but didn't get an answer. Then he turned the galley. When the Turks saw it, they threw the letter tied to a stone on board. It was from the Sultan.

The council didn't need to ruminate long over the contents. Suleiman gave notice of his decision to take the isle of Rhodes into his possession. If they turned it over freely, he gave his oath that all the inhabitants great and small could remain in their faith, their customs, their work, and their time-honored way of life. If any wanted to leave, they were free to do so with both goods and family. If any wanted to enter into the Sultan's service, he would be welcomed with better conditions than those he had formerly offered. The Sultan waited for an immediate and affirmative reply to this offer.

"In any case, you may be assured that Our Imperial Majesty is already on his way to you with all that war requires, and then the decision will be determined by God. We have desired duly to inform you of this so that you will not be able to say that you were not rightly summoned, warned, and informed. We will then raze your castle to the ground, not leaving one stone on another, and let you and yours be slaves and die a violent and sudden death, according to the Almighty's will, as we have done with many others. Therefore, you may be fully and certainly advised. Given by Our Imperial Sovereignty in court at Constantinople, the first day in June."

This was the declaration of war. One could only answer such a summons with cannons.

The Archbishop

Day after day they waited for the Turks. Every evening Fra Giovanni would speak to his brothers in the order for a short while. He had an unbelievable memory, almost as good as the Archbishop's. The only difference was Fra Giovanni remembered Bible verses and could cite the prophets, while Monsignor Balestrini had an inexhaustible penchant for citing Cicero, Ovidius, Vergilius and Petrarca.

Fra Giovanni did not speak in vain. There was seriousness in the air. As Bosio said, "one was invited to the wedding." The knights knew enough about the Great King's wedding to think about their wedding clothes. They went to confession more often than usual. There was an increase in self-assumed penance. Perhaps because the order's rules stated that a brother who was found in open fornication would be excluded, while a wretched sinner, whose mistake had not been discovered, would be able to hand the matter over to God, provided that he imposed upon himself a proper penance.

One morning after mass, Monsignor Balestrini, the Archbishop, called upon brother Giovanni. The Archbishop was preparing the sermon he would give the knights on Sunday, Holy Trinity Sunday. He wanted to hear what brother Giovanni would have said to them. Might the brother possibly suggest some good word to proceed from?

"Monsignor should maybe begin with a word of admonition," the little Italian said cautiously while looking at him with his round childlike eyes.

"For example?"

"Maybe that which is written in Jeremiah in the second chapter: 'For they turn their back to me and not their face, but when trouble comes they say: "arise and save us!" Surge et libera nos!'"

Monsignor threw both hands up:

"But I should encourage them! Strengthen their courage, the will to fight, and faith in victory! One can't speak that way."

"Reverendissime, I do not mean only this. Later one can go over to the other."

"For example?"

"Maybe it is written in the next chapter: 'Return, O faithless sons, and I will heal your faithlessness. Behold we come to you, for you are the Lord our God.'"

The Archbishop looked to be thinking.

"I shall think on the matter" was all he said.

Sunday came. The evening before, one of the brigantines, which had gone out on reconnaissance, reported that the Turkish armada had passed Mytilene. All the Religion's knights and serving brothers stood solemn and silent under the dark blue star-strewn wood roof that stretched over San Giovanni's slender pillars. Monsignor spoke.

It was a beautiful speech. "Lucullentissima oratio" thought the judge Fonteyn, who sat among the honored guests up front. His Right Reverend swept over history; he called forward from memory the council and the fathers' victory-rich fight, the great threat of the infidel, and the glorious task of opposing the tyranny. He pointed to his bishop's cross and said that even he sought to annihilate the unbelievers and all their work. So now he wanted to give some good reasons why they should be certain of victory. God has many reasons to punish, but he was a forgiving God. And the first among all the saints, the Baptist himself, the Holy forerunner fought for his own order. How strong were the defense works! How infinitely better now than in d'Aubusson's day! And they had still won a glorious victory in his days. Monsignor spoke warmly about the walls, the artillery, and the boulevards, and not least about their unrivalled leadership.

The Grand Master squirmed and thought: the walls are good enough, but I would rather hear about another fortress. The one written about in the Psalms: "In the Lord I have my refuge and fortress, My God in whom I trust" (Psalm 91:2).

The long speech was finished. The Knights moved about again. They were seized by the final word about the two possibilities: be victorious and honored all over the earth, or fall and win the martyr's crown—in both cases an imperishable honor.

Amirelen d'Airasca, the Italian Pilier, went up and kissed Monsignor on the hand, thanked him for the beautiful words, and assured him that that all were built up and satisfied—molto edificati e soisfatti.

In the sacristy Monsignor turned to Fra Givoanni.

"Did you notice that I gave them an orderly admonition?"

"What do you mean, your Right Reverend?"

Monsignor looked irritated.

"You didn't notice it? I said that God forgives when men begin to be better and more watchful of their obligations, so as we now are doing, noble knights—I said—as I should wish that you always did, *quod ut semper faciatis velim*! You didn't hear that?"

Fra Giovanni looked at him with his child-like pious eyes, almost hopeless.

"I heard that, Reverendissime, God grant that they take it to heart."

He knew that he ought to say something else: You only said that, your Right Reverend, to calm your own conscience, not to awaken theirs. But courage left him.

They Are Coming!

THEY ARE COMING.

The rumor spread like fire in grass on a late summer day. A man had seen them from one of the towers up on the mountain: a forest of masts in the bay behind Simi. Everyone rushed to the walls by the sea and hung over the breastwork. But there was nothing to see and nothing happened. If one went up on the old acropolis where fallen pillar stumps jutted up among the thistles, one could see the masts when the haze lifted. Only the masts. The rest were hidden behind the water's reflection. But the Turks seemed only to cross back and forth along the coast. Slowly, they moved this strange forest of naked treetops, which rose up out of the water.

In the Grand Master's palace, they knew the reason. It was only the first detachment, approximately thirty ships. They had made an unsuccessful landing on Lango, burned their fingers, and continued.

Life began returning to normal again. On land, the ripened grain was cut, carried to the city, and then up to the castle. In the Mandraki, there was a steady stream of small boats, heavy laden with refugees from the islands.

"They're coming!"

This time it was a false alarm. It was only the thirty galleys. Everyone knew that it wasn't the great armada. Still, they looked out cautiously. There were not many on the walls who had seen so many boats at once.

It was Tuesday, exactly one week since the Turks had first been sighted. And it was Saint John the Baptist's day, one of the year's great feasts for the Johnites. Everything was celebrated as usual, the high mass in San Giovanni, the long procession through the city with all the knights in their black capes with white crosses, the long litany, the wax candles, the Baptist's picture under the canopy, and the great standard—all as usual.

People ran along the walls and squares so as not to miss any spectacle. The Grand Master continuously read reports discretely brought to him where he followed in the parade, first in line behind the Baptist's picture, quietly and happily smiling as usual.

The squadron glided past on the other side of the point and continued to the south along the island's west side.

In the evening, one knew that the enemy lay outside Fanés. Some detachments had been inland and burnt the grain that hadn't yet been harvested. There was no question of a great land invasion.

The next morning the Turks were gone again. They had sailed back to Simi in the night.

On the boulevard d'Auvergne, the clang of the stone hewers' chisels was silenced for the first time in half a year. A group turned out the last load of stone flakes and the broken pieces. The Auvergnat langue prepared to take possession of its new boulevard. The cannons that stood ready on the curtain were rolled out on the new platform.

There it lay now like a massive mountain, prominently imposing in the moat where it made a great curve to the west to take itself around the massive bastion.

Chevalier Chalant supervised the placement of the pieces. André Barel was in command of a group that would put the culverin in place on the north side. They were all just about to lift it together to get the front wheel up in the right circle of stones that marked the piece's place when someone came running.

"Was macht ihr da? Die Mauer gehört uns! Our wall! Verstanden?"

It was a serving brother of the German langue, and he was not alone. In fact, there were two standing with him carrying crossbows cocked and ready. And now one of their knights came running.

"Abite! Weg von hier!"

The chevalier spotted them and came over.

"What's going on?"

In broken Lingua Franca, the German tried to explain that this piece of wall—he pointed to the encircling wall before the Boulevard's north side—was allotted to the German langue. Because it still remained a boulevard outside, it belonged to the Germans according to all regulations, precedents, and privileges.

André looked at the German, a little broad shouldered lord with red cheeks, full in the belly and lips, with an energetic wrinkle between the eyebrows and very straight in the back.

Chalant tried to work with him. He suggested that one should still be able to put the cannons there, at least until later. But the German fastened his eyes on him. Impossible! Such could establish precedent.

"Ich darf unsere Hoheitsrechte nicht aufgeben."

Meanwhile, the sweaty workers a little ways away had pried the piece into place. The German saw it. He ran over and shoved the closest Auvergnat away, waved his people over, and began to roll the cannon back. At first it was a tug of war, and then it came to blows. People rushed in from all over the boulevard. The Germans were helplessly disadvantaged. They retreated to the breastworks and stood there burning with anger and bitterness. One of them bled from his lips. The knight had drawn his sword. Reinforcements ran from the German wall.

"Madmen!" someone yelled. "When you have a hundred thousand Turks within sight! 'Cento mila turchi!'"

It was d'Airasca, the admiral. He had come by to look at the new boulevard. Because he was an Italian and therefore impartial, he successfully got the exasperated men to at least break apart from each other. Then he bade them go before the Grand Master and the council to settle the matter. Until then, the cannons should stay where they were.

Everyone was satisfied with this. The Germans stood, silent and resolute along their wall. The Frenchmen turned their backs to them and went back to work.

D'Airasca found the Grand Master in the tree garden where he inspected the second of the four reserve cadres that he would place behind the Spanish and English walls under the command of Sir John Buck. Even the Marshal took part in the inspection. It could hardly have turned out better. Three Grand Crosses were already gathered. The only thing left was to go directly to the ordinances, and after a half an hour when the inspection was over, there was a quorum for council.

The Grand Master seemed to take the scandal calmly. He knew that it was the drawback of one of his greatest tasks: the langues jealously guarded the right to protect their particular sector. Each langue had its traditions, its customs, and its ambitions.

And the langues could happily have those. Precisely because of these, they were able to make the impossible possible. The absurd consequences he would have to take in the bargain. It belonged to his tasks to coax them to the right.

Speedily and Solomonicly, the council arrived at a decision. The matter would be submitted to the Religion's highest authority, the general chapter, sometime in the future when it was possible to assemble. Until then, the Auvergnats would defend the whole boulevard. But in the contested area, no other standards would be placed other than the Grand Master's and the Religion's.

One of the writers immediately wrote down the decision: after hearing from the procurator of the worthy Auvergne Langue, as well as the procurator of the Worthy German Langue—and so forth, until the final comment: "and neither of the parties could establish aforesaid delay as precedent, more or less, as certain for better right or other grounds of what part it was whatsoever, over and above that which by the dispute was originally submitted."

The lords were soon finished.

It was the last decision of the council that the protocol recorded that year.

The next morning the Turks came in earnest. It was again a great feast day, Octovan of Corpus Christi, and again it was celebrated with all the usual ceremonies. As usual, the Grand Master carried the sacrament in procession around the church and allowed all the usual prayers before he placed it on the altar again. As soon as it was over, he went up into the palace to go through the reports that streamed in all morning.

Already at daybreak, all the city's church bells rang to signal that it was time to take position on the walls. People from the vicinity came in an unbroken stream, carrying over their shoulders all sorts of spades, scythes, and crowbars. The donkeys could hardly be seen under burdens of bedclothes and household goods, and so the women with children on their shoulders, children on their backs, and children by the hand. It sounded and looked like mourners at a funeral, the women coming in with unkempt hair and the children dirtied with soot and trail dust.

Because it was good custom to share another's misery, the women in the city began to complain and cry in the same manner. Just like it was at a great funeral, the streets were full of groaning and lamentation.

From the walls, masts and sails could be seen coming up from behind the horizon. It was futile to count them. Then the ships came forward. The whole sea was covered. They were all types that were sometimes seen in the harbor at Rhodes: galleys, ketches, galiots, galleons, carracks, paranderies, mahons, brigantines, fusts, and eskiras.

They held course directly for the city, and the nervousness climbed for those on the walls. Finally, prolonged rolling drum rolls were heard echoing from the palace, from the barracks, from Saint Nicholas and all the towers. The alarm bells rang and tolled. The gates to the palace went up and out rode the Grand Master in his best Italian armor with the gold chasing on the helmet and the breastplate practically glittering in the sun. Behind him came the bodyguards and the musical entourage and the first company of reserves under himself, d' Amaral. The trumpeters sounded their signals, other trumpeters answered along the walls, and out of the domiciles, barracks, and lodgings streamed knights, slaves, and citizens out into the city, fully-equipped. The mourning women finished pulling their hair and looked curiously at the splendor. The farmers who shouted and quarreled, scuffled and crowded, quieted and let themselves be moved to the side. They too stared with wide eyes. At first everything was chaotic. All marched around each other to different places. It was a muddle of nodding helmet plumes and swinging halberds. But then the streets emptied. All knew where they should be. In a few minutes, they were up on the walls and boulevards or gathered in the reserve's parade grounds. It was remarkably quiet. Only music played. All the flags went up. They fluttered and smacked along the breastwork, red and white and golden yellow against the blue sky.

During this time, the armada changed course and sailed west around the island's north point at a safe distance down along the coast. It disappeared behind the mountain of Trianda.

There was time for siesta. The people slept in the shade behind the breastwork. Nothing happened. But when the sun began to go down, the armada came back. Maybe they found the west wind too harsh to throw anchor. They were trying to get over to the other side of the island.

The endless row of ships rounded the point at a respectful distance with sails swelling in the wind and long streamers that pranced in elegantly beating loops against the sky. The music corps played. The Janissaries' white hats contrasted against the blue sea, and the people by the railings shouted their battle cries.

The trumpets and drums answered from the city's walls and towers and a thundering "Saint Jean" bellowed from thousands of throats. It was the Religion's old battle cry that used to ring out on the battlefields in the Holy Land.

"It is just like a great festival," said the war judge to Gianantonio Bonaldi. They had ended up together on the Italian wall by the ocean beach along the east and had an excellent view.

"Almost as it was when I came here with His Eminence a year ago. War can be very beautiful."

"The first page in a book is often the most beautiful, Lord Doctor."

In the same moment, a cannon shot thundered not too far away. Dr. Fonteyn held his ears in fear and shut his eyes. The big piece over there had made a long scoot backwards, the smoke still engulfing it.

Bonaldi watched inquisitively over the sea. He was able to follow the big cannon ball. A white splash came out of the water.

"This side," he said, "by a long shot."

But the Italian wall did not yield. This time they lowered the cannon barrel and attempted a ricochet. The cannon ball fell gradually, skipped on the water and lifted itself again almost as if someone played ducks and drakes with it. But it didn't reach either.

"Think if they shot back," said the judge.

"Such happens in war, Lord Doctor. But not right now. Those are galleys out there, and they have to turn their nose this way before they can do anything. But was it not fun? Lord Doctor, those bringing letters will always be answered."

High up in Tour Naillac, the Wolf stood with two comrades and a writer. They watched and discussed and dictated.

"One big galley, say nine-hundred . . . Up to nine-hundred, but it is Janissaries, not that. Then we have a galeas, one of the biggest. What do you think it carries, Pietro?"

"Maybe eleven-hundred."

"Then we will write that. And next . . . a big trunk in the paranderia. Good little people on deck. She certainly has cannons and stores. What should we write?"

"Best to specify what she can carry."

Then we guess," said the Wolf. "Two-thousand salmi—what do you say?"

"Write two-thousand five-hundred salmi, do you hear? Don't count it together with the men."

They watched, counted, and added until the twilight made all observations uncertain. Then they reported to the Grand Master.

The answer was read: Soldiers, sixty-four thousand, excluding rowers and seaman. Of them at least eight-thousand Janissaries. A lot of supplies, at least nine huge boats able to carry five-hundred cannons with all the tack.

The Wolf finished:

"It would also be the first delivery. I guess that they have more coming."

The Art of Survival

D R. APELLA SIGHED. HIS hardest hour had come, the hardest in his life.

Deep within his being there was an instinct stronger than all others: the will to survive. Perhaps he inherited it from his fathers, who patiently developed the art over centuries of persecution. Despite everything, they managed to save their lives from horrid fates and were able to pass on the art of survival to new children of Abraham.

He remembered his childhood home in Smyrna, painted in violet like all the other Jewish homes, scorned by sons of the prophet and despised by the Christians. His father had patiently born all wrongs, coaxed, compromised, adjusted, and yet always remained the same. He made endless sacrifices to help his son study. So he too became a doctor, and it was his misfortune.

He remembered the evening in Constantinople when he was called to a strange little office near the seraglio. It took a good hour before he realized that some of the kingdom's mightiest and most dangerous lords were in front of him. He played as dumb as he could. But they mercilessly put him in the vice and forced him to understand. He was to be sent as an agent. He would gather information as a loyal subject of the Sultan—that is what he was, right? It would not be unprofitable for him if he survived. The Sultan always paid *after the service*. They looked at him knowingly.

So he had to survive. He tried to win some time. He wanted to know what it meant. But he could not escape. First, he had to answer, yes or no. He answered, yes.

So they developed the plan.

The Sultan needed an agent in Rhodes, a cunning and broadminded man with opportunity in leading circles. Everyone knew Rhodes had a shortage of doctors. He would move there and open up practice. Of course, all the Jews had been banished from there already at the turn of the century—as always, they were accused of spying and general unreliability—but he would certainly be accepted if he presented himself at the very beginning as a convert desiring instruction for baptism.

He tried to win time. He had to complete his training. It was allowed. He thought about fleeing. But where would he run? The threat of deportation would hang over him wherever he went in Christendom. And then where would he go if he had certain death waiting for him under the half moon? He needed to survive.

So he came to Rhodes with very useful instructions. He took reports that were then carried via Chios, the mastic island under the protection of the Genoese, whose neutrality was respected by all.

It had gone better than he had thought. There were many bad people and good people, as in most places. The knights were in a class by themselves, different than the others. They could play the bully, but they could also be very charming. And you could only admire their capability.

Even the baptismal instruction he had suffered through. He had long ago shed the hair he had when he was baptized, but he had discovered something that the fussy and talkative Dominicans never had informed him of. This Jesus was a Jew. Peter was a Jew, Jacob, John, Andrew, Phillip, Thomas—all were Jews. This admired Baptist that all the knights held as their order's patron was Jewish.

He took strength from that when the day of his baptism that he feared could no longer be postponed: It was a Jew, a compatriot, one of his own persecuted people, one whom they bullied and killed, who had commanded it. And it was more Jews who had carried this wonderful custom out into the world. However crazy baptism may be, it was still something that belonged to his own people. It was not a concept that belonged to these heartless persecutors alone.

Because of this, he was able to send his reports without great risk and without scruples of conscience. He reported the things that happened: what had been razed and what had been built, who left and who was appointed, how many people were enlisted or were demobilized, and what the gossip said about the plans concerning foreign policy. The Sultan was able to get most of this information himself. He never thought of himself as a black traitor. He certainly had no obligation to these Franks, who never gave his own people anything but trouble. But he was still a doctor, and he was so with his whole heart. Now he thought about all the men he had successfully treated. There were many of them here in the city by now.

But now it happened. He had feared it all this last year.

He looked around the room. The door was closed, the bolt in place. Cautiously, he unfolded the piece of paper.

It had been inserted in the chink of the door, invisible from the outside. He had no idea how it had gotten there. It was written in Turkish with the Arabic script that he knew well since his earliest years of study.

He read it again.

"Beloved, I long for news from you. Send me a greeting, from your window straight to me. I light my red lantern there. I want to know how it is with you, if my gifts come and how they are received. If any of yours are sick then let me know. My heart burns with longing for news. You know the reward of the faithful, just as you know the fate of the unfaithful."

He laughed bitterly. It was so thoughtful of them to give it in the form of a love letter so that the knights would think that old Apella had a Turkish lover somewhere among the prisoners—if the letter had gone astray.

So—they wanted to know how their gifts were received. They would soon begin to bombard the city. And if any of them were sick—that meant that they wanted to know the number of casualties. When it came to the wounded, he would know better than anyone else.

He entered the outbuilding they gave him to send the message over the walls. He wrapped the paper around the shaft of a bolt, tying it down with string; then he would put the bolt in the crossbow and shoot. He stored the crossbow in the closet. For safety's sake, he had had sometimes gone hunting for deer and rabbits in the hills above the city or went target shooting with the knights to their great satisfaction. So there was nothing suspicious about his crossbow.

But now, after so many years, it would be used as it was meant to be used since the beginning.

He went to the window. He lived up high, and had a remarkable view over the houses before the Auvergne wall. He could think of it in the dark. Did a match not light there? Behind the wall the terrain of the mountain rose up. And there in the dark, a bit outside the Turkish encampment, a red lamp lit.

He pondered. He needed to survive. And going to the Grand Master to confess everything was too risky. It was silly. His sense of understanding told him that the Sultan had every reason to win this duel. The day the Janissaries broke into the city no one but those under the Sultan's protection would be spared.

Throwing the protection away meant almost certain death. It was a risk to secure it, but a reasonable risk. He had to take it if he wanted to survive.

He took a little piece of paper and wrote in Turkish:

"My lover, I have received your letter. I will come some time this evening when I have a worthy gift to give you. Hang out your lamp when the time is convenient." He took a deep breath and shut the door. Then he picked up his crossbow, lashed the paper around the bolt, pulled the bow taut with the screeching crank, laid the bolt in the bolt groove and blew out the light.

Slowly, he opened up the only shutter and aimed at the red lamp. It was eerily quiet. The bolt's hiss had to be heard over the wall. But then someone beat a drum roll, and a dog barked. He fired the shot.

July 1522

CHEVALIER BAREL INSPECTED HIS two cannons.

He was a knight now, him, little brother André, who had just turned nineteen this last year. The Grand Master had permitted all the novices to be dubbed knights as soon as it was no longer important to finish out their year as a novice.

André stroked a hand over his new surcoat with the white cross and quietly fingered his sword hilt. He had left his golden spurs at home. They would only have laughed at him if he had strutted around with such antiquated things here among the cannons.

He would never forget the high holy days in the church this past year. His time as a novice had been useful. He now knew that there was seriousness behind all the pomp and ancient rituals the Grand Master read.

It is written that he who desires to be received into such an honorable society as the Hospitallers has does well. "But if you do so because you see that we are well clothed and ride on stately steeds and have all of life's necessities, then you receive it badly. For when you want to eat, you will be forced to fast. When you want to sleep, you will have to be awake, and when you want to be awake, you will have to sleep. You will be sent to places that do not please you. You will give up all your desires in order to fulfill another's order. You will have a rough time in many ways in this order. Are you willing to subject yourself to all this?"

He had answered that yes, he was willing, and he meant it.

The newly fledged Chevalier stepped up on a powder keg and looked over the breastwork at the Turkish encampment. He did it with a nonchalance that was no longer advisable. There was not much to be afraid of. The Turks over there did everything dubiously and awkwardly. They needed two weeks to come on land. One could see from the walls the powerful flotilla in the bay of Paramboli. Huge boats came and went day in and day out in unbroken ferry traffic from the mainland. People came on land, many people. Gropingly, they made their way over there, just out of range. They had set up their camp and took shelter behind an earthen wall. But they had hardly ventured into the broad cleared-away area from the moat where all houses and gardens were carefully leveled to the ground weeks before the invasion. As soon as they attempted to, they were met with fire from the walls.

The knights had launched attacks many times. It was a job for experienced men, and André had to watch from the walls. There was always panic among the Turks at first. Their field workers ran for their lives and their Azab, the light infantry, were beat unhesitantly and badly. Then the order of the Janissaries came in closed ranks under nodding heron feathers. Then the knights would slowly draw back, overpowered. He had been there to cover the retreat with his cannons many times.

But now there were no more attacks. The Grand Master wanted to spare his people. The powder needed to be spared. But as soon something cropped up within range, the cannon thundered from the walls.

Chevalier André looked at the tents in the camp, some conical, others stretched long, some brown and faded gray; most were colorful, some lined with gold fringe. It was said that others were poor. There had been many deserters, a few of the many. Some were surely dispatched to spy. The deserters often said the same things. The soldiers sulked and were disappointed. They had believed they were going to Italy and were going to have the richest plundering. Then they ended up on this mountainous island where everything was deserted, and the best a man could find was a rusty frying pan in a deserted house. Every single onion and every bit of cheese had to be shipped over from the mainland, and the food was old. There was loud grumbling; and Mustafa, the supreme commander who answered directly to the Sultan, had all he could do to transport the siege works.

At least the last information checked out. One could see that with his bare eyes.

Preian de Bidoulx, the commander of Lango, reported to the Grand Master heated, unshaved, and fresh from the sea. He had convincingly requested to come to Rhodes in order not to miss "si bonne affaire." So he had been given permission if he could still make it through the blockade.

He was able to do that, and it had not been particularly hard, he said. He had hidden in a bay on Simi and studied the Turkish blockade boats' habits. Then in the cover of darkness, he just slunk into the great channel where the boats go day and night between Marmaris and Rhodes. Cautiously, he followed the Turks almost down to where they anchored and then turned and followed the same lead back. Then all he had to do was cross back in front of Saint Nicolas. No one expected that a ship coming from that direction would turn out to be the enemy.

The Grand Master listened intently. It followed that the blockade was broken. He had counted on it. With the powerful west wind now during the summer, a relief flotilla had every prospect of breaking through. He built his plan based on that.

He explained. The night after the Turkish armada passed by, he had sent two fast boats with a special envoy to the Pope, Emperor Charles, and King Frans. They would report that the siege had begun and that it was now life or death. If Christendom wanted to keep its lock on the Eastern Sea, then one could not allow the Grand Turk to go undisturbed as long as it was possible to stop him. Also small reinforcements could be important. The Grand Master appealed and pleaded. And then all the brothers of the Order were issued orders to report without delay with all they could scrape together of people and necessities.

"When can we have them here?" Bidoulx asked.

"Possibly as soon as the end of August, probably in September."

"And until then?"

"We endure. Brilliantly, if the Turks continue in this tack."

They immediately went out onto the walls. Bidoulx was doubly welcome for all he knew about cannons. One had his worry. Most of the men were inexperienced. Their aim left a lot to be desired, and they often missed. Then there was yesterday's incident on the English wall.

They stood before the piece that had blown up, a practical culverin cast a year or two ago in Lyon with a relief of a fire-spewing basilisk on the bore. The piece had cracked right over the powder compartment. Two men had died on the spot. You could still see the blood on the stones. Why?

The powder charge was normal, the master bombardier informed them, as is called for. He was a renowned man who could be trusted in his tasks.

"And well packed?" asked Bidoulx.

"That the Chevalier can be certain of," said one of the slaves. "We thrusted eight times."

The Frenchman nodded.

"There we have it. I have seen it before. The powder wants to have space to move and dance; otherwise, it sparks the wrong way. Four times and not too hard."

"You can go through it with them," said the Grand Master. "All are commanded to gather together after Vespers."

Three days later—it was the nineteenth of July—Bidoulx was called to the Auvergne wall. Brother Raymond Rogier, the commander, asked to introduce his youngest colleague, Chevalier Barel.

"New in service, I see. Congratulations."

Bidoulx looked at the greenhorn with his one eye, as usual.

"What's going on?"

"The Chevalier has made a little discovery," said Rogier.

André felt a little upset. What if it all turned out to be nothing?

"See there," he said. "Just left in the edge of the hole, the little earth wall. It has grown over night and it seems to be just a wood roof on the upper edge. Can it not be . . . ?"

He hesitated. Bidoulx didn't.

"Ma Foi! A mantle. Are you loaded?"

André nodded.

"Then we will aim precisely where the forest is, where it opens up."

"It is wide," Bidoulx said, "I wonder how many pieces they can have there? How many do you have covering this section?"

"Three," answered André without needing to think about it. "This one here, the six over there, and the one on the Spanish wall."

Rogier looked satisfied. His people honored him in front of Bidoulx. They conferred and gave their order. Then they waited.

The high summer sun burned relentlessly. Helmets, harnesses, and hip plates were as hot as hearths. The soldiers had to insulate so as not to burn themselves. It was warm, but one got used to it.

"Now," whispered André, who never let the earth mound over there out of sight.

Slowly, like a drawbridge, he raised the giant-like wood flap. In the deep forest peeped three or four cannons. Bidoulx pointed them out competently.

"Passevolanter or sacres. Not too much, but we shall not be fastidious. Fire."

The black smoke hid everything. But on the boulevard one could see that they had hit. When the visibility cleared, it seemed they had split the boards in a heap over the Turkish cannons. Some moved about the remains, but no Turk dared show himself.

The next morning the mantel stood there again, and they began from the beginning. Evidently the Turks had planks to spare, like people.

That same day Antonio Bosio sat in a little fish boat off the coast of Crete. He had slipped into a bay with a sandbar just before a sheer steep cliff where he sat completely invisible.

He waited. All had gone just as he had planned. The duke and the signori had said no to the Grand Master's polite request to borrow Gabriele Tadine da Martinengo, the famous defense work architect, for a few months. It was a brisk and impolite no, intended to be heard by Constantinople.

Before it reached there, brother Antonio had snuck in the back way to the noble house in Candia where Martinengo lived. They talked about what would happen if they were denied. That is why he was now here waiting.

He slept his siesta in the afternoon heat and was woken by steps in the sand. It was Matteo, an old friend he had in the village on the other side of the point. Where didn't he have old friends? And he had important news with him.

Two riders from Candia had come. The one had a red livery with a gold lion on the stomach and a big trumpet in his hand. He had blown a clattering fanfare in the middle of the siesta, and the other announced on behalf of the duke that a certain Gabriele Tadini, called Martinengo had absconded and was suspected of traitorous conspiracy. Therefore, all his goods were forfeited and would be confiscated. He himself would be searched for. He who found him would get twenty gold ducats, and he who kept him hidden would be hung.

Exciting things were about to happen and they did. Horse hooves stamped in the back. Three lords rode down in a gallop and jumped out of their saddles. The first was tall, broad-shouldered, slender, with deep-set eyes and an enormous nose. It was Martinengo.

"They are after us," he said.

"Then we split," said brother Antonio. "Welcome aboard!"

"No, they are coming by sea with a galley. They know that we have to have a boat waiting somewhere."

"Then we will go by land. May I ask the lords for a little help?"

He loosened the stay and took down the mast.

"And so a little further up on land. May I ask for a lift? Yet a little closer to the cliff there, and then get in with all you want to have with you, for we must ask Messer Mateo to let the horses disappear in the forest."

"And now we build ourselves a little tent," he continued. "Like Peter on the mount of Transfiguration."

He had loosened the big lateen sail from the pole. It had once been reddish brown, but the sun and salt had given it the same color as the rocks on the shore. "May I ask the lords to crawl in? It is good for us to be here. Lord, the Baptist, keep your hand over us."

Martinengo looked at the arrangement first. His eyes glistened. The sail covered precisely that part of the boat that could be seen when the galley made a little excursion into the bay to look around.

They crept in just in time. They could hear the oars beat and the hammers clang against the gong. The galley rowed on by.

"Now we only need to wait until they row back past in the evening tired and angry," said Bosio. "Then the sea will be free, until we see beloved old Rhodes and the Turks. Maybe the lords will give their names? I missed them in the haste."

"Yes, they are Scaramosa and Conversalo, and they are lifelong friends."

The twenty-second of July. Martinengo had successfully made it. After a couple hours, he knew almost everything. He had been up in the campanile and seen the Turkish lines, their ditches and earthworks, which now stretched around the city in a circle from the bay by Akandia to the beach at Saint Nicolas. He established that they would soon have their heavy batteries clear and that the chief part of them seemed to be south of the city. He went around the walls, stepped down on the boulevards, toured all the casemates, and inspected every cannon aperture and its field of fire. He inquired of all that the defectors said.

"Many thousand miners from Bosnia and Valakiet? That means that they will concentrate on tunneling and blasting on a grand scale. What do we have for counter measures?"

He was already saying "we." The Grand Master noticed that and answered:

"When we heard how they breached Belgrade easily, we had Bidoulx make preparations, which consisted of digging out the moat's bottom and those shafts. They are like listening posts, and from the holes we can start countermines."

Martinengo thought.

"The risk is that they pour earth down and fill the approaches for us. Then they put snipers to guard it and make it impossible to move about down there in daylight. We ought to have a cover, an underground passage along the whole moat a good piece from the walls. It would be in the way of all their tunnels. Do we have people?"

"Plenty just now. The builders are just now finishing."

"Then we must take the opportunity. When they begin to shoot in seriousness, we will have all we can do to make repairs. Where should we start? Can we go look?"

He was already on the way.

In the hospital the men were busy dressing the first round of wounds, some saber cuts and many bullet wounds. The Turks were good with guns of all types. And they shot well, better than anyone had believed.

Shooter Franz helped the surgeon, brother Gierolamo. He wetted the opium sponges and held them to the noses of the injured. Some slept after a little while. Others knocked the sponge away and said that it smelled poisonous. Then brother Franz would point a little cautiously to a shot-up leg or show them master Geirolamo's saw so that they understood that the bitter smell was not the worst. He innately objected to using such means. He reddened every time he was forced to it, but he knew of no better way.

Doctor Apella stayed more and more with the wounded, though it really wasn't his obligation. Brother Geirolamo was glad to do it. The doctor knew a lot about dressings and bandages and had a keen sense when it came to deciding if one should cut out a lead bullet with the saw or let it remain and fester until it was easier to work it out.

The doctor often stayed till late in the evening. The chaplain had read the evening prayers, the infirmary had done his prescribed rounds, but the doctor remained sitting next to someone's bed with a little screened hand lamp beside him on the floor. It looked as if he was afraid to go home.

One evening, he sat by a young boy from somewhere in the district of Bologna. He had taken a pike in the chest, the lung was injured, and the matter had taken a nasty turn. The doctor knew that it was a hopeless case.

Suddenly the boy asked:

"Doctor, is it true, what the Monsignor said?"

"What is that?"

"That we can be sure of heaven if we die in this war?"

The light of the lantern illuminated the boy's face. He had big anxious eyes that said: tell me *the truth*. The doctor was glad he was sitting in the dark.

"Why do you ask me about this?"

"Because the doctor is a Christian. A real one."

The Doctor was quiet, swept in his darkness.

The boy continued.

"The Doctor doesn't do like Father Dominique: only pass by. The doctor cares about a wretch . . . and didn't Jesus do that too?"

"He did that," the doctor answered. He could say that correctly. The boy had just said what he had thought many times. This was precisely the difference between the Christians and their Lord. Jesus cared about wretches.

"But the doctor hasn't answered my question."

That was when the doctor groaned. What should he answer?

"The Monsignor is right enough . . . "

"Are you sure?"

"Yes, that is true . . . but you must sleep."

"I just can't do that because I want to know how it will go for me."

The doctor paused. He must say something.

"You ought to ask Jesus. He knows better than me. You said just now that he cares about wretches. Try to think about him."

"Does the doctor mean that I should pray to him? Though I am as I am? Does the doctor believe he will hear me?"

 What should he answer?

"You could try."

And suddenly something fell into place, which he ventured to say.

"Do you remember that there was a thief who hanged next to Him at Golgotha? He heard him."

The boy looked at him, thoughtfully.

"I shall try, doctor."

The Spades

THE DAY AFTER—JULY TWENTY-EIGHTH—BEGAN eventfully. Cannon thunder from the Turkish flotilla could be heard on the walls, rolling salvos and lots of smoke as if there was some grand sea battle. The whole bay was full of festive fluttering banners. The salutes continued on land, right up to the Turkish encampment. The air began to quake with drum rolls and fanfare, and the ground shook under the feet of parading troops.

Suleiman had come.

When doctor Apella arrived in the hospital courtyard, sweaty after walking through the hot alleys, Shooter-Frans stood in the doorway prepared to report. He looked sorrowful.

Four died overnight, more than in a long time. Of those, three were wounded. Two had bullet wounds and one was stuck in the lung.

"The little Frenchman?"

"Yes, doctor, and he asked me to say something. He was thankful for what the doctor had said."

"What I said?"

"That he should not forget Jesus when he would die."

The doctor looked so puzzled to Shooter-Frans that he was embarrassed and wondered if he had said something dumb. But the doctor looked right past him and went up through the door.

It remained calm for three days. Then everything began to happen at once. The ground before the walls began to move. The earth lifted itself. The ground tore in black zigzag lines. Spades threw up stone and earth. In front of the joint between the Spanish and English walls, something began to rise, looking more and more like a mountain. Another just as high raised itself in front of Carretto's tower by the Italians.

Men shot from the walls as much as the pieces could stand. The men sweated and swore, loaded again, burned their fingers, dipped sponges in water and gave themselves a bath. Cannon balls plowed their way through the moats. The earth sprayed in black cascades. Human arms stretched themselves in the air as bits of board flew through the air and the wounded screamed. But day and night the ground continued to move. Shovels scraped, picks clanged against the rock, the earth rose up, purposefully without interruption day and night.

Sir John stood and watched on the breastwork of the English wall. His faithful sergeant, Richard Craig, stood next to him a step down, where he ought to be.

"Inconceivable," said the Turcopoler. "Can you believe it, Craig? In one week they have now shoveled and mined and piled up the earth over there. Have you noticed an interruption?"

"No, Sir."

"But how do they keep it up?"

"They get relief every seven hours."

"How do you know that?"

"Wait, sir. It is not long now."

They waited and shot for a while. Again, the earth and stone shot up into the air and formless objects followed. Were those bodies? Or bits of them?

Suddenly, they heard something like a half-choked shout for joy, a sigh of relief uttered by a thousand men.

"They are being relieved now, Sir."

John Buck listened. One could not hear a second's worth of interruption in the shoveling and scraping in the tunnel. The spades must have fallen directly out of their hands and into the others. How was it possible?

"Sir, I have thought about the matter."

"What then, Richard?"

"If they continue in this manner, then they will be high over our heads by next week and will be able to look down on us. Then we will be in for it."

John Buck scratched his head, irritated. He didn't think much of this new manner of war, nothing for a gentleman.

But when Martinengo came up in the afternoon, Richard got sympathy for his worries.

"You have to build cross walls here, within the boulevard so that one can move under their protection to and from the curtain to the batteries."

"Lots of work, sir. Can we get a work detail from the arsenal?"

"Some maybe, but most of it you will have to do yourself."

"With *soldiers*, sir?"

"Precisely. Make it clear to them that their lives depend on it. It is better to have the walls finished before you have to run the gauntlet of their muzzles."

Richard understood.

"All right, sir. We will do our best."

Martinengo was now a chevalier. From day one he had said "we" when he talked about Rhodes. After three days, he spoke about the Religion as if he belonged to it, and on the seventh day he asked if he could join. He wanted to be taken into the Holy Order of St. John.

The decision came quickly. Really, he had traveled here to carry out his work in this place where there was more to learn than anywhere else in the world. But then he had been completely taken up by the life within these walls. He wanted this life for himself.

And it was granted. All of the normal rules were overlooked. He was dubbed the second of August by the Grand Master himself in the Church Santa Maria della Victoria in the presence of all the order's brothers who ventured to leave the walls. As a gift of honor, he received the bamboo staff that old Carretto used to carry as his field insignia.

The Fire

FIRE CAME FROM THE earth embankment. Behind shielded defense, the Turks stamped, packed, and rolled their artillery pieces forward. Heavy, revolving wooden protection was set up during the night supported by massive oak poles. Dug in, crouching, pressured against their wills, the Turks waited for the right moment for their artillery to flash up there on the walls out of their spiteful stirring apertures. They raised the lid and let the shot go. But often the Christians' shot came first. Their cannonballs slammed straight into the artillery placements and crushed the planks, the pieces, and the bodies. Mehmed himself, King of Cannons, Suleiman's friend, son of the Topdji Pascha, who made the world's best artillery, had both legs smashed and bled to death in his tent.

One figured that two out of three battery placements would be blown to bits. But in the night, the Turks worked, cleared, sawed, plugged, shoveled, and buried. In the morning they would start from the beginning again.

The walls too had their casualties. The Turkish fire became more violent every day. The enemy found out where there were dead angles. There was always some corner where one could place his bombardier so that it was next to inaccessible.

Then they spewed fire with the same precision and the same tenaciousness with which their shovels worked.

The Germans took the first real firestorm. The stone balls as big as watermelons came howling and thundering against the wall. It tottered and quaked with each hit. The earth filling behind it was insufficient. Every time the wall was hit, it looked as if the whole curtain would fall and take people and cannons with it down to the moat. But the Germans up on the crown did not budge from their pieces. Inside the wall all available people worked. The Grand Master was at the head. They pushed with braces and stays; they stacked stone and dumped their wheelbarrows. At the same time, they shot all they could with the artillery on the palace walls and defense works. The men up on the curtain crouched under the whistling of the stone balls and loaded and shot under showers of stone splinters. Finally, the Turks had enough and gave up the attempt.

The next attempt was against Saint Nicolas. It was during the second week of August. Over the commercial port's water, stone balls swarmed in, battering the walls from different angles according to the rules of the art. First they came diagonally from the left, then diagonally from the right—like boxing and punching a face, first on the left cheek, then on the right, then on the left again without interruption until the beaten man can no longer stand. Some of the stones found it hard to endure. They dropped out of the wall and smashed to pieces, and the balls continued to heave against the area with the certainty of a victory yell. But the breach in the wall was never big enough for more than one man on horse to ride through. And a new wall, just as repudiating and implacable was peeking out from behind it. The Turks gave up the attempt.

Meanwhile the fire increased day by day along a line south of the city from the sea around the English boulevard along the southwest all the way up to the Auvergne wall. The whole stretch was bulging with batteries. They were demolished, but they came back again. Garrisons were mowed down, but others took their places. Cannon thunder rolled and the black smoke rose from the hot balls like out of a volcano all day long. Of course, the further the heavy pieces could be carried forward, the harder they hit against the walls. Finally, they were just before the moat in deep pits coming from the counter escarpment, the stone lined walls that lined the moat's outer edge. The whole area there was strewn with trenches, cannon placements, and shooting defenses. The moat opened to small black holes where one of the stones was broken loose and fell down into the pit. In the hole you could catch glimpses of long matchlock rifles with an uncanny accuracy.

Richard was right. They were in for it. His men were finally induced against their wills to build protecting walls when the Turks began to pick them off as soon as they left the breastwork to go and fetch a water bucket or a basket of oakum. It was dangerous to work. Now they worked and toiled every night to repair everything that fell during the day.

Commander Juan Barbaran stood on his wall, that which held the Aragon langue, though they all considered themselves Spanish. He called to confer with his Maestro Bombardier, Rostam. They looked down on the boulevard where the men lay pressed against the breastwork, pinned by heat and powdered by stone dust that rained over them with every new bombardment. The moat was filled with black smoke, but soot belched through it from flashes of light on the other side, almost sixty steps from the Boulevard's front side.

Everything down there seemed to be in splinters. The new embrasures were changed to pieces of stone, blown to bits, split and stacked up again in new uneven banks. Demolished cannons with cracked carriages, fragments of buckets and ramrods, dented shields and armor bits lay strewn everywhere. On the north side a piece of the wall had fallen and just in the angle between the boulevard and the wall lay so much fallen stone and spilled earth that a man could climb right up to where they stood.

"The storm is coming. It won't be long now," said the Spaniard. "We have to get many crude pieces to shoot with scrap, big charges with good spread."

Rostam beat regretfully with his hands.

"The Italians say the same. And the Provençals, and the Englishmen. We can . . ."

In the next second he was dead, crushed by the heavy bombard ball that hit him almost the same moment they saw the flame from the barrel. The Spaniard, who was thrown down by the air blast, could hardly believe it. He calmly covered the bloody remains with a riddled flag, sent a report to the Grand Master, and waited for the bearers. It could happen to anyone on these walls.

And two days later it happened to him.

The Spanish Wall

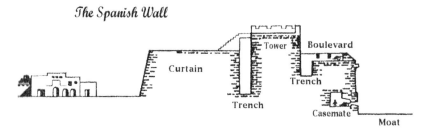

The Sultan's Cauldrons

THE GRAND TURK HAD yet another scourge prepared. He commanded his mortars.

They were dug in in the back lines like giant cauldrons half hidden in the ground. The bottoms were filled with powder, then oakum was packed on top of the powder, and then two men would sink a smooth cut round ball of granite into it. The ball was so big they could barely get a grip around it in order to lift it. When the shot was fired, the ball climbed up into the air on fire and flew in a weak arc up over the city. Then with increasing speed and a crescendo of evil-filled whining, it would crash among the houses and people. The first ball fell in the beginning of August. By the end of the month, the castle had recorded over seventeen-hundred hits.

The war judge, Fonteyn, stood with Doctor Apella in the long colonnade outside the hospital. He greeted a good friend. The doctor was going out also. They walked down to the city together, leering at the battered houses and stepping over heaps of wall stone that the old men and boys kept clearing. The walls in front of them thundered with cannon fire, and distinct gunshots sounded like cracks of a whip through the rumbling. The war judge wrapped himself in his long cape. Pearls of sweat glittered along the folds of his full neck.

"Say, Lord War Judge . . ."

The doctor hesitated a little.

"Have you ever witnessed an interrogation under torture?"

"Of course, every week, possibly many times in a week. It is one of the duties of my office. I have to ask the questions and determine the treatment."

"And what is the treatment?"

"At first, a little on the rack with a hundred fifty pounds at the feet. That is sufficient for most."

"And what then?"

"Then I take the big weight with the winch on both hands and feet. Then the joints begin to loosen and separate. By then, most begin to speak. If not, then one can always use the branding iron."

"How long can a man hold out?"

"That is a question of discernment. Of course, it isn't punishment. That comes afterward."

"But what if he confesses before it even starts?"

"Then he might be spared torture as long as there is no reason to believe he isn't holding anything back. I think they should always be tortured."

"And what if he, in fact, has nothing to confess?"

"Then it is recorded in the minutes and is properly noted."

The doctor nodded, almost frightened of the judge, this fine humanist so brilliant with his Latin, lover of wine, music, and spiritual conversation. How could humans be like that?

Then they separated and the war judge disappeared down to the harbor district followed by his faithful butler, the moor Gasparo.

A half-minute later, they heard an ominous whistling that climbed to a piercing howl and finished with a fearful crash. The doctor ran over to see what had happened.

It was one of the huge mortar balls. High above, it had slammed into the wall of a house and ripped it apart so that you could see the room behind it through the cloud of dust. The street was full of stones, bits of limestone, and whirling smoke. There was one dead in the midst of the wreckage. It was the moor Gasparo.

The war judge must have been thrown away by the impact. His black cape was dirty. His face was a whitish gray.

"But it is impossible, Doctor. Dead? He can't be dead. He was alive just a minute ago . . . So fearful . . . Living one minute and dead in the other . . . How can that happen?"

"Such happens in war" was the only thing the doctor could find to say. But then he prayed. There was something in him that had to come out.

"I would rather go out like him than be tortured by the Lord War Judge."

"Angelo, lovely child, little child, don't cry. Look at Gregoris. He doesn't cry. . ."

Anasthasia bent over her twins in the bed. The powerful crash had awoken them when one of the huge stone balls crashed down into the neighborhood in the middle of the night, possibly a hundred feet from their house. There were shrieks of despair and the goats bleated.

How she hated these mortars! There the mortar ball lay the day after in the wood splinters, round and pompous like an egg in a nice warm nest. And all around it lay shards of the poor clay pots and wooden plates and tinplated dishes which were gifts to the housewives on the day of their wedding and were their only adornment on the way.

"Angelo, shame on you. What will Papa say if you are scared of the Turk? Quiet, little boy, it is not dangerous. It is only a present that the Sultan sends on his birthday. A big, big ball for Angelo to roll in the street, out in back, boom and bang and whoops! And then we roll it up again . . ."

She had thrown the boy up over her, where she lay in the bed, and sang to him. He laughed.

Anasthasia wondered who had screamed. Had someone been injured? It was a great wonder—a real wonder for which they thanked God every day—that more men had not died. In the beginning they thought they were all goners. But soon they learned that the balls did remarkably little damage. Apparently, it was not so easy to hit a man from above. And even if a house was razed, as a rule, the first floor remained. It was worse at night. But people showed resoluteness despite all this. The Grand Turk, the Tyrant, would not get them on their knees in this manner.

"Angelo, so now are you well again. Sleep now. In the morning we shall build a soup kitchen for the Turk, so fine a cook with so many cauldrons. There, mom will cook black soup, tar soup, and sulfur porridge and warm tar. And Papa will offer it to the Turk when he comes. Nothing for a little boy to taste."

The boy slept, and the smile faded from Anasthasia's face. She looked tired and haggard. So she kissed the twins and pulled a warm blanket over herself to try and sleep.

Doctor Apella prepared his third report. This time he didn't care to continue with any pretense of a love letter but wrote directly about the matter in plain text.

"Two-hundred fifty wounded and at least seventy dead since the last report. Total count, six-hundred thirteen wounded; one-hundred eighty dead. The count is greatest due to fire from small-bore weapons; second, from cannon fire. Mortar fire in the city is of little effect. Total at most twenty-one dead and twenty-eight wounded bad enough to need medical attention."

The figures were important. He wrote them with a hidden meaning. The Turks themselves could figure out that every dead civilian cost them approximately forty stone balls, each the work of a master at cutting stones. He kept it all before him what he had seen of the realities behind these figures: The girl with the crushed hips, the young farmer who had to have his right arm sawed off, the housewife who lost her nose and eye and was doomed to be the ugliest woman in the village, the whole lot of lifelong tragedies. Neither did he attempt to separate from the iron grip that lay over them all and brought them all together every time the well-known howl was heard above them. If the Turk wanted to adjust his fire, that was his affair.

He could rejoice in his poor wretched ways.

He said a little about the repairs on the German wall and the great digging work that continued in the Auvergne section. It was very hush-hush, but so much one knew: everyday there was so much dirt and newly-broken stone carried out.

He rolled up the paper, loaded the crossbow, put out the light, and shot. Just then the red lantern flickered. The report reached him a couple seconds later. It ought to have taken away the sound of the bolt as it flew over the wall.

The Miners

IT WAS UNBELIEVABLE THAT the Turks had held back from storming for so long. They had made scalable breeches in three places. There was only one possible reason for their delay. They wanted to keep digging in under the walls to mine them and let a few key points fly into the air as a last preparation immediately before the attack.

Martinengo sketched, measured, supervised, adjusted, and counseled. His work was the most requested from the island and the stone cutters from the city. They quickly recognized whom they had as a leader. They followed him blindly after one week.

The tunnelling continued in under the Auvergne wall alongside the moat. There the tunnel split up. One branch went north up to the German section; another went in the opposite direction along the Spanish wall toward the English boulevard. There it turned east to go down to the sea along the English wall. The tunnellers were finished up to that point. They had stools with listening posts laid out in regular intervals in the direction of the enemy and tunnels back to their own lines.

The men had been forced to work. Martinengo had appealed for volunteers. So Father Gennaios had reported, a little Greek priest with olive gold complexion, melancholy eyes, and small shoulders. He was not the only one of spiritual standing; there were also Franciscan and Greek monks. But Father Gennaios was by far the weakest. He dragged the heavy wheelbarrows filled with earth despairingly. When there was no one around to see it, he sat down in the dark and panted.

One day he was close to going up. He had crept into a side tunnel to a listening post. It was not yet manned, but the listening instrument was set up, a washbowl with water and a drum. Every time the ground vibrated—

and it did that ceaselessly because they picked and dug for burning life forty or fifty feet from there— rings formed in the water. The drum was Martinengo's invention. It only had skin on the topside. It was stretched hard, and right under the skin hung a little bell that gave off a little ring when the skin vibrated. It sounded quite beautiful here in the dirty dark underground.

Father Gennaios looked apathetically at the little drum. Sand and bits of stone had fallen on the drum skin. Through all the shaking, the light grains had begun to make a pattern of rings somewhat like those in the water washbasin.

The watch came. He looked, listened, and turned to the drum to beat away the dust.

"Tired?" the soldier asked.

Father Gennaios nodded.

"Yeah, it doesn't hurt that a spiritual man can feel what it is like to work."

The priest was finished being sorry. He only got up and left. He would have to acknowledge his defeat and ask to go home, being declared incapable.

He went along the tunnel. There stood other drums waiting to be set out, all more or less dusty and all with the same pattern in the dust.

He stopped dead. This dust—it was insane to clean it! The rings in the water went away. The bells rang only for those who stood within earshot, but these patterns remained. One could come in the morning and see what had happened during the night.

He went straightway to Martinengo, who, true to his habit, inspected, measured, and ordered the work to continue. The Venetian followed alone. His eyes lit up.

"Splendid," he said. "Such a worker like you is worth his weight in gold."

When he heard that Father Gennaios was a priest, he asked him to take charge of the supervision and reporting from the listening posts.

Already, in the third day, Father Gennaios had something to report. He had set out his drums in some new places along the tunnel before the Provençal wall. Late at night before the ground began to shake under cannon fire, he inspected them. There was an inescapable decision to be made, so he sent for Martinengo. He looked, compared, and put his head to the ground.

"They are very close," he said. "We have to hurry."

It was easy to see the results from the Provençal wall. There was a little chapel, maybe a thousand feet from the wall. The Turks had dug a tunnel right up to it. But no one could figure out what to do about it. Today the problem resolved itself. Martinengo had strengthened his tunnels with a division of Cretans. He disappeared among the tunnels with powder kegs and the long trumpets with bellows that were used to blow fire. One noticed a light thrust in the ground, and after a few seconds a pillar of smoke with powerful violence rose up from the ground over by the chapel. Within an hour ,Martinengo's men began carrying up armfuls of Turkish picks and spades.

Father Gennaios felt sick. There were many people who had held those picks. Surely many of them were conscripted. They were probably all Christians. Why should one need to use the reason God gave him in this manner?

The third of September had been murderously warm. The sunlight and the Turkish fire made life next to intolerable for the Englishmen on the boulevard. Finally, evening came with food and relief. The men had just handed their pieces over to the night shift, when Martinengo came up from the barbican. He spoke in a low voice with Sir Pemberton, who had the command.

The English man turned and looked at his people.

"You can eat here," he said shortly. "There is a good deal we have to do yet this evening before we can go home."

The men muttered. They wanted to know why. But Martinengo only said that they had to trust him just now.

They sat and chewed their bread and cheese and drank their portions of wine grudgingly. They had sat down together apathetically, and no one made any attempt to move.

Pemberton and Martinengo had gone over the boulevard's furthest end. They stepped and measured. Martinengo stopped among the second and third batteries from the left end.

"It has to start here," he said.

He adjusted the first stone. Sir Pemberton laid the next, went forward to the next one, and put a crowbar under it. The men came alive. They could not believe their eyes. What had happened? Sir Pemberton broke stone?

Pemberton looked up.

"Yes?" Nothing more was needed. The men got up and grabbed their crowbars. The reinforcement workers came with their stone. They kept it going along. Only late in the evening did Richard come home.

"We have built a whole new wall, right over the top of the boulevard. Martinengo was there the whole time. But he did not say what it would be used for."

The First Attack

THE FOURTH OF SEPTEMBER was just as warm. When the shadows finally grew long, the Grand Master came with the brothers who belonged to the staff and the bodyguard to read Vespers and Compline in the little church in front of Porte Saint Athanase. It was right behind the English wall, and the Grand Master had his quarters here ever since the situation began to be critical.

It was almost intolerably close. Antoine de Golart sat and watched the Grand Master. How much energy did this man have? At night, he visited the posts; by day, he received reports of losses and new Turkish batteries. He dictated letters, listened to complaints from citizens, and ordered and inspected new injuries on the walls. He never slept more than a couple hours at a time. He should have been completely out of it. But now he read the Psalms and seemed to do it remarkably well. In the field, the daily offices could be replaced with an Our Father, but the Grand Master had still not made use of the possibility. The prayers were prayed as usual while the cannons fired and prayers little by little became fewer.

Now after Vespers, Antoine would escort the Grand Master to Pomerolx's house in the French auberge. The assistant lay very sick. A few days ago he had gone to the crown of the barbican to inspect some approaches. He had slipped and fallen down. He was brought up unconscious, but he recovered and claimed that he had only been scratched up a little. He had not bothered to dress his wounds before late in the evening and now he lay with a high fever and incredible cramps.

It was Thursday. The Vesper Psalms dealt with the incomprehensible ways God acts on behalf of His people, whom He saved from all their enemies in the harsh desert, incomprehensible to all human calculations. It wasn't hard to see that the Grand Master took the words to heart.

Compline would follow immediately, and the Chaplain had managed to say: *Deus in adjutorium meum intende* (Make haste, O God, to deliver me) when an earthquake lifted the floor and the whole house shook. The quake was followed by a fearful thundering, as if the whole wall outside had turned into the mouth of a cannon. It was dark around them; stone and earth hailed down on the church. The roofing tile above was heard as it was crushed.

The Grand Master continued where the priest had stopped: *Domine, adjuvandum me festina.* Make haste to help me, O Lord.

Then he said:

"Amen, so be it Lord. And now we go do ours. Come, my brothers."

He went to the door with longer strides than normal as he put on his helmet. They hurried out into the street in under the archway and out onto the other side. Then they followed along the wall in the shadow of the barbican in order to swing left past the Tower of Mary out onto the boulevard.

With a blink of the eye, Antoine figured out what had happened. The Turks had run a mine under the Englishmen's boulevard. Smoke engulfed that area and it was covered with bits of stone. But there was a gaping hole, and this hole was already full of Turks. They rolled up over the de-molished mess. They had already reached the crown of the wall. They had planted their flag among the stones. For the first time ever, the crescent moon waved over the walls of Rhodes. One, two, five, seven sections.

It was a good way down the wall. The Turks had a dangerous ad-vantage rattling, clattering, panting. They flowed and streamed through the middle gate and pressed up the stairway and finally to the plateau of the boulevard. The fight raged by the newly built cross wall four feet from where the ground blew apart. The stone pile began there and the Turks already had a firm footing. New columns crowded in the moat and pressed in the back. Martinengo's emergency wall made a heavy line holding them back.

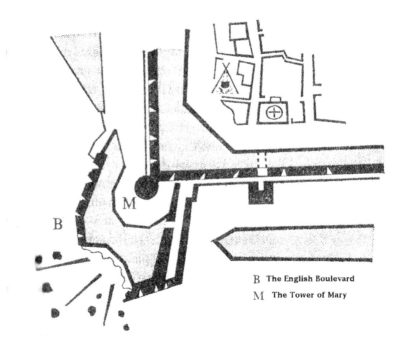

B   The English Boulevard
M   The Tower of Mary

In two hours the fight progressed to hand to hand combat. For the veterans, it brought back the old nostalgic feeling of steel against steel, saber cut against armband, sword edges biting into brigandines and mail. For the greenhorns, the fight seemed like a breeze from hell with the howls and soul-embittering cries of distress, blood, and curses.

John Buck came up with the reserves. Today he had a full armament and his visor was down, steel from head to toe. This was a war for a gentleman. So ought a knight always find battle. He cleared and slashed with the two-handed sword, groaned and stank, sweated and swore. The cannons spewed fire from the wall behind them and from all flanking boulevards and outworks, dispelling the Turks in the moat. When the twilight thickened and they had enough, they drew back fighting and disappeared in their tunnels and holes down in the earth's inner bowels on the other side of the moat. And within the same hour, the cannons over there opened up with fire.

Outside his quarters, the Grand Master received his reports: Henry Mansell who bore the Grand Master's standard was shot in the head but still lived. The galley captain d'Argillemont lay dead with an arrow in the eye. Fourteen others were on the dead list, all well known by the Grand

Master. Then came the wounded, eighteen, and finally the enlisted men, who were taken in one lump.

One thing remained. It was Sir John who said it.

"Your Eminence, I am sorry that I have the duty to inform you: an hour ago the Grand Commander brother Gabriel de Pomerolx died of his injuries.

This was the first time Anasthasia's soup kitchen came in use. Because they were right next to the wall with their backyard directly facing the wide connecting path that followed the wall's inner side, it was determined that there should be a soup kitchen set up there. The kettles came with a great store of fuel. Barrels with tar and pitch rolled in. Buckets and pots were lined up. Then came the chef, an old woman who had been there in 1480 and knew all the recipes. She had three women helping her. All lodged among the fuel and barrels.

When the fearful explosion shook the city and the small stones beat against the kettles, the younger women let out a high-pitched scream. But the old woman from 1480 set them to work. They made a fire and began to open up the barrels. They anxiously listened to the noise on the other side. Up on the wall, they got the order to keep the pitch cooking. One practically hauled up the first pot for safety's sake. But the boulevard would be kept, and no Turks got close to the wall.

The next morning Anasthasia went up on the wall. It was a dizzying undertaking. The wall was fearfully high, and there were no stairs here, only rope ladders. It was best not to look down while creeping over the edge at the top. At first, Richard had to hold her hand, but now she did it on her own.

They had gone over to the breastwork.

"Yeah, there they are," Richard said. "They are Janissaries. That means they had planned on breaking through. Otherwise, they would not have sacrificed their best men."

Anasthasia looked hesitantly. The Janissaries were hated and feared. They weren't even Turks. Every one of them had been born to Christian parents. It was the Tyrant's worst form of tax. His old under-officers would come and inspect all the boys like horse traders and pick out those who looked the healthiest to be raised as Janissaries.

There they were now, all mowed down, lying in impossible positions and firmly stuck to the ground.

Anasthasia swallowed. They all could have been like Angelos and Gregoris twenty years ago. Some little mom in Albania or Bosnia had carried them to a priest to be baptized, and now they were here, dead.

"But Anasthasia, do you mourn? Spare your tears. You have red eyes and there are worse things to mourn."

Anasthasia was not very sure about that, but she was quiet.

The Grand Master made his morning rounds on the walls. He began with the Auvergne wall. Chevalier Fournon, the Chief of Artillery, reported and was thanked for a remarkable job the day before.

Martinengo came up out of the casemate.

"Yes, Martinengo, what is it you need today?"

"Old accounts, Your Eminence."

"What do you say?"

The Grand Master was used to his architectural defense needing the most unusual things: fine sand, small bells, silk string. But old accounts?

"What will you do with them?"

"Come, I have something to show you."

They went down the casemate, a huge vaulted room with four small holes, all pointed south so that the moat over by the Spanish Boulevard was easily covered.

Martinengo pointed to some very dirty gray packets wrapped up in paper, which lay neatly stacked up along the way. His eyes glittered under his bushy eyebrows.

"It is Fournon's invention. Powder loads made up before hand. They only need to be driven into the bore. Frightfully clever when the moat is full of Turks."

The Grand Master inspected the cover.

"Where did you get the paper from?"

"That is just the problem," said Fournon. "This is why we need stacks of old receipts."

"Can't you get those in the secretary's office?"

"We tried, Your Eminence. But Soliciano spreads his arms out as if he is protecting his children, saying that he can't afford to give a single little piece of paper. One can never know if in the future there won't be a dispute over some little patch of ground in Bretagne and then he will know precisely what it has yielded through the years."

The Grand Master looked grim.

"Greet the Vice Chancellor for me and tell him that we have a little war going on. I am now invested with extraordinary powers. All clean accounts are to be laid out. You have only to choose those you want and march away."

The fellow's eyes lighted in the dim light. At last they had overcome the paper dragon, his old archenemy up in the palace.

The Second Attack

EXCITING DAYS FOLLOWED. THE Turks were digging everywhere. The drums tracked the digging. Martinengo listened and calculated. It was hopeless to break into all these tunnels and take the fight down there. There was another way. You simply let them finish digging and loading without disturbing them. But when the mine blew, the gas would be released through well-calculated side tunnels, often in the face of the Turks who were ready to storm.

Over at the English boulevard, the Turks were still successfully running down an arm of the wall. Then they stormed again five days after the first attempt. This time it took three hours to throw them back. Layers upon layers of newly dead men lay in the bottom of the moat, some wearing expensively embroidered coats. They did not spare their people, and neither did their officers spare themselves. The Sultan had decided to squander. The galleys went to and fro over the sea, carrying new people, new supplies, and new powder.

Thirty knights and serving brothers had fallen, and they could not be replaced. Not now. Every day the lookouts on the palace spied for relief. They ought to be here by now.

Success was to be rewarded. The day after the attack, Richard Craig was called down to the Grand Master's command post. He received a reward of ten florins for his resourcefulness and his courage yesterday and was named on the spot to take command of the Turcopolers.

That evening Anasthasia held a feast. The little house and backyard were full of guests: women in the soup kitchen, some neighbors and friends, five English archers, a group of Cretans, and fellows from Rhodes. Richard took more and more of them under his command so that the dwindling garrison on the boulevard could be reinforced. He got along well with them.

They drank and sang. It was a little foretaste of the wedding feast to come when the war was over. The Greeks sang about Anasthasia in the manner of an old ballad. They sang about a bride who was like a porphyry pillar in the emperor of Byzantium's palace with a golden capital and glittering stones around the forehead. They sang their soldier ballads, sad songs from years gone by, when poor boys enlisted with the Venetians or the King of Naples.

> My beloved, will I ever see you again?
> For now I leave to Frankish lands.
> Somewhere waits a battlefield foe,
> Maybe a grave on the shore sands.
> The sea surges dark,
> Kort-Oglu lurks behind the point,
> With powder dry and breastplate hard.
> But the heart therein is frail.
> My beloved, will I ever see you again?

The bit about Kort-Oglu the boys made up the year before. The songs always changed themselves a little according to the changing times.

They continued.

> My Rhodes, will I ever see you again?
> For now I leave for Frankish lands.
> Somewhere waits a foreign cove,
> A castle I have never seen,
> The sea surges dark.
> Long running are my hourglass sands.
> As my heart beats brave,
> yet it mourns when not seen.
> My Rhodes, will I ever see you again?

Anasthasia looked at Richard, who for decency's sake sat over among the fellows. Her eyes saw what he was thinking.

"You will never go back to the land of the Franks. You will stay with me. My heart does not mourn. It has never been so happy."

Doctor Apella sent his fourth report.

Casualties since the last attack, at least three-hundred fifty dead and four-hundred thirty-two wounded. Total wounded, six-hundred eighty-nine. Of them, one-hundred fourteen have died. The complete number of those dead is around six-hundred fifty; forty-eight of those are knights.

How much did these reports mean to them? Some of the results of the reports he made were obvious. The Turks had shot down the campanile when he reported that the artillery fire was directed from up there. They had also adjusted the mortar fire. He took a little pride from this.

He made some additions, reporting on the climbing shortage of wood and the daily expectation of reinforcements.

He felt a bit more uneasy than usual, though, as he extinguished the light and opened the shutters. Not only because he risked his life. He had no choice but to take the risk if he wanted to survive. No, he began to falter on the decisive points. Was surviving really the most important thing? Here these knights and simple boys from the land died, truehearted and voluntarily. He felt something between envy and pride when he thought of his compatriot, this selfsame Jesus, who after fifteen hundred years could still inspire such courage in men. They certainly didn't give a fig for most of what he said so long as they lived . . .

No, now he was wrong. This hospital that he loved and in all seriousness called the best in the world was their work. Apparently, all this was a present day effect of this Jesus.

Among the four books he got of particularly officious acquaintances since he was baptized, he had put three on the shelf or would leave them lying out only so that they would see that he was reading. But the fourth he had read. It was the New Testament. With fierce satisfaction, he had established how little the Christians concerned themselves with their Christ. They ran to all these saints that were not even mentioned in the New Testament. They swarmed before the Queen of Heaven, who wasn't mentioned in the New Testament either. But they never thought of reading the Sermon on the Mount. One could find here in the New Testament the most damning statements concerning their madness. Time after time, he discovered that he himself could take refuge here where he had Jesus as his compatriot.

He shot, lit the light again, and sat down to read.

The Shadow

THE GRAND MASTER SET foot in his palace for the first time in over a week. The Chancellor, the Marshal, the Admiral, the Turcopoler, and the Castellan were all called there. He had the doors to the foyer shut, posted a watch there, and then closed the inner doors to his workroom himself.

He had two serious worries.

First, the powder was beginning to run out. The report from the arsenal came like lightning from a clear sky. If the rate of consumption remained where it had been during the last couple weeks, the stores would last twenty days at best.

"We had stock for a year?"

He looked questioningly at the Chancellor, who was responsible for the matter and made the reports.

As usual, D'Amaral looked straight out. He looked hurt and grieved.

"With normal consumption, the stores were enough to last a year. This must be the result of irresponsible waste."

There was some truth to that. Certainly, with limitless access, the men shot to their hearts' desire.

New rules were sketched in a hurry. No firing on uncertain targets. No firing without orders. There were strict restrictions outside of a storming.

Fortunately, there were substantial stores of saltpeter. The mills would immediately begin to grind. Were there enough horses for it?

"You can take mine," said the Grand Master, "all fourteen of them."

"Even Phaeton?"

"Even Phaeton."

Few things could have made a deeper impression. Now it was really serious.

The other worry remained.

"We received a report with the boat from Lindos late at night. They wanted to warn us. The deserters have told them that the Turks are well informed about everything here in the city. They know our casualties and know what only a small circle of us know."

It was painfully quiet.

"Brother Waldener has something particular to report?"

He looked at the Castellan.

The German began thoughtfully. There is a red lamp. It is always in the same place. And there are curious bolt shots, always aimed at the light. As yesterday—over the tower on the Auvergne Wall. At about ten o'clock. Chevalier Barel had been there and was completely convinced. It came from within the city. From the over city."

The silence was oppressive.

The Castellan received orders to go through all the details with Chevalier Barel. If the red lantern is seen in the evening, one should determine the exact position and find a line of sight into the city. Then one should follow the line and test all conceivable tracks.

They departed with deep uneasiness, almost without even looking each other in the eyes.

The Chancellor was full of bitterness. He had locked himself in his room.

So they suspected him of treason? They wanted to declare him guilty because they squandered away their powder? Naturally—treason was blamed for all lost wars. But they could spy however much they wanted. They could stand there with long noses.

He had done his duties despite escalating unwillingness. Anyone could see how the walls were smashed asunder and the garrisons dwindled. Soon the last great storm would come. Then they would all die.

He was not scared. He had felt so many scimitars sweep by his face that he could take that slash to the throat that would prove his last without blinking. But it irritated him to have to follow this Phillip Villiers de l'Isle Adam and his fake glory. Had he never met this man, his life would have looked much different and better.

The Third Attack

ANASTHASIA HELD HER EARS. The noise from the other side of the wall drove her crazy. It was now the third time in less than two weeks that the Turks stormed. She had heard their piercing war cry screamed by only one ecstatic dervish. Then the cannons thundered, followed by a crackling clatter of hooks and muskets and the whirling wind of the arrows. And then the crash came when the attack columns heaved themselves against the steel clad defenders behind the emergency walls built of blown bits of rock. It sounded as if a giant continuously tore a roof plate in two and smashed it together. So it had been going now for three hours.

The fire burned under her kettles. Yet they had only carried up two pots. That meant that the fight was still out on the boulevard, which was separated from the Tower of Mary by a deep moat and the wall. Her black soup would not be needed before they crowded down into the moat. But then much more would be needed.

The worst was this continuous shooting. They had their sharpshooters in position, and they followed the fighting with their long guns plucking men off one after one. No amount of courage helped with them.

By evening it was quiet. She climbed up on the wall. Yes, Richard lived. They had seen him. But in the barbican the dead were laid in two rows. The wounded had to be helped first.

Late at night Richard went home with his free pass, very tired and very serious. Sir John was dead, shot through the head when he opened his visor to dry off the worst of the sweat and wipe his hands. And he was not the only unlucky one. Preian de Bidoulx had fallen, shot straight through the throat. He was dying as they carried him away.

Richard talked reticently. Then he just lay there and stared at the ceiling. It was quiet for a long time. But she could not let him sleep yet.

"Richard . . . "

"Yes, my child."

"If the Turks break through . . . "

"That won't happen."

"But if—do you promise you will come home and kill me and the children?"

"Quiet, Anasthasia."

"No, Richard, I will not be quiet. We women are people too. I will not be tossed around among that mob and be raped by one after the other. And the boys will not be taken to be Janissaries!"

"Quiet, Anasthasia. Why torture ourselves? We will beat them."

"But if . . . "

"That won't come to be."

"Then you can promise . . . "

"What?"

"That you will kill us before we fall in the hands of the Turks."

Richard stared at the ceiling. Then he changed the tone.

"There is nothing I can deny you. You know that. You extortionist, let it go. You can have it as you like, if it will comfort you now. I promise."

The Traitor

THE LIGHT WAS ON at all times in the hospital. It should have been quiet a long time ago, but they were all still working. Brother Frans wandered about miserably. All who could stand on their feet had been sent home. Bunks and mattresses had been squeezed in between all the beds and into every corner. But still they came with one stretcher after the other. He had begun to lay them out in the open halls by the garden on loose straw.

Brother Gierolamo worked resolutely. Doctor Apella had almost become his assistant now. Both the other medics, who otherwise remained invisible in the shadows behind the little Jew, had been accustomed to tend the running work always with their own hand while Doctor Apella stood with his sleeves rolled up, drying a spurting blood vessel or supporting a leg that had to be given a splint.

The Grand Master came in the middle of the night. He was on his usual rounds among the watches. Tonight he made it to the little hospital. Doctor Apella reported.

"Forty-eight new, six dying, the ward is full."

Of course, that did not need to be said. They hardly had a place to stand among all the beds.

"And Henry Mansell?"

"He lives, but it is in God's hands."

"And Preian de Bidoulx?"

"He has not bled out, strange enough. The shot went straight through his throat, but the spine is unscathed. He is unconscious."

The Grand Master looked around.

"If there is anything I can do for the Doctor, just let me know. The Doctor knows that I am thankful, for all this . . . " He made a gesture to the beds on the floor. "And for an example that has done me good. We old

Christians with all our ugliness can need a reminder from someone who comes from the outside."

It was harder than anything for Doctor Apella to send his report. In the morning he came home dizzy and threw himself on the bed. He was unable to sleep, though, and began to read. Then he stopped on the verse that had been following him now for the whole day: "He who wants to save his life will lose it." It was a word from Jesus, his compatriot.

Oh, this Jesus of Nazareth! Could he not leave him in peace?

He shook himself. This was a mere whim. He was overworked, under the weather, half tortured to death by so much work. He would let reason take the lead.

Lose my life? No, he would survive!

He sat down and wrote, counted on his fingers, went right to the figures and finished the report. Then he made it dark in the room, opened up the shutters with the usual cautiousness, waited, and shot.

He was startled. Did someone move down there? When he lit the lamp and began to eat, there was a knock on the door. He could hear steps; heavy steps, many steps. They came up the stairs. Then the Castellan stepped in with the watch. To their surprise, they found Doctor Apella standing there completely still, absent-minded, on the floor. He nodded to himself and mumbled as if acknowledging.

"He shall lose his life . . . "

The accused confessed openly to the three war judges. He spoke about his long activity as an agent and about his last five dispatches. But he denied that he had any accomplices.

Doctor Fonteyn demanded he be examined under torture. This bit about accomplices ought to be examined more closely. But the other two overruled him. The crime demanded the punishment for treason: To be hung, put on the wheel, and quartered.
The Doctor looked almost relieved when the sentence was read.

"Does the sentenced have a wish?"

"Yes . . . A priest. Brother Giovanni."

Fonteyn looked confounded. The first could be allowed.

"But it must be our predetermined priest, you see—this week Father Dominique.

"Then let it be," said the Doctor.

But then it seemed as if he had thought of something.

"Lord War Judge . . . His Eminence the Grand Master has once promised that he would hear me if I had any particular wish. I ask that the court carry my request that I may talk to Fra Giovanni."

Dr. Fonteyn now looked even more confused and shook his head. But the others saw that it was proper. A runner was sent down to the city while the condemned man was carried back to his cell in the palace.

It wasn't a very long time before Brother Giovanni was there. The key rustled. Then the iron gate opened and closed again.

They were alone. The priest sat by the doctor on the bunk.

"There are lice here," said Doctor Apella pardoningly. "It makes no difference to me now, but . . . "

Brother Giovanni's childlike eyes looked curiously at the man sentenced to death. Was it bitterness? Gallows humor? No, rather, consideration. In the last moments.

"The Doctor asked me to come?"

"Yes, there was a problem. But first . . . "

And so he told his story, just as he did before the judges. But he added what he hadn't told them, about his desire to survive and about the word of Jesus that cut him to the heart: He who will save his life . . .

"And now I want to know: that I now lose my life, why will I want to save it—is it a punishment? His punishment?"

Brother Giovanni shook his head.

"Not a punishment, Doctor. A consequence. So it goes."

The Doctor was quiet.

"If nothing unfortunate had happened and the Doctor was able to keep his life with the Turks, then the Doctor would have been lost—to Jesus, I mean."

The Doctor nodded slowly.

"And he would have been sorry for that. Therefore, he wants to hinder that."

"But now I lose it in any case?"

"No, the Doctor shall save it."

The Doctor shook his head, pensively. "Not I."

"Listen, Doctor. It is time that the Doctor turn around and see who has been in the Doctor's company the whole time."

The Doctor looked up curiously.

"I mean: here the doctor has walked with Christ next to him so close that it has been like a light and others have seen it, everyone but the Doctor himself."

The Doctor looked down again.

"Impossible, this whole time the only thing I wanted to do was to save my life."

"Not only: there was a tug of war in the Doctor as within us all. Between the two manners of living: to save life and to lose it. And it was Christ's manner of life that won more and more. Remember, Doctor what he says: whoever does what is true comes to the light so that it may be clearly seen that his deeds have been carried out in God—by God, through God."

The Doctor stayed quiet.

"And now the light is here, Doctor. The Doctor only has to turn his head a little so he can see him. The Doctor's Jesus."

Now the Doctor nodded almost unnoticeably.

"And what does he say—in such a case?"

"Whoever believes in me, he shall never die. He does not come into judgment. He has passed from death to life."

"But all my unfaithfulness? All the times I took the sacrament without faith?"

"Those he has long ago suffered for. He has only been anxious that he might forgive them. Now will the Doctor give him joy?"

"Can I do that?"

"Yes, like the prodigal son when he came home. This, my son was lost but now he is found. Now we must we rejoice and be glad. It is he who says it."

The Doctor nodded. Now he looked up right before him.

"Then you also were righteous . . . "

"We are never righteous," said the priest almost frightened. "Only Him, He is always righteous."

The Doctor nodded.

"Behind all this foolishness there was also a greater truth."

And so he said hastily.

"And this I am glad for . . . Dare I now ask Brother Giovanni to come again in the morning with the sacrament? And possibly follow me the last part of the way?"

It had been cold. A stinging northeast wind blew from the sea. The Turkish mountains were beautifully covered with the morning sun, so plainly that one thought he could take them. Brother Giovanni, shivering, swept his long black coat around him when he hurried back to the Italians' barracks from Padellan where the gallows were raised.

At the table sat some brothers with their bandages and crutches. They looked up.

"So, how did the traitor die?"

"As a true Christian."

They looked at him puzzled.

"I could wish for a death like his," said the priest in a low voice.

"You don't mean that? Quartered and put on a pole?"

"We shall all die in one way or another. We all need forgiveness for all that we have done. The most important thing is that one may keep his hand on Jesus when the time comes."

"And you think he did that?"

"I think that," the priest said with conviction. Then there was nothing more to say about the matter.

The Great Storm

THE DECISIVE MOMENT WAS coming.

The enemy's batteries were all in action. It was inconceivable that people could cause such a thunder and sweep the earth in such darkness. They crushed, splintered, and ground the walls asunder while mutilating the men with unmerciful precision. Everyone said: "Nothing like this has ever happened on all the earth since the beginning of creation. And may it never happen again!"

The fire weakened in the evening of September twenty-third. It was once again possible to catch a glimpse of the Turkish camp and hear the sounds from there. The camp was anything but dead. The muezzin never went quiet. The dervishes howled louder than anything. The heralds trumpeted and gave the battle cry that was taken up by a hundred, a thousand, ten-thousand hoarse voices. It rolled like thunder out over the camp and in over the city's sunder-shot walls.

"What are they saying?" asked Anasthasia when she clambered up on the wall with limestone splinters in her hair and with a basket of bread in her arms.

"Some battle cry for in the morning," Richard said evasively.

"Yeah, but what?"

One of the boys from the land looked at her, dumbfounded.

"Land and houses for the Sultan, goods and slaves for us."

"They have been given a pass to plunder," he explained.

"Quiet," said Richard. "There won't be any plundering here."

The Grand Master had come to the English wall. William Weston had command and reported.

"We are thin, Your Eminence. Buck is dead. Askew is dead. Russell and Rawson are also dead. Pemberton, Aylmer, and Sutton are wounded. Pemberton can stand on his legs, but his arm is in a sling."

The Grand Master searched his memory. "Maybe you can have Buet and Baron from Saint Nicholas."

"Thanks, Your Eminence."

"But otherwise you know how it is. They will storm the breaches in the morning, in four places, or five, if they dare to try the Auvergne. And we can count on an attempt at St. Nicholas simultaneously, as you know well . . . "

The Englishman nodded and the Grand Master continued.

"I have scraped up a few reserves, but we have to conserve. Also, you should only ask for reinforcements if and when they are really needed. Not a minute before. But neither a minute late. I trust you."

Meanwhile, Martinengo made his last inspection on the Spanish wall. There was the wound in the heart, the great breach. It offered an open path straight into the city.

He had dressed the wound. During the night and days, they had built a whole system of emergency walls and traverses that enclosed the threatened place behind a new ring of walls. There were cannons and harquebusiers overlooking it all from well-hidden nooks and crannies among the piles of stone, in the windows of houses behind them, and up along the roofing tiles a bit further away from the windmills that dominated the gate to Koskinou where cannon aimed right into the breach.

Martinengo made the sign of the cross. All that stood in the power of men was done. But there was a limit to what men could do.

Two hours before dawn, the Turks began bombarding so fearfully that the ground trembled. The walls quaked, and the sky was red with fire. Soon the moats, the barbicans, the boulevards, and walls were engulfed in an impenetrable black and pungent haze.

No alarm was needed. Everyone waited by the cannons and behind the stately formed piles of scrap stone, their guns resting in the apertures. The fire cracked under the kettles, the pitch bubbled and simmered like scalding water.

They came at dawn. Just as the cannons went quiet, they broke up through the black smoke from out of the holes and tunnels down along the paths in the moats. They ran up over the stone mounds, the piles of dead bodies, and wall remains, howling all the while. There were Jayalars in loose formations, blue Janissaries in tight columns, Syrians, Anatolians, Bulgarians, Albanians, and the self-conscious Mamluks fresh on the scene from Egypt, determined to show that they were able to do what all others had failed to do.

The defenders waited until they saw their columns clearly in the smoke, only some ten paces from the walls. They knew that the holes behind them were packed with people and that every cannonball, every bit of shot, every stone splinter had to hit its mark. As the howling fire swept out like columns from a volcano, the men down there were swept away. But others came to replace them. Bolts and arrows, lead and scrap loads hailed from the walls. The cannons were loaded again,;the powder-packed oakum and bags of scrap were shot into the crowds of men who trampled each other. They only pushed harder. Every door was filled. They filled the streets to the brim like rain in a gutter. Where did they all come from? There were so many people that it was impossible to shoot them all. It just wasn't.

So they advanced with defiant, threatening fiery screams of triumph. In a final effort, they set their pikes in holes, high behind the wall's crown, and fired rifles by company in three step formation. If anyone pushed back, he was pushed forward again by the man he pushed. If anyone fell, he was kicked and trampled by those who followed.

Again the piercing, crushing, pounding, shrilling sound came as if from a smith shop in hell, full of screams of death, hatred, and agony. This time it was heard in the city's furthest corners, in the hospital, in the prisons, and even down in the cathedral's crypt.

The Italians fought heroically and in desperation out on il Terrapieno, the great embankment that stood in the moat like a precipitous plateau between two flooded ravines. The whole southern spur had been razed and the Turks thronged there. No one could see a stone block or a foot's width of ground. Everything was covered with thronging columns of men fighting, climbing, fencing, and struggling. There were traverses thrown right over the defense's small plateau where the knights were fighting. And right there in plain view of all stood Lodovico de Morso, who had fled to Crete, swinging his two-handed sword like a logger swings his ax. No one would ever again be able to say that he was scared. Gabriele Solerio and Jacabo Palavisino, his two comrades in the escape, stood right by his side. If anyone thought that they had tried to escape, here they could see for themselves!

Lodovico fell, Gabriele was carried away blind, but the line held. It held there even after another hour.

It was just as hard over at the Provençal wall. They had already stood up against the superior force for two hours.

"We ought to have reinforcements."

"It won't be much longer."

"Where is la Roque?"

"Wounded and carried away."

"Is Morgut not coming with the reserves?"

"Soon enough, man. We are still standing. Look at the Italians. Are we weaker?"

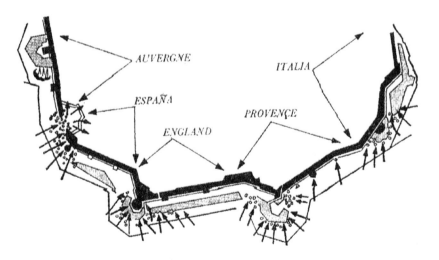

It was critical, though, at the English wall. The boulevard, beaten asunder, seemed covered with a mat of Turks. The holes around them were like an early summer meadow covered in flowers that glitter in the sun and explode with color. The howls, yells, and rejoicing were deafening. Six standards had already been planted on the wall's crown.

In this sea of men there was only one empty space: the little plateau of what was left of the boulevard. There the wounded and dead were left, surrounded by a heavy fighting line along the wall. The Englishmen could soon be counted on fingers. Among them stood Frenchmen and Castilian knights called from their up-to-now un-assailed walls. There were also Cretans and Rhodians, simple people with open helmets and cheap breastplates, who thrusted their pikes with sure hands.

The Grand Master anxiously sent his reserves in from the barbican, never more than was needed to hold the line unbroken. To place people in reserve behind it was the same as allowing the Turks to pick them off one by one.

Up on the wall, Richard Craig led the fire among his Cretans. He still had a dozen of his English archers. They had their great day. Their long bows flexed and shot, six, eight, ten times a minute. However much the crossbowmen sweated and cranked, they could not make up for even a fourth of their arrows. He followed the confusion down there in the maelstrom with a trained eye and tried to send his arrow shower where it was most needed. But what did it help?

Anasthasia bore buckets, fed the fire, and prayed. She was afraid. For the first time during this war, angst overtook her. The battle had kept on for over three hours now, and it looked as if things were taking a turn for the worse. The alarm was deafening. There was a new tone of assured victory in the Turkish howl, a rapacious roaring like from a wild animal smelling its prey. It was the worst over by the Spanish breach. There they were certain to break through. And there up on the wall, the men needed to have pitch and tar, simmering oil and boiling water without end. They screamed and threatened. They requested that someone come up and help them haul up the pots and cauldrons.

Anasthasia climbed up the rope ladder. With one look she saw how bad the situation was. The Turks were down before the walls. The English men had shot up all their long arrows. They hurled down pots of boiling water, heaved stones, and lit long crackling sulfur strings that fell into the screaming crowd, entangling men who could not escape. And the Greeks cranked, aimed, shot, and cranked again, bathing in sweat with distorted faces.

"Where is Richard?" she screamed.

They pointed to the Spanish wall and attempted to scream over the noise.

"The Grand Master took him. They have broken through over there."

Anasthasia began to run. The Spanish quarter of the wall was only a few paces from the place where Richard had his post. It was hardly three-hundred feet long. In one weak corner it went into the city, and then turned out again to the Spanish tower and the boulevard. She ran by the wounded lying on the ground or sitting up against the breastwork. She hopped over piles of stones and cannon carriages. She only had eyes for one thing, the maelstrom over there behind the tower. The great breach was there, surrounded by a resilient line of provisional walls. It was a real maelstrom full of Turks. A forest of banners fluttered from the conquered piles of stone, and the wild joy in their yell betrayed that they saw victory within reach. And worst of all, they had also planted their banners down on the boulevard. She could clearly see the Turks standing behind the breastworks.

She tried to push her way in among excited men trying to turn a cannon. The bloody carried away the wounded, screaming at each other. The smoke from the black powder was thick, and she was deaf from the firing.

Down in the maelstrom, she discovered the Grand Master's standard surrounded by hand-to-hand fighting. It tottered, hands fought for the staff, blades sparked against each other. And there in the crowd, in the midst of this skein of wrestling bodies, stood Richard. He stood—with one knee to the ground with a parrying dagger in his left hand raised like a shield from the hacks that hailed down upon him. He lifted his sword, tried to come up, stumbled again and fell. In the next minute, help was there in the form of steel and red coats with white crosses. The Turks yielded a few steps.

She threw herself over the edge of the wall, hurried down the rope ladder, and ran between the living and the dead. There—they carried him and laid him on the ground. She threw herself on him, felt his clothes wet with blood, embraced his head, cried out his name, kissed his mouth, and listened for breath.

He was dead. She let go of his head. It slipped down on the ground, heavy and dead.

"Get away from here," someone yelled. "Up with you, they are coming."

A strong hand took her by the shoulders, dragged her up, and shoved her away.

"Away with you, run for your life."

She threw her arms over her face, looking only at the ground before her as she ran through pools of blood over outstretched bodies among an angst-filled trampling of fleeing feet.

"Angelos, Gregoris . . . "

There, just over there, only minutes away from here, only a few minutes from the Janissaries.

The Grand Master toiled and got the tottering line to reform. Everyone could see the standard far forward and knew that the Grand Master himself was fighting like the others. Martinengo's cannons began to work. The Turks grew thin again and began to hesitate, looking about.

Just then, when the Grand Master's men began to gain ground again, Anasthasia came rushing. No one had seen what had happened, but all saw that she was wearing Richard Craig's bloody surcoat with the English leopards and his sword in her hand. Without looking around, like a mad woman, she rushed at the nearest Turk and cut him down, swung the sword, met another and another. Then she fell, run through by the nearest pike before anyone could grab her and carry her to safety.

They laid her dead body next to Richard Craig and ran back to disappear in the maelstrom again.

"Chevalier Bourbon."

"Your Eminence?"

"Try to see if our people in the casemate are alive. Maybe we can press up through there and take the boulevard back."

It was the fourth hour. Around the Spanish breach, the defense ring shut again. If they only had the strength to keep going, it might fix itself. It was heavy work to divvy out thrusts and hacks with all their power, time after time, clad in steel plates that could weigh twenty, thirty, or forty pounds.

Bourbon took his men. Through the underground tunnel, they made it into the boulevard's basement with the hidden batteries and were greeted with joy by a handful of artillerymen who thought they were forgotten and left for dead. They took them along, pressing cautiously up the stairs to the inner trench, and peered up to the boulevard. No Turks to be seen. They stormed up the next flight of stairs. There, friend and foe had fallen on top of each other. The artillery on the Auvergne wall had swept away the intruders. Those who were left fell, their banners torn down. The artillery had trained their cannons on the sea of Turks in the breach down before them. The first shot had been greeted with a shout of joy from the wall on the other side of the gaping hole. The pages kept turning themselves.

André Barel wiped the sweat from his forehead. The sun would soon reach its midday high. It was warm up here. It must have been even hotter for those standing in the midst of the hell over there and on the embankments this morning. His own men began to tire, even though it was a cakewalk to swing cannons and load and roll the pieces in place again, compared to standing down there and hacking with all your strength.

They had received their share of the storm's fire in the morning, but their wall had never been breached. They had all been able to shoot undisturbed into the sea of people over there. The Spaniards were their neighbors. The breach was in sight and all that came up out of the holes and pits over there on the Turkish side had to pass in front of the mouths of their cannons. In the morning he had thought that all would be lost. He had expected orders to draw back for one last desperate fight at the palace for the last two hours. But now he began to regain hope. His amazed eyes marked the difference. In the morning the Turks had rushed forward like hunting lions. Now they crouched and crept behind embankments of earth. They stood and hesitated in the opening of the tunnel mouths before they ventured out. Their confidence began to fade.

It wasn't that remarkable. The whole moat was covered with the bodies of those who never reached the other side. With every step, the reinforcements had to climb over them, and this was a work of the Auvergne langue, a good work in its way. But, yes, he didn't want to think about it. Not now.

"Your Eminence?"

"Yes, Marquet."

"The men no longer have their strength. They have kept it up for six hours. For every enemy they do away with, there comes a thoroughly rested man in his place.

"I see that, Marquet. Now, I will play my last card."

The last card had been forgotten behind the city walls by the arsenal. The evening before, the Grand Master had led half of the garrison from Saint Nicolas there. If the fleet came under attack, they should return. But they hadn't needed to do that. They were still there. The Grand Master ordered them forward.

He had used all the other reserves with the Italians and Englishmen. The line stood. The Turks' losses were appalling. The defense's architects rejoiced triumphantly. They had spent hours calculating the angles and setting up their flanking batteries.

"But if it all goes bad now . . . "

"Then we have nothing left," the Grand Master filled in. "That is why we waited until now. Now I think it is the right time. God help us."

And it was the right hour. When the Turks were forced back and their columns clogged the breach, the loss of men became so fearful that Suleiman gave up. He followed the battle from a platform made up of ship masts, sending in new people and throwing in small reserves. Yet with escalating uneasiness, he saw the attack stagnate and break up. A rout would put a stain on his glory and break his troops' morale.

He let the trumpets sound the retreat.

Sir Thomas Pemberton could finally think about going to the hospital to have his wounded arm dressed. He had fought the whole day with his left arm in a sling. His Englishmen had fought to the last man. Now that it was over, the ghastly truth was clear. Buet was dead, Baron and Roche likewise, and Craig, the indispensable Craig, with at least half of his archers.

He got up to go. His arm was bursting with pain. But still—he ought to go give notice of his death to the brave girl behind the wall that Richard Craig would have married.

Sir Thomas turned to the left in the alley and went over to the soup kitchen. Among the broken up barrels and the empty kettles, by an enormous glowing heap that kept falling over, sat an old woman with disheveled hair and dead eyes staring off into space. She hummed some ancient dirge.

Sir Pemberton asked about Anasthasia.

The woman stared at him.

Did the lord not know that Anasthasia was dead? Died in battle. Died in her husband's own bloody clothes.

Something almost prophetic came over her. She could have been a prophetess in a drama.

Pemberton crossed himself.

"And the boys? Who is taking care of them?"

"Anasthasia has already taken care of that."

The woman looked at him with her penetrating eyes.

"There they lie! There, *There!*"

She pointed to a fire. And so she told.

When it was the worst and all were taken up with handing off buckets and pails, Anasthasia came rushing. She was crazed and disappeared in to the boys' room, and there . . .

The old lady could hardly get it off her lips. But Pemberton understood. She had put them to death.

"She came out like a crazy woman, threw them on the fire, and screamed that no Turk would put his hand on them. Then she ran in again and came out with the silk cloth that kyrios Richard had given her and the necklace and perfume bottle. She threw it all on the fire. All, kyrie, and then she ran."

Sir Pemberton turned away from the pile of embers. He dared not look there as hardened he was. He only wiped his eyes and left without a word.

The Tower of Margat

A SPIRIT OF TENSION remained in Rhodes.

It was not any great Te Deum. It certainly was a great victory, a victory that still shined. This little city was victorious over a world power. Everyone was sure to thank God for it in the churches. But then the requiem and masses for the dead were read without end. All the auberges were transformed to hospitals for knights and serving brothers, while the common people lay in their barracks and all the elderly women and children who had been shot or suffered from bruises and saber cuts were led to the churches or to the court buildings down on the square.

Shooter-Frans worked out in the city. He tried to be a medic on his own and bandaged, splinted, cut, and sawed. He felt fumbly and helpless, and there was not enough anesthesia by his calculation.

The extent of the misfortune was clear when the Grand Master received the final report. Of the common soldiers, approximately half were out of commission. Of the knights, two thirds were dead or so badly wounded they could not stand on their own feet. Almost all the rest had some minor wound: lost fingers, saber cuts in the face, and moderate stabs in legs and chest.

But there was still hope. The Turks had suffered losses too, so terrible that no normal troop could bear them. And it was well known that dysentery and other diseases ravaged the camp worse than in the city.

There were more deserters than usual. They came with remarkable news. Suleiman had an inquisition among his Generals. Mustafa, Supreme Commander, was sentenced to death. Pir Pascha, Vizier, performed the execution and was then immediately sentenced to death, even him. All the pashas had gone to the Sultan's magnificent tent, threw themselves at his feet, and begged for their lives. That, in any case, was the rumor in the camp. And all expected orders to board the ships.

They also made their own observations from the walls. The cannons were quiet. Small groups of Turks cleaned up, burying rubbish and the dead, and carried away damaged material. Or—was it really damaged? Was it not the beginning of the departure?

The Chancellor had had a sleepless night and a terrible day. Yesterday, he expected to die, but today completely different possibilities opened themselves, the most terrible he could conceive. If the Turks departed, then l'Isle Adam would become a new D'Aubusson, a hero celebrated throughout Christendom, held in immortal glory despite all his mistakes, despite the fact that the victory was due to nothing more than undeserved luck and pure accident.

If the Turks departed now, the history of war would mark their greatest mistake. If they only knew! It would be fate's bloodiest injustice, if now, after they had pushed the fork so far down, they would give up without taking the apple that was all but theirs.

Did such accidents really control people's fate? Only meaningless chance? No—there was still something else: Will, one's own will, the strong man's ability to subdue his fate.

It was written in the stars that he would obtain his will, if he only dared to cast the bold throw. There was nothing he wanted as much as to hinder this Phillippe Villiers de l'Isle Adam from being crowned with everything, even with this undeserved glory.

And the bold throw? There was only one thing to do.

He wrote a short, factual report, militarily concise and correct. He pointed out how incorrect it would be now to abandon the siege. He undersigned: "One who wants to live in peace under the crescent moon."

He hadn't thought the last through. But suddenly it hit him that this was a great possibility for the will that turned fate: The possibility to have life when all others vanished. It was possible. But only on one condition: that he put himself and his expertise in Suleiman's disposal. As so many others had done.

He called for Blas Diez.

"I am going out for a minute. Get me a crossbow, the little one that I use to hunt with."

He put the bolt in order. For security's sake, he bound a red string around the paper and let the ends hang free.

Blas Diez, as normal, did not question anything. He could be trusted in all seasons. If his master told him to stand in the door of their house and shoot down the French Prior when he went through the gate across the way, he would do it.

It was dark. They went to St. George tower within the barbican of the Auvergne wall and down to the cellar. A watch greeted them. It was empty by the cannons. No Turks would come at night, and the artillery-men enjoyed a well-deserved sleep in their quarters by the wall.

In the stairwell they stood together with a small dark form that roved about. The Chancellor shouted harshly, and Blas Diez lifted his lantern. They found it to be Father Gennaios inspecting his drums. He looked frightened and vanished.

The Chancellor shot his bolt and turned back, calmer and more satisfied than he had been in a long time. At home he saw the former proprietor's coat of arms with the motto: *Firme Fe*, a firm faith. Normally, it irritated him. But this evening he felt full of a new confidence. He knew what he believed in.

They drank wine in the Auberge d'Auvergne. This seldom happened because their stores had become scant. But this evening no one cared to conserve. André Barel had just come home from a promenade along the wall and had had great things to tell. It was no doubt that great divisions were moving, and that they were drawing back in the cover of darkness southwards on the road to Paramboli where the transport lay.

Men toasted and drank despite the fact that so many of the brothers were dead this evening. They had not died in vain. The men let loose and were not ashamed of it.

It was only old Dumon who let the cup sit. He just sat and looked out in front of himself as if he disapproved of it altogether.

"Pierre, what's the matter? What are you brooding about?"

"The Tower of Margat . . . "

They stared at him. The Tower of Margat? They had had enough of towers and walls at least for this evening.

"Have you not heard the history?"

He began to tell them.

"It happened long ago, back when we still fought in the holy land. Things started to go bad. So it went for Margat. It may have been one of our best fortresses, just as strong as our Krak. It was high on a precipice like our walls here, only three times higher. And way out on the spur was the key tower, the impregnable Tower of Margat.

Then Kalaun came with his Mamluks. He was the Suleiman of that day. But we were able to hold our own. We were able to do so by making attacks. We burned their siege towers and their siege engines. So we thought that they would have to retreat now. And there was a great feast that night.

But the next day, an old fine lord with jewels in his turban came carrying nothing but a walking stick in his hand, saying that we had to capitulate now. He said it was our last warning. Understandably, we laughed. He just told us that there was something in the vicinity that we absolutely had to see. He invited us as politely as could be for a visit. As many or as few that wanted to come—to exchange hostages was understood. We decided to send a couple of the brothers, and the fine Saracen took them around the mountain that the Tower of Margat stood on. He then took them down a shaft and into a giant cellar they had made under the floor. The roof was supported with large beams, and there among them lay dry brush, soaked in wax and tar. And now all they needed to do was set fire to it, then the roof would break up and the tower would fall down into the cave with all the brothers. That was what you did at that time."

"Yeah," finished brother Pierre, "so there was nothing else to do but capitulate and depart. And that they did."

"They could have stood and died in the ruins," someone said.

"That is understood. It is just the choice one has to make."

"But the relief," someone yelled. "That too is a possibility?"

"Yes," said Chalant, who sat there with his arms in a sling. "If the Turks don't depart, then it is our only chance."

Victory or Death

FOUR DAYS HAD GONE by.

André Barel stood on the breastwork and followed every movement on the other side attentively. Even yesterday there had been signs that could be explained by a departure. People were picking up spades, helmets, and guns out of the holes, piling them in bundles and taking them away. But today they began to repair the wood by the breastwork, and newly dug sand came up out of the tunnels. It was a bad sign.

When six days had passed, the stench from the moat was almost unbearable. People tied linen handkerchiefs rubbed with garlic, cumin, mint leaves, or whatever they could find in front of their noses. There was no longer any hope that the Turks would depart. The Turks would remain and the corpses in the moat would stay there. Suleiman had changed his mind.

People speculated regarding the reason. Had someone persuaded him? Some traitor? An Albanian had escaped the day after the attack, a clever and cunning fellow, who happened to be furious about some reprimand he had received.

The confirmation came on the tenth day. One of the slaves, a Hungarian, took the risk of escaping rather than being sent among the dead in front of the approaches. He said that the Turks were building a little provisionary castle for Suleiman up on the side of the mountain. He planned to stay until Rhodes fell, all winter if needed.

On the twelfth day, hopes were raised up again from the hopelessness and stench. A brigantine, captained by a Brother Bresols, had come during the night with the good news that relief troops were gathering in Neapel and Messina. The Grand Master let the news travel. People began to breathe easier. It was as if the stench began to depart.

"Blas, this evening, you will go with this paper like last time . . . "

Did the amicable Blas look a little hesitant? Maybe it was best to talk to him.

"You can be at peace, Blas. Nothing will happen to you that won't happen to me. I promise you. And I plan to live next year too. I don't say anything evil about anyone, but they govern like madmen here, straight into the burning and the destruction of us all. Therefore, I am now arranging a lifeline to come and pull me up on land. And I promise you that you may hang onto it with me. Do you understand?"

Blas bowed his head slightly. His unchangeable humble butlerishness got a little weak shimmer of satisfaction. He left.

D'Amaral adjusted himself with a feeling of contentment. He knew his people. He had always thought that the amicable Blas became a Christian only to escape becoming a refugee, and that he accomplished a lot with a quiet reservation—just like himself. He thought about Blas.

Again he felt the same enchanting feeling of peacefulness. No god who looked through the window. No petty judge to fear. There was only an endless space where the stars made their way as witnesses to the mysterious unknown powers, powers that created opportunities and possibilities and gave them to those who knew how to take advantage of them.

The Grand Master had listened to Chevalier Bresols, took note of everything, reflected and meditated. It was already determined that Brother Bresols should return with the same brigantine in two days after he had gained enough sleep. He would do everything he could to hasten the reinforcements. He would tell them that they should come in small groups. That even a handful of people could make a huge difference and that they should bring powder with them, as much powder as they could scrape together without delaying themselves more than forty-eight hours.

They ought also to be able to come as early as the beginning of November. Rhodes could hold out until then.

But then?

He had never had more than one thought: victory or die, with emphasis on victory. It had been the theme in all his speeches, in council, among the knights and before the citizenry.

But if the emphasis now displaced itself—from "victory to "death"? The whole of his life he had been prepared to die. He was eighteen the first time he heard the lead weight of battle sing past his head and bury itself in other bodies with a dull thunder. He was prepared every time he met an enemy ship and saw the row of barrel mouths and conical helmets over the rails, and now, every day anew. They continuously asked him to spare himself, to not go into the hail of bullets, to not lead the attacks himself. But he had refused. Just as he had refused to flee up to the palace again and sleep in a bed instead of lying on a straw mattress behind a stone wall by the Spanish breach.

He knew what it cost. He could never get rid of his fear of death. It had to be conquered anew every day. Just like the desire to save himself or the desire to tell people off, to find scapegoats, to say poisonous remarks if they disapproved. He had trained himself so long in the art that it began to be a second nature. But only a second; his old nature remained, and it gave him more than a sufficient amount of sin to confess when he confessed before Brother Giovanni.

The Sharpshooters

THE TURKS HAD BEGUN to move again. The spades scraped. The earth tunnels moved. The enemy came closer, digging in deep under the protecting roof of beams and earth.

During the calm of the day, they cleaned the barbican at the foot of the Spanish wall and carried all the broken stone in through the breach. Now the little defense with its wall and its own shooting apertures were defensible and hardened.

It was a mistake. The Turks attacked and were beaten back. Again the cannons on the Auvergne boulevard swept straight into the moat. But so the Turks began to patiently and systematically to scoop down sand in the holes. It ran out of the holes on the other side, it thudded and rustled, and, all night, every night, through squeaking spades a wall grew up directly across from the moat. It protected the Turks from the evil black eyes on the boulevard d' Auvergne. The rampart was strengthened with a wall. A covered path ran under it. The Turks now had tunnels right up to the wall's foot. And then the barbican fell.

The defenders tried to heave powder charges and floating fire down over the Turks. They were massacred and burned; the acrid smell of sweaty flesh blended with the sickly sweet stench of dead bodies. But the Turks held. They covered the barbican with joists and raw ox hides that were inaccessible.

Then the defenders tried to open holes in their own walls in order to shoot the Turks. They shot back. It became a nerve-racking game of hide and seek where a man crept behind the walls, looked through apertures, and tried to be the one to shoot first.

It was the eleventh of October in the dawn.

Martinengo had slept a few hours and came to inspect the night's construction work. The artillery duels had begun again. Both sides were dug in. They placed their pieces as far within the earth embankments and stone piles as was possible. Martinengo kept everything in his head, with every piece in the right place and every aperture properly balanced. He was everywhere, drew explanatory sketches, gave orders, and commanded.

The night's work was going well. The builders could have made it even better if they had more wood to support it with. But every beam that splintered was irreplaceable.

Martinengo looked and bowed. The apertures were right, just as he had thought. The first covered the high parts of the stone mound over there where they must emerge. The other two covered the next sector. When he looked in the third, it happened as so often happened before. There was a whining whiplash, a whistling and a report—and then the ill-omened impact, not sharp and pointed, not metal against stone, but soft and dull.

Martinengo fell flat. His helmet rolled over the stone. With a half-choked yell of dismay, the men turned to him. He was shot through the right eye. His whole head was bloody.

"He lives," someone said. "The ball went out again. Here by the ear."

A stretcher was fetched. And they lifted him up and ran. People stretched out behind the stone banks.

"Who is it?"

And it went like a cry of angst from wall to wall, from breach to breach, through the streets and alleys.

"Martinengo is shot."

Brother Frans had become a soldier again. The whole city had been finely combed, searching for reserves, when he reminded someone that he had been with the artillery. So they fitted him with a breastplate, leg bands, and overcoat again. And now he stood in the basement of the boulevard d' Auvergne. Now he truly was the old Shooter-Frans that everyone laughed at.

He had never been much of a perfectionist. But in the hospital he had at least learned to pick things up off the floor. There was good use for that art here. Oakum and tattered paper wrappers, cannon balls and leather gloves lay strewn about the stone floors. He stacked and sorted cannon balls, put powder packets in a tidy pile, and swept the rubbish in a corner.

His comrades poked fun at him until Chevalier Fournon gave the men three and four credits at the morning inspection for their good order, and ordered the first and second batteries to follow their example.

A few days passed. A couple of men had been wounded up on the boulevard. Then they discovered that Shooter-Frans could apply dressings. It made him popular. No one knew when they might need his help. He could hardly be the one everyone made fun of, but he was never called anything but Shooter-Frans.

The camp had snipers again. The Turks attacked down by the English Boulevard two days in a row. You could hear the noise and shrieks but were not able to see anything. Then the wall gave way. The only thing that could be seen was the silent fight for the Spanish wall. This was always in front of them in continuation to the Auvergne portion to the left of the moat when they looked through the long apertures. The Turks could not be seen. They hid quietly behind the earth embankments as they shot up directly across the hole and under the wood covered with ox hides over there by the wall's foot.

The fighting continued there. It was right up against the city's walls. The Turks could take it with their hands. Now it only needed to fall down.

The Turks dug themselves in under the wall. The earth was thrown out of the hole. They used it to strengthen their protecting embankments. In order to keep the magnificent wall from collapsing on them, they supported it with large wood beams. Finally, the wall rested on nothing but a system of crossing braces and supports. The Turks filled the spaces in between with twigs. Then they set fire to it all. Then they went back and waited, ready to storm in through the rat holes and mole paths on the other side.

With endless strain, the Auvergnats peeped through their apertures. The smoke belched, flames shot out. They cracked and popped. The wood burned, but the wall stood, until finally the fires sank altogether into a pile of ashes. Then a black hole gaped from the wall and the stones over it were black with soot. But the wall stood.

A cry of relief went up from the boulevard. People clapped their hands and gave the old wall applause. They had a true love for it. It was a wonder what one could feel in this way for a stone wall.

The Turks did not give up, though. They took a day. Then they were ready with the next device. They tossed huge anchors through the air, the type used on board big freight ships. They were shot with particular siege engines, a type of giant crossbow. They sailed through the air like dragons with a coarse rope trailing behind it. Most hit the crown of the wall and fell down into the moat. Some made it over the breastwork and jerked when the rope could not run out any further. In the same second, the rope was tightened. One could not see how it was done. The Turks were hidden behind their embankments. But there must have been hundreds of hands that held on and tugged.

Several anchors hopped back over the breastwork and broke down in the moat. But some were set with their teeth biting hard into the wall's crown.

The men up there tried to hack the rope. The Turks anticipated this and met them with such a hailstorm from their sharpshooters that no one could stick his head over the edge of the breastwork.

So they kept it up for a good hour. With almost endless strain, the men watched through their small apertures. Now it was the fourth anchor, then came the fifth, and it sat there. Now the Turks began to wind. Somewhere behind their earth walls, they must have set up a winch. The rope stretched to an extreme, the men at the winch screamed and wailed, and the rope shook with every new power pull of the lever. The wall wailed also. It twisted and turned like a man on the rack. The men on the walls suffered with it.

Fournon wrung his hands in his helplessness. Here his round cannon balls were worthless.

"Brother Frans, run down into storeroom and see if there might not be some bar shot left. Maybe we haven't shot it all up."

He knew that they had, but he wanted his conscience to be at peace, knowing he did what he could.

"We'll try with shot," he said. "The coarsest kind." They loaded and shot. It was hopeless. A couple of the ropes looked a little shabbier, but other than that, nothing.

During this time, Brother Franz groped around with his lantern down in there like a bandaged storeroom keeper. He lifted and searched. There were cannonballs for many calibers, powder barrels, and empty room, a lot of empty room. But no bar shot. Not any. There was old scrap, wheels to gun carriages, sponges to poles, wood barrels for the water. And in one of the barrels lay an old chain with a weight on each end.

He remembered that they shot with similar chain shot at enemy ships to cut down the rigging. It couldn't hurt to try it.

He tried to lift it but had to put the lantern down and take it with both hand to pick up the huge clumsy thing. In the sunlight he groped around to find the stairs. Out of breath, unsteady and flushed, he made it to the casemate.

"There wasn't any bar shot, but . . . will this be of any use?"

Chevealier Fournon jumped for joy. "Frans! The Baptist himself has sent you here!"

Then he gave a stream of orders that he halfway worked out as he gave them. "We take four . . . Double pack . . . pack it just right . . . In with the oakum . . . and now . . ."

He put the balls and chain in himself as careful as if he put a gold necklace in its case.

So—now they could aim. Shooter-Frans helped. Fournon commanded, just so . . .

Then, just before the shot, they glimpsed through the sight a cloud of their own black smoke.

Fournon ran to the aperture to see when the rope would be tightened straight.

Frans saw the little hand signal that meant "fire," but he did not hear the order. Then a whining report came through the firing hole that filled the whole casemate. The shot had gone straight over the cannon. The man with the match was shot through the breast by some Turkish sharpshooter. He went down on the cannon and swept with him most of the priming powder. The match hit the ground.

Before he really knew what he was doing, Shooter-Frans had bent down and reached out for the match. He blew life into it and drove it down in to the last remains of powder over the priming pan. The piece roared, spewed smoke and fire, and hopped back. It tumbled, rolled to the side, and flew by Frans, who had to grab hold in order not to fall.

Then he bent down in the smoke and got a grip under the arms of the man who was shot to lay him out right and see if it was profitable to bandage him.

Fournon had been able to see from his aperture that the shot was just right. Then the thick powder smoke covered everything. But up on the boulevard there was a joyous yell that spread all along the wall. The yell was joined by the winners like a roar of victory celebrating a great achievement. And over on the other side came an answer of embitterment and grief.

Everyone rushed up to look. In the moat lay the ropes. All five were cut, nappy and bristling at the end like slack cow tails.

"Who shot?" yelled the men up there.

"Brother Frans," said Fournon. "He is the one who found the load and fired the shot."

So it happened that Shooter-Frans, who in distress laid his dead comrade properly on the floor, was now being thrown up to the roof of the casemate by victorious Auvergnats. He was told that he was an honor to the Religion, that Provençe and Auvergne always belonged together, that he was now an honorary Auvergne, and much else.

Then came an order from out of the bodyguard. The Grand Master wants to see the shooter who fired the master shot at the ropes. He will have a reward.

So they brushed off the giddy Brother Frans, beaming with joy, and winked at him when he limped up onto the wall.

A minute later he was dead. Another sniper with a long gun had been waiting in just that opening of the breastwork. The shot hit him in the temple. Shooter-Frans fell on his back and lay there with a happy smile on his face.

"Absolutely meaningless," said one of the men, who took him to the hospital.

"He was loved enough by God," said Brother Giovanni, "that he was vindicated already here on earth. And so he was able to go home. Can one ask for anything more?"

Harder than Dying

"GIVEN THE THIRTIETH OF October, 1522."
The Chancellor reluctantly wrote the date under the finished draft. He knew what it was to sit and write letters to Spain and France—pleading letters to indifferent princes, harsh letters to slow brothers of the order. Even if the letters successfully made it through the blockade and the fall storms, they would not get results. In any case, not before the Janissaries' scimitars raked straight through Rhodes.

Anyhow—the Grand Master wanted to see the draft. Who would he send with the letters? Where was Blas Diez? He had not come back from the wall yesterday evening. Had he taken the matter into his own hands and fled to the Turks? It would be understandable. A man only has one life to live. Though, it may have been better if he had let his own master cast the die.

There was a knock on the door and the Chancellor looked up. There stood Didier de Tolon. He was in command of the great breach. A couple of other lords watched behind him, all in armor. Do you expect them to attack today? He looked at them suspiciously.

"What affords me the honor?"

"The Lord Chancellor is wanted at the castle."

This wasn't right. If anyone was to call the other, it was the Chancellor.

"Tell him that I will be there in about a half an hour. I am busy now."

The lords at the door had made their way in solemnly and dressed so as to show that they were officially serving the order. Tolon continued with remarkable coolness.

"We are under orders to bring the Lord Chancellor to the castle immediately."

"Orders? From whom?"

"His Eminence, the Grand Master."

The Chancellor gave him a long look, inspecting as from above. He appeared indifferent and haughty. He just looked at them and said:

"All one can expect. So as one is steered at the present . . . "

The sun began to sink down the backside of Mt. Stefan, and the men on the Auvergne boulevard made their way into the shadows behind the shot-up merlon. Bitter experience taught them how visible the evening sun made them.

Wherever two or three of them gathered together, they talked about the same thing. Their Chancellor had been taken to the castle. There was something real shady about this business with Blas Diez too.

They had caught him at night. Right here down in the casemate with a crossbow in hand that he had hidden among the rubbish down in the underground storeroom. He had shown up here many times, but the watch always thought he was carrying some message from the Chancellor. Of course, the Grand Crosses' servants were not the first to be suspected of treason.

But now that the Chancellor had been escorted to the castle—escorted there by many high lords in full equipment—it looked more than bad.

"What is the punishment for something like that?"

"You know very well what it is. Hung and quartered."

"You mean that we might see the Chancellor's left butt cheek suspended by a pike here on the wall?"

"Shish, people, we don't know anything . . . "

Two days later, Preian de Bidoulx sat on the small stone bench of a window in the great hall of the French auberge. He still had a sizable bandage around his neck where he had been shot, but the wound had closed itself. It was a miracle that he lived. There was but one greater miracle on Rhodes at this time: that this Martinengo was still alive and looked like he would recover. Though there was an empty hole where his right eye had been.

Bidoulx had been to Vespers in San Giovanni—which at present was seldom possible for the sake of the service. He had popped in on the way back to hear the news. The Bastard of Bourbon sat on the bench across from him holding his crutch. Antoine Golart stood on the floor with his arm in a sling. Bourbon spoke quietly so as not to be heard everywhere in the room.

"He had a Turk that he sent to Constantinople a year ago. The Turk came back remarkably fine and well dressed."

"Yeah, I saw that myself," said Golart. "It looked quite peculiar."

"And he was responsible for the stores of powder," said Bidoulx. "It should have been more than enough for a year. I wonder if he said that in good faith?"

"And he is said to have told a good friend already at the election that this would be the last Grand Master of Rhodes."

"That is true. Commander Luis was at the examination. He was the one who heard it."

"Just how long has this been going on?"

"What if he advised Suleiman to come?"

"Well, in any case, he was the one who convinced him to stay."

The trial dragged on for four days before the court was finished. The judges crowded in the little room in Messer Lomellino's house just before the great breach where the Grand Master had had his quarters for two weeks now. His straw mattress was folded up in a corner. The table was encumbered with paper. Blunt iron shoes, shin guards, knee buckles, helmets, and plain clothes hung in the hall. The three wartime judges, the two Grand Crosses, and the assessors filled most of the free floor space.

"Has he confessed?"

"No, Your Eminence. As much as we tortured him, we have not got a word out of him. Not one."

"What then is the court's evidence?"

"First, Blas Diez's full confession."

"Then it might be mere fabrication to throw the chief guilt on someone else."

"There is a body of circumstantial evidence, Your Eminence. The threats he spoke to Commander Luis . . . "

"He hardly would have said that if he really had been in collusion with the Sultan."

"Then there is the inexplicable contact with Constantinople through a well remunerated slave . . . "

"That also happened so openly that I have a hard time believing that it was an issue of treachery."

"Taken all together, your Eminence. But there is still the more deci-sive evidence. Father Gennaios saw them together in the Auvergne bar-bican with a crossbow and an arrow with a paper tied with a red string. It was the day after the great attack."

"Why didn't he report it immediately?"

"Because it never occurred to him that the Chancellor might be out on some less than praiseworthy errand."

The Grand Master thought for a bit.

"Have you confronted him with Blas Diez?"

"Naturally, Your Eminence. He heard it all. Though it hardly looked at all as if he heard. Then he just said that Diez was a scoundrel, un vigli-acco. Diez took a lot of abuse from him and said that the Chancellor had promised that he would help him and pull him out with a life line—what-ever he meant by that."

The Grand Master sat again thinking quietly. They could hear what he was thinking. Then he took the pen and quickly wrote his approval on the sentence. Blas Diez would be hung; the Chancellor, executed by the sword. Both would be put on the wheel.

The night of the sixth of November, the Grand Master slept in his bed in the palace, which was unusual. He had spent the greater part of the eve-ning in the castle's chapel to the right of the stairwell. Then he visited the watches on a couple sections of the wall as usual, slept a couple of hours, and then went to the chapel again for Matins with Brother Giovanni and some other knights, who hobbled in very silently, just a few crutches scraping and hitting the stone floor.

The Grand Master was sitting immoveable at the moment. The splendid missal was open in front of him, the missal he had made at home in France. Every page was framed with a wide border of flowers looped together in blue on the bottom. Every border was adorned by a drawn sword and by his motto: *pour la Foy.*

For faith . . . He had never doubted. He had given himself, his youth, and his best years. And now he thought he would soon give his last and hardest and be laid to rest somewhere, but not like his predecessors among the stone halls of San Giovanni with a splendid epitaph etched above them, but in some mass grave among the other plundered and trampled corpses.

He was ready for it. But before then? He felt himself collapsing. Outside, the Turks began the bombardment and the chapel's small glass panes shook. The Turks would splinter and crush the walls again. And then the walls would be patched together again during the night by a handful of workers, from whom one was still able to get more out of than there really was to work with. The enemy would dig a few more ells, and yet another wall would fall into their underground tunnels. Their marksmen would pluck off a few more of the wall's defenders. And yet he would still be able to find the means to inspire them with courage, to stand there as a firm wall to be leaned on when they could no longer manage to hold themselves up.

But if that wall fell now? The last days had demanded more than he could manage. For the first time, he had consciously withdrawn from his duties in the preceding days. He had refused to preside over the ceremonies in San Giovanni, when Andrea d' Amaral was brought in—broken by torture but unbroken as he wore a Grand Cross with a face of stone and with an air of superior contempt—and was deprived of his order's uniform and his knightly insignia.

And now out there, at this hour as the sun was coming up, that same Andrea d'Amaral, previously a knight of the order of St. John the Baptist, was brought to the place of execution.

The Grand Master waited. He talked to God as Elijah once did.

"Lord, it is enough. Take my life. They have murdered all your prophets and fighters. Pomerolx is dead. John Buck is dead. And now d'Amaral has died this terrible death. He will be run through and put on a pike like a criminal of the worst kind. You know, Lord, I cannot forbid it. Justice must be carried out for us all. It is enough. Lord, take my life."

There were steps heard on the stairs and he went out. It was Tolon come to announce that the sentence had been executed.

"Did he say anything?"

"Nothing. Father Dominique held a picture in front of him, but he just turned away."

The Grand Master walked by the workroom before he went back to the breach. The Turks shot their heavy bombards the whole time, and you could hear everything breaking about a thousand paces to the south.

The Grand Master went through the office. Brother Fancesco, the artist who used to help the architect Zuenio, was sitting there.

"What are you doing today, Brother Francesco?"

"Drawing the new plafond for the English wall. To be erected when we rebuild the boulevard. I would really appreciate it if Your Eminence would approve a new motto.

"A new motto?"

"Yes. I have a proposal. It builds on the four initials in Your Eminence's name, Filippo Villiers de l'Isls Adam. F—V—I—A: *Fortis Virilisque In Adversis*, firm and manly in opposition. No dull motto for our Grand Master," he said.

The Grand Master was quiet and introspective.

"*Domine no sum dignus*. Lord, I am not worthy."

But—maybe it was not a report, but a reminder? Not a request, but an order?

"I approve it," he said.

Father Giovanni waited in the workroom. The Grand Master started right away.

"Brother Giovanni, do you have a word of encouragement for me, to help me carry on?"

"Not I, but the Savior."

"And what?"

"When you are old you shall stretch out your hands, and another will dress you and carry you where you do not want to go."

The Grand Master was quiet.

"I am willing."

"Is the Brother Grand Master?"

The Grand Master looked ponderously at the little priest.

"Yes, I believe I can say that. I have expected death everyday for weeks on end."

"And it might be ugly."

The Grand Master looked a little more puzzled and asked:

"Does he not say that we shall be ready to lose our lives for his sake?"

"Yes—to the end, but first that we shall take up our cross every day and follow him."

"Yes, to death. And it is probable that he has decided this for us now if no reinforcements come."

"But if they don't come, then the Brother Grand Master must drink his cup to the dregs. Not leave it half drunk."

"What do you mean?"

"I mean that brother Grand Master must be willing to live to the end. See all the horrors. Share the extreme disgrace. Not leave the dregs to those who stay behind."

The Grand Master looked at the priest again. Could he read his thoughts? How did he know that his Grand Master had just prayed: "Lord, take my life?" The priest continued:

"I only mean that a father does not desire to leave this earth so long as his children need him. To give his life is a grand sacrifice. But it is greater and better to live and remain."

"There are risks one must take in war," the Grand Master said, half-pardoningly.

"Yes, and such as one must not take. In matters of the first type one can pray: 'your will be done.' And be certain that the Lord listens. But you can't do this with the other sort in which one might put God to the test."

Again, there was a loud crash in the great breach. The Grand Master got up.

"I have to go now. Thanks for the admonition. If it is His desire, then I will carry it with me to the very last."

Winter Rain

GIANANTONIO BONALDI PULLED THE tattered cape over him. He was freezing. He could hear the rain smack in the water pools in the garden. A little rivulet had seeped in and wetted the straw where he lay. Laboriously, he moved closer to the wall. His swollen fingers ached. A stone had fallen on them yesterday.

He shut his eyes again. If he had the strength and dared, he would have unstrapped his breastplate and scratched his back. In three days he had not been out of his armor, and the lice ravaged him unmercifully. They were completely inaccessible within his metal shell.

Out there, the shovels scraped in the wet gravel. Was it their deepening the tunnels, or was it the Turks digging themselves in closer? It wasn't very far to their first rat hole. This is why he had to sleep here in this all but dilapidated house among all the snoring, groaning men and the stench of their bodies.

He remembered the evenings when he paraded with his friends and his garrison under fluttering streamers through cheering crowds and ear-deafening rejoicing. He had worn the same breastplate then, new and polished to a shine over a red buff coat. Now it was dented and rusty, scratched by pikes and notched in the brim by saber cuts.

The war had become a dirty groundwork, a fight for loamy holes with stinking puddles. The Turks had quit storming. They dug in instead. They had pushed through the great breach and into the city. They were met by a new wall or rather a circle of pits, walls, berms and defenses that spewed fire on them. Then they had gone underground.

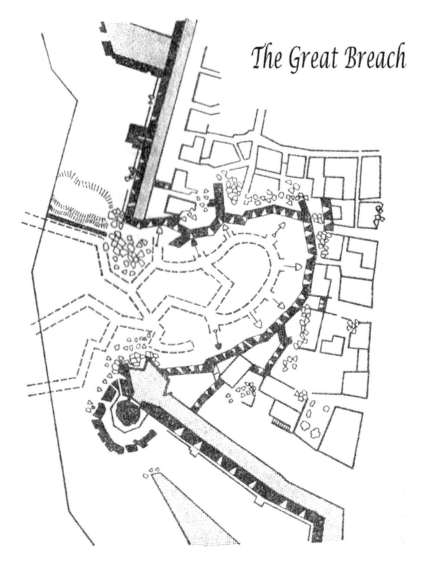

The Great Breach

Only their molehills were visible. Here and there a prickly row of wood ends poked out of the ground. We ought to have charged forward and thrown them out of the breach—if only we had the people. We could have shot their defenses to pieces, if we only had the powder. Now we sit and wait, shooting only when we are sure to hit and are sure not to be hit if we expose ourselves.

The Turks must have lived like frogs in a swamp when the rain rushed down and filled their holes. But they were able to change out their people and let them rest. They could replace every board that was shot. And their cannons played continuously, spraying muck and stone pieces over our artillery mired in the clay.

Bonaldi listened. That must be their shovels he heard, maybe thirty feet away. They dug themselves in under the wall, the third wall in a row— to make it fall. Sooner or later, maybe even tonight. He had the cannons move back and moved the harquebusiers from the most exposed places. He tried to think of something else. He crept on his knees, tiredness ached in every member. He was sick, and his hands felt a swelling boil of physical pain.

If Bosio was still here! But he was in Rome or Naples or maybe in Marseille to request help. And he was needed there more than here right now, if he was able to get through alive.

He woke up and noticed that he had slept. He felt warm again, pleasantly warm and relaxed. It was a delight just to rest and get some shuteye.

Then the wall was razed like a landslide by the edge of a winter stream, and in the next second the alarm rang like a bell. He stumbled to his feet, got his men up on their legs, and staggered out. But there was no attack, only the scraping of shovels.

Soaked by the rain, they turned back, but they couldn't sleep any longer.

It rained continuously. The water ran in small rivulets between the stones in the makeshift walls and gathered up in pools on the ground. The pools floated together and grew into lakes. These came halfway up to the men's knees.

André Barel and his people kept busy making channels in the ground and leading the water to the lowest holes in the wall, which changed to babbling and gurgling drains where the water ran out and continued down into the Turkish tunnels. The men sneered and jeered. Today the Turks would have something besides storming to think about.

André straightened up and felt the rainwater run down his back plate. It was cold, but it relieved the itching. He had relocated here down in the pit with his two culverins when the Turks finally succeeded in shooting down the old wall that stood across the spades and ropes of both mines. The breach had widened to an unfathomable gap. Defense lines ran throughout the city with makeshift walls between gables and shooters in the barricaded windows. Little by little, the houses were torn down and the stones stacked up. It was a lap work of encircling walls around the open field of supported earth as the Turks conquered. Day and night they worked on expanding their territory with the help of the spades.

Everything was soaking wet and thoroughly drenched now: clothes and boots, wood boards and bread. Still the Turks shot. The wood roofs over their cannons seemed to hold tight, and the shooters stayed in their caves in the mountain on the other side of the moat. There they could keep their lanterns burning. They sent their greetings from there, watchful and persistent. Huge stone balls ploughed dikes into the water-drenched ground so that the clay spewed and the laboriously stacked-up stones flew about. There was nothing else to do than to crouch down and creep together in some drenched corner between the walls stones. The powder had to be spared until it was really needed.

One hour after dawn came the first loss. A black stone fell on one of the men, and he was carried away with crushed legs. A half an hour after that, another man fell out of the working party with a bullet through the head. He was a Turk. No one took it too lightly. He was irreplaceable. Before noon, two more had fallen, both so badly injured that the chaplain came and gave them their last rites. Brother Giovanni was there within a few minutes. When he was finished, he stayed. The Turks shot hard, and he could be needed again. He sat next to André Barel behind the great stone cairn.

So it was that brother André found an unsought chance to ease his heart. He was bitter. It was hard for him to express it, but brother Giovanni listened and seemed to understand. It wasn't just the disappointment and the lost illusions of a magnificent life of a knight. It was deeper. Essentially, he was bitter at his own illusions about the world he grew up in, all the false conceptions about glory and chivalry where grand lords all dressed up in protective cases ride around simple people and pierce them with a sharp lance. And in the worse case, they themselves were captured and ransomed for hard cash gathered by their poor landsmen. In a way, he thought of it as a type of justice that he sat here in the clay like everyone else. And he saw that his brothers in the order did it without grumbling.

Essentially, there was more chivalry in that—like Bonaldi just now with dirty and bloody hands helping to dig toward a forecastle under a raised wall—than to sit like his brothers at home watching a floating plume with metal roses clattering over a silver glittering horse while breaking a lance in front of the dames who watched with amazement. Fundamentally, men here never got this distorted conception.

He tried to clothe all this in words now and make it clear for Brother Giovanni, while the rain water dropped from his helmet, and Brother Giovanni looked at him with his childlike eyes, possibly a little surprised, but still more approving.

"I should wish," finished André, "that I get so much power that I could change the world."

But then Brother Giovanni looked almost frightened.

"Those who believe that they have the power to do that are the most dangerous of all."

He nodded toward the breach.

"Do you think Suleiman doesn't mean well? He has power and he will change the world. He believes that he rules better than our Christian princes. And he is right about that in many respects. Now he wants to make the whole world happy. So he sacrifices some hundred thousand wretches here in the clay. Sure, he thinks it is regrettable. But for the sake of good . . . It is for the future. He knows how it ought to be, and he wants to see that it is so."

"But how do you want to do it then? You can't just be happy the way the world is."

"No, who could do that? And the worst is that not even God has the power to do it. Not before he makes everything new. But still he has some sort of wonderful care for us failed creatures even though we all end up doing evil. He has given us an opportunity. This is why he has still not let the Day of Judgment come upon us, but he holds on, repairs and patches, just like we are doing with this wall, even though the devil shoots the whole time."

"How do you mean that he patches?"

"He forgives. He brings every last one of us to shame and repentance."

"But it is not enough to change the world?"

"Some is always enough. There is only one thing you can really change, and that is yourself. And, of course, the more who do it make it more and more clear that something has happened in the world."

"But it takes a long time. We ought to be finished with the regrettable things now in our time."

"You will have a better world without repentance? There is no such thing. Otherwise, God would have applied this method a long time ago."

Someone yelled for Brother Giovanni, and the conversation broke. Brother André was not really happy. He was willing enough to begin with himself, but he would like to continue with the others, with coercion not with lamps.

One-hundred sixty-nine—he made it to one-hundred seventy before the hour.

André Barel was lying on his back in the hospital's great hall counting ceiling beams. The doors up there were closed because it was cold, but his eyes had adjusted to the half dark. He was motionless on his straw mattress with a water mug between his bed and the neighbor's. The floor was completely covered with mattresses, and only by the foot of the bed was there a small path. He had a fever, a high fever. The bandage around his chest was sticky. They had picked out all the stone slivers now, Brother Gierolamo said. But it stuck and burned every time he was changed.

In a half slumber, he listened to the rainfall. He saw it drop in pools where he dug with a pick and made a little flood, and suddenly the sun shown, a lovely sun in April over the meadows by the beach of Loire. He dug a deep channel in the sand between green tufts with a crooked tree branch. It would be a mill.

And there was Henriette, his big sister. He could hear her cackling voice with the caring irritating inflections.

"André will be a Hospitaller, Knight of Rhodes, Chevalier de Saint Jean. Little brother will be a baille. He will be called worthy trustee. He will have a thick round stomach and ride in the falcon hunts and have three servants to help him out of the saddle."

So they had thought when it was decided that he should travel over the sea to serve with his spurs in the church's service. He himself had thought the matter to be approximately like that. And now he was here.

Would they ever know what happened to him over here? Other than that he belonged to the many who died when Rhodes was taken by storm? And if he came home, would he ever let them think about what happened in this war?

"Good recovery, André. It is your lucky day today, the vigil of Saint Andreas."

Through the veil of fever, he saw Chevalier Chalant, his arm in a sling but otherwise healthy again.

"If it helps at all to call on Andreas," André said, tired. "D'Amaral also calls upon him."

"All the more reason to have the good apostle make us some special service. I have asked him to help you with your legs."

He winked and went further on. André sank into feverish dreams again. He heard the alarm of some great Turkish attack, jayalars howling, the Janissaries' penetrating war cry and the ringing of steel on steel.

He woke. He could still hear the alarm. He turned sleepily to look at his closest injured comrade.

"Are they storming?"

"Yeah, at the breach, and by the Englishmen and down by the Italians. They have kept it up for more than an hour now."

André shut his eyes again. The alarm and the shooting increased, or maybe it was only so in his feverish brain?

He heard the bells ring in Sainte Genevieve. Saw cherry blossoms waving white against a blue April sky. The bells in the castle towers chimed in. It was Sunday morning. They should go to mass.

No, here he was with his mattress on the cold brick floor. But the bells rang. All the bells in San Giovanni, in Sainte Marie du Chateau, and down in the city. Someone hastened by, one of the serving brothers. He put his helmet on with a half run along the small path between the beds.

Yes, so. It was a great alarm that signaled extreme danger and called everyone to the walls. The bells also rang when there was a breakthrough. André shut his eyes again. If the Turks broke through, there wasn't much left. Surely they would cut his throat here where he lay. Men as badly wounded as he was were useless as slaves.

He folded his hands. A great calm came over him. He was not alone. He knew that, but that needed to be clothed in word. Here was some-one who went around between the sickbeds. Just like on the streets in Capernaum. He stayed and bowed down. His breast had a great wound too. His hands bloody. It seemed that he knew all about it. When those at home could never understand. He had been through it, the cold and rain, dirt and vermin, beaten and wounded, the fear of death and defeat. He was the God who descended down into all this. He was very near. It was good to have such a God.

When André woke again, Chalant was standing there again with his arm in a sling looking at him.

"Saint Andreas thought about us," he said.

And so he told him.

When it looked most hopeless, the heavens opened up and it rained as it had never rained before. The Turks' tunnels changed to flood baths. They came together and became impassible. The dam they built across the moat with so much toil to protect them from the Auvergnat cannons sank down in the water. They had to run the gauntlet before the apertures on the boulevard d' Auvergne again. Even better, they slogged forward through the mud, and the Auvergnats shot with wild glee because they no longer needed to sit by as powerless observers. So the assault was broken altogether.

"So, you see, Saint Andreas feels that he is our protector. I will remind him of you again."

He bowed benevolently and went. André shut his eyes again and prayed. Saint Andreas was well enough. But he knew someone better.

The Oath of Chivalry

IT WAS WHISPERED IN the city. No one ventured to say it out loud, but all knew it. A negotiator had come to the Auvergne wall, a Genoese from Chios, a certain Girolamo Moniglia. He had spoken of a free departure, about the possibility of saving life instead of dying for a lost cause. Those on the wall told him to be off with himself.

It was whispered to the Metropolitan. Roberdo Peruzzi and other rich citizens stole up to him at night by the back way, one after another. The man on the wall had come back. He had asked to talk with their friend Matteo Via. He had an important letter with him. But Matteo was sick and the Genoese would not leave the letter. So he let it slip out that it pertained to greater persons than he and Matteo. It carried a greeting from the Sultan to the Grand Master. Again, the men on the wall told him to be off with himself and sent a shot after him to show what the people of the city thought.

But could they be satisfied with this? This was something that had to be talked about. The gates were watched and the doors were closed carefully at the Metropolitan's.

Meanwhile, the Turks continued to shoot as usual and the spades never ceased to screech and scrape. Now they were even in front of the Italian wall and quite a ways under it. By night, small boats stole into the harbor from Ferakles and Lindos, from Lango and Saint Pierre, loaded with men, cannon balls, and powder. The Grand Master emptied his castle and took his last reserves home.

A couple of days passed, and the negotiator showed up again without a flag or a letter, but certainly with the Turks' approval. He was greeted with complete silence. The Grand Master had forbidden all conversation with the enemy: a city that begins to negotiate is half lost already.

There was even murmuring among the knights. There were men in the circle of the Grand Cross who closed their doors and received secret visitors. In the latest hours of the night when they made their rounds on the wall and visited the watch, they stood together with other wanderers of the night. They would sit in the shadows and whisper in private.

So it happened that the Grand Master was visited by the Metropolitan, two Grand Crosses, and two noble citizens just a day before the end of the first week in Advent.

They got a clear and very determined "no." Capitulation would not be entertained. The Knights of St. John had been a Christian shield for four hundred years. During that time, they had always been able to take the hardest fighting. It was their call and their glory to sacrifice themselves. They had received their goods and their property, their reputation and their place, not to enjoy them, but to be able to give their lives in the hour of need. In a world where all failed to win the life, they were called to show that you could lose your life with joy when you have Christ. Maybe they could wake the blind rulers of Christendom while there was still time before the yellow crescent moon flew over St. Peter's Cathedral and the Vatican, over the Cologne Cathedral and Notre Dame.

The lords were quiet and left. But the Metropolitan came back, this time with a great delegation of important citizens. This time he spoke at length. He respected the willingness of the knights to die as a sign and a sacrifice. But he was under obligation to speak for his flock, for the poor people, who would be hacked in pieces, defiled, and traded as cattle. Here there were fathers who cared for their wives and children. Wasn't the Grand Master father of them all? What will he answer to the mothers when they stood with children in their arms and looked up to him as their only hope?

Now it was the Grand Master who was quiet. He only replied that he would talk to God about the matter. They took their leave with that answer.

The next day was the eighth of December, the day of the Holy Virgin's Immaculate Conception. The Grand Master permitted a greater procession than ever to be arranged and led it to San Giovanni himself. There he delivered a solemn promise before all the people that if the Madonna saved this city with her intercession, he would build a church here to her glory with the name Immaculata Conceptio. He ordered this promise to be noted in the council's protocol book that had now gone untouched for months.

When the grand procession wound up on the Grand Rue, André Barel was lying on his mattress listening to the litany. His fever had broken. Whether or not this was because of Saint Andreas' intercessions or Chevalier Chalant's, the sickness had passed and he knew that the danger was over for now.

He felt very secure. The certainty of Christ's presence did not leave him. In some strange way, he felt he was being carried by an endless mercy.

That evening Brother Giovanni went on the evening rounds. He talked about the great festival in the church and about the Grand Master's votive promise. André asked unsuspectingly:

"But why don't we go directly to Christ?"

The priest looked at him with wide eyes. But there was no heretical criticism in the nineteen year old's look, only a childlike wonder and a confident trust in the Lord Christ. Brother Giovanni nodded indiscernibly and said almost with a sigh.

"We might should have done that."

The council was convened on the ninth of December. The Grand Master related what the city delegation thought. What does the council think?

The answers varied. Many thought that a knight shouldn't listen to such talk. That it was reasonable for the merchants to want to save their lives. But it should not influence those who bowed to the oath of chivalry.

"The oath of chivalry—what was it?" someone asked. "Was it not that knights should protect widows and the defenseless? Did they not bear their weapons for the sake of the poor? Were they not Hospitallers? They should sacrifice their own lives, but not those of others."

While they talked it over, there was a knock at the door. All was quiet. Who dared disturb them?

The watch commander looked bothered. A deputation of the city's foremost . . .

They were admitted and spoke bluntly. They talked about their families and their people. If by some miracle of God's revelation, they were able to depart freely, then they ought to take it. If the knights want to die with sword in hand, then they at least ought to allow the citizens to send away their wives and children. If they were denied this, then the citizens were ready to take matters into their own hands.

They left a letter. It was signed by all the foremost men in the city—Genoese, Florentines, Frenchmen, and Greeks. Then followed a long and painful silence.

When the deputation had left, the council heard from their foremost experts, the one-eyed brothers in arms Martinengo and Bidoulx. They demanded an absolutely unvarnished report.

Preian de Bidoulx began. The black bandage he now wore around his neck to cover the bullet wound could be seen above his breastplate. He spoke shortly and directly to the matter. With the reinforcements from the castle, they had approximately fifteen-hundred men who could still stand on their own legs. The slaves and working people were almost all dead or wounded. Only with the most forceful exertion could he get together enough people to move a cannon. To repair the improvised walls while they were being shot down was out of the question. By way of ammunition, there was maybe enough for another attack. If one wanted to know what he meant, it was that the city is lost.

The Grand Master turned to Martinengo. The bandage around his head had shrunk to a white bandage covering his temple and a patch for the right eye socket that was empty.

He reported on the walls. The enemy had now continued to tunnel approximately two-hundred feet within the great breach. The Spanish tower was in ruins. The boulevard had fallen. The defenses razed. The Turks were up to the curtain. The Provençal wall still stood without any great breaches, but the boulevard and the towers were shot to pieces. Two thirds of the Italians' defenses had fallen. They were only holding on to the spur way out into the harbor. Carretto's tower was crushed but held together, though not without great sacrifice. Further out east, the enemy's tunnels reached up to the curtain, which had been undermined.

What did he make of the matter? Indefensible, if relief does not come soon.

The deliberation was long. Everyone spoke. Many said the same thing. They themselves were ready to die. But the people in the city, that was another thing.

Some talked about the holy relics. Would they fall into the hands of unbelievers? Would the Holy Virgin of Philerimos, the holiest among Madonnas, she whom Saint Luke himself had painted, be defiled and shamed by the Turks? All knew that the Grand Master carried an almost fanatic love for the little Madonna. He had taken her from the mountain cloister, brought her to safety in the city, and moved her again to protect her from the cannon balls.

So the council voted. The result was to not dismiss the negotiator if they were made an offer.

And the Turks did offer. In secret, the rumor made it down to the Turkish tunnels and reached one of the Paschas. The next morning a white flag of truce fluttered over the chapel Lemonitra. A white flag went up over the Koskinou Gate.

Two Turkish officers stepped up out of the tunnels. Martinengo and Bidoulx went to meet them. Without many words, the Turks handed over a letter from Suleiman himself.

Early in the morning, the Grand Master, who slept even less than usual, called for brother Giovanni.

"It is the same thing again. I need a word in order to work. Do you have anything for me?"

"I have one. But first, Brother Grand Master has to be ready for that which the Savior gave him last time."

The Grand Master looked curiously at his chaplain.

"To allow myself to be led to where I did not want to go? I am ready for that. I am willing."

"For what, Brother Grand Master? To die?"

"Yes, also to die."

"But to live?"

The Grand Master was quiet, and the priest continued.

"To continue—despite everything? To believe without seeing? To go into the darkness with God—only God?"

The Grand Master looked up.

"I believe I am willing. Even for that. God help me."

"Then I have a word for the Brother Grand Master again today. It is written by the Prophet Isaiah. 'Who among you fears the Lord, and obeys the voice of his servant? Let him who walks in darkness and has no light trust in the name of the Lord and rely on his God.'"

The Grand Master repeated it thoughtfully, half to himself.

"Walk in darkness . . . Not see light . . . and still trust. Was this His will for me?"

"I believe so," said Brother Giovanni. "And don't forget what it says. Rely on God in the midst of darkness. Brother Grand Master needs it. There will be so many now who will need to rely on Brother Grand Master."

The Sultan's letter was a proposition for capitulation, signed by Suleiman with golden letters. It promised free departure for as many who wished, with goods and weapons, as much as they were able to take. But all that the Religion owned in land, fortresses, and subordinates should be given over to the Sultan. In this matter the Sultan's proposition demanded immediate answer. If he did not receive an unconditional yes, the matter would take its course. No one would be able to think about escaping, whether man or woman, whether dog or cat.

The council met in hours. The reinforced council was called in. There were so many question marks, so much that one wanted to know. On the next day, one did not dare draw out any longer. Two negotiators were sent right away, Peruzzi and Passim, the first a judge, the other, one of the few knights who spoke fluent Greek. They disappeared behind the Turkish lines.

After a few hours, two noble Turks came climbing over the holes and offered themselves as hostages. Simultaneously, they recommended three days truce. The men stopped shooting and breathed out easier. The Turks were serious.

The next day, the judge came back. In the morning, Suleiman received them in his opulent red tent. He had denied any knowledge of any letter or proposal of negotiations. They took it calmly. It was protocol. The besieged were the ones who were to ask for negotiations. This they did also. And the Sultan gave them his offer, just as it was written in his letter, with the addition that no walls were to be made and no reinforcements carried into the city during the negotiations.

And Passim?

The supreme commander, Ahmed Pascha, kept him. He would not come back before the third day. But he would be well cared for and richly treated to food and drink. He had spoken much with the Pascha about the siege. As good soldiers, they understood each other. He had asked about the Turkish casualties. Sixty-four thousand in battle, answered Ahmed, and forty to fifty thousand by disease. But none would believe that they were weakened by it. Passim swore he had seen between eight and ten thousand tents.

That day—it was the fifteenth of December—two new negotiators were sent to Suleiman. They asked for continued truce and a few days respite. They made the request cautiously, with many explanations about the involved situation in the city to which belonged eight langues, two churches, and a citizenry of at least ten nations. Suleiman did not honor them with an answer. In their presence, he gave the order that all the batteries should open fire.

The people on the walls who had dared to climb up and stretch out in the December sun were in a hurry to disappear into their crawl holes again. Even the Turks made their way into the tunnels unwillingly. They needed not hurry. There was hardly a reply from the walls to the hailstorm of cannonballs that smashed against them.

In the city blasted the great alarm and the bells rang. Merchants repented. They remembered what had happened in Belgrade, and they told the Grand Master they would rather die with him. He thanked them, and they manned the walls. On the second day, the Turks stormed the Spanish Barbican but were thrown out again. The next day they made another attempt and were successful. The shovels scraped against the wall again and the spades broke loose the stones in the bottom layer. The nights were cold, a little too cold for the citizenry on the walls. They watched thoroughly frozen, disinclined to everything. One deserted to his home to his warm bed and was hung by the house gable. But more followed after. It no longer helped to be strict.

The Grand Master called the citizens' leaders and went to talk with them. How was it with their will to die? They excused themselves on grounds that they did not know that they were so low on ammunition. And the Grand Master sighed.

He wanted to win time, at least another day. Reinforcements could come anytime. Three nights ago the faithful Galliga had slipped out into the sea again, loaded with people from Crete and with wine infinitely longed for in this city where most now had only drunk cistern water for two months.

The Grand Master made yet another attempt to negotiate. This time he sent Peruzzi alone. He went with the treaty which Bajazid, Suleiman's grandfather, had prepared. In it, he had cursed whoever broke the commencing peace. Ahmed read it, ripped it up, stomped on the bits, and heaped words of abuse and insults on the poor Peruzzi.

Passim made a third attempt. Would there be any thought of compensation to the Religion for the fortresses that would be left? Ahmed answered that the proposal was an insult. The Sultan demanded a simple yes or no. Nothing else would reach the Sultan's ears. Simultaneously, he sent back two men who were captured carrying earth to the English boulevard. He had ordered their ears and noses cut off, hacked off their fingers, and stuck a letter full of threats in one of their jackets. The letter was just as bloody as the poor letter carriers.

The bow was close to breaking. The Grand Master knew it and gave in. He approved the capitulation and sent Passim to the Sultan with the yes he demanded.

But he still dared to take one risk. He allowed two merchants to accompany Passim and negotiate on behalf of the citizens. When Suleiman got his yes, he showed his munificent will to his new subjects. Five years tax free, the right to freely emigrate within three years, and best of all, freedom for all future time from the hated human tax, the obligation to give their sons to the Janissaries.

It was the twentieth of December, the day before the Fourth Sunday in Advent.

In the evening the Grand Master retreated to his palace again. He had not lived there since July. He slowly went up the wide stairs and through the dim halls. There were helmets and mattresses on the floor. The watch had stayed there when the wounded were taken to the hospital. There were rolls of parchment piled up on the table left scattered when they were searching for Bejazid's treaty. The chairs were completely unorganized around, just like they were when the reinforced council finally separated.

He entered his workroom and sank down by the desk. Sheets of paper and drafts lay stacked together with maps, sketches over mine paths, test bolts they tried to cut from old roof beams, and a dirty bit of material with two flecks of blood.

Brother Giovanni came with the usual report from the hospital. Six dead today. The Grand Master looked at him and made a tired gesture to the piles on the desk.

"You see. Here is my ash heap, and here I sit like Job."

"And there is a great honor, Brother Grand Master."

"An honor?"

"Yes, an honor that only comes to God's elect. In the ash heap one only has God left, and just there one can show that it is sufficient. It is not all who are suitable for this task. But God knows whom he has chosen. Was there anything more, Brother Grand Master?"

"No, little Brother Giovanni. It is enough for tonight."

La Ritirata

WOULD SULEIMAN KEEP HIS promise?

Everything looked good at the beginning. As the citizens desired, the Turk moved his people and his tents a couple thousand feet away from the walls. Their tunnels were empty and abandoned. Only a few watches stood, posted by their cannons.

Three or four hundred Janissaries marched into town with an Aga at the lead, quietly, in exemplary order, and seemingly indifferent. They took up the barracks and only set out a couple symbolic watches.

Everyone breathed a little easier and set about with their remaining worries.

No one even thought about the fact that it was only three days to Christmas. The shops were crowded, and the streets were strewn with the stone and shattered household goods no one cleared away. Through the open doors, you could see people digging in their chests, taking down tapestries from the walls, and drying their tears with cloth.

For the most part, the worst was over.

For the knights and all their people, the matter was clear. For the foreign merchants, there was hardly any choice. But it was hard. Many of them were born on Rhodes, and this was their real homeland.

It was worse for the Greeks. Leaving Rhodes meant handing over everything for an uncertain future. Staying might mean not having any future at all.

Just one night after the capitulation, the Grand Master began the work of evacuation. That night, he sent Martinengo and a pair of other knights away in secret because they were more than tempting for the Turks to keep. Even Father Gennaios was offered a place. He declined.

"The shepherd should be with the sheep," he said. "If we could take them all along, then I would also go. But if even a few have to stay, so must I."

"But the Turks will force you into their service if they find out how you helped Martinengo. And if you say no, they will flay you alive."

"God will not use me much longer. The distress will be as a blink of an eye and weighs light, even if it doesn't feel so while they are doing it."

The Grand Master could only ask if there was something he wanted as a thank you for good service. He asked for what could be left in the pharmacy. And he was promised that.

In the harbor, they worked day and night to get the great boats seaworthy. There stood Preian de Bidoulx with his black band about the throat leading the work. They cut poles, took down tattered rigging and torn sails in order to patch others. There was nothing in the reserves. Everything was broken, and the shipyard likewise was a plundered bone shop.

Where would they get rowers? All Turks, Moors, and Saracens had departed in joy, carrying and supporting their wounded friends. There weren't many buonovoglie, paid rowers, left. The Grand Master announced that all who freely made themselves rowers would get priority for their families and their luggage when it came to share the little storage available on board.

They began to stuff the last room—the shelves and closets—with the archives. Valuable documents from the Order's first years, rolls with clanking seal capsules, yellowed parchment with minutes and letters were piled, packed down, and carried onboard, but much had to be left. The overexcited Vice Chancellor was wringing his hands when he ran and searched for the Grand Master in the palace, in the arsenal, in the hospital. The Grand Master must have information, and he had it.

The auberges began to empty. Chairs, tables, and beds were left. Chests were taken, but only if they were used as packing cases. Only the clothes, books, bowls, and dishes that could carried in a sack or a tied up sheet were taken.

It was harder for the affluent. There were many beautiful homes in the city. It wasn't possible to let all their carved cupboards and rolled up carpets to be carried on board. Most were left. Some were given away to friends and faithful servants. Many were sold for a song. A few stood abandoned on the wharf and disappeared in the night's dark hours.

It was worse for the churches. The Grand Master got involved. There was no thought of taking all the beloved pictures of saints. Statues were sacrificed. Among the paintings they could only take the most famous: Philerimos, Lemonitra, and a few others. Relics, church silver, and some attire were packed in their chests. That was all. The rest was left behind.

Father Giovanni was among those who packed. He had been entrusted to take care of the Madonna from Philerimos. They had put her in the church floor, in a heavy wood door, and would cover her with sackcloth. He looked at the small face with the long nose and the melancholy veiled look. It looked as if she stared higher, past and over them, dreamy and absent.

"She didn't hear us either," someone said.

"She was not good enough," said the thick sexton disrespectfully, as he swept the sack over her.

Brother Giovanni pretended not to hear. He wondered to himself if one did not ask the impossible of the little virgin. If one did not make her into something which neither she nor her blessed life fruit ever meant that she should be. Was it any wonder, then, if someone prayed to her in vain?

The Sultan had granted twelve days for departure. The first four were gone, and it was Christmas Eve, the vigil of the Savior's birth. That night, mass was celebrated in Roman and in Greek rites. It was crowded in all the churches. Everyone knew what the Turk generally did with sanctuaries.

On Christmas morning the unpleasantries began. During the past days, the idle Turks had come closer to the city where they lingered around outside the walls. Now they came in through the Koskinou gate and began to look around. They came in small groups, self-conscious and haughty. They treated the people they met as if they didn't exist. Soon one saw them everywhere: in the squares, in the harbor, even within the convent. They walked into the churches, pointing at the saints and laughing at them.

Then they began to pick among all the things that were left out to be packed. They grabbed clothes and material, weighing candlesticks and tin mugs in their hands. Then one of them didn't put a candlestick back but let it disappear in his wide pants. The owner protested, but was beaten about. He crawled away with a bloody lip and escaped out into the garden, hiding his daughters in bushes behind the garden shed, while the Janissaries portioned out his possessions and left.

The example spread. First, the Turks took what was out in the open. Then they began to break open chests and cupboards. When the doors were closed, they tried to break the lock. If that was too hard, they went to the next house.

Chevalier Chalant walked over the square outside the hospital. Three Janissaries blocked his way. He turned away. They reached for his sword. He still had his right arm in a sling. With the left, he took a hard grip on the Turk's hand. But it was six hands against his one. They grinned scornfully, drew out his sword, tested their own, nodded approvingly, stuck the point under his throat, grinned again, and began to push him to surrender. He let it happen. It was an insult to his honor as a knight, but he had learned much this fall. There could be a sort of victory in accepting defeat.

Inside the hospital's big yard, the Turks had first started to gather. When their numbers were sufficient, they went up the great stairs and into the hall. Lunch had just been brought out on the famed silver dishes, the Religion's pride, the symbol of the purity in the hospital and the respect they showed to the sick.

One of the Janissaries bowed down, reached for a bowl, bit in the edge, and remarked that it was silver. He threw the contents in the face of the patient, stuck the bowl under his arm, and reached for the next.

There were many who wanted to share the plunder. Porridge fell on the floor. The bowls stacked up on each other. The Turks took the covers off the beds to make sacks. Or why not take the mattress too? The sick were left on the floor, the mattresses gathered up with the straw shaken out. Bitter voices protested. The Janissaries laughed and continued.

There was a blind knight at the door, a little Aragonite. He had his eyes shot out. His whole head was a big bandage. When someone took the food bowl from him, he beat in unconscious anger around him. He found a leg and pulled the thief down. The silver bowl clanged on the tile floor, and the Janissary screamed bitterly when the blind man gripped his throat. His comrades rushed over, picked the Spaniard up out of the bed, carried him out in the open hall outside, looked around for a place to throw him, and threw him over the rail. With a dull thud, he hit the garden's stone plates and moved no more. They turned back and gathered up their booty.

One of the serving brothers came rushing up the Grand Rue upset and out of breath. He wanted to warn the Grand Master.

It had already been done. Chevalier Chalant, Passim, and two other lords came half-running out between the gates. They were on the way to the castle where the Janissarie's Agha had his quarters.

The Aga shrugged his shoulders. He had no orders for a case like this. Neither did he have enough people to patrol the whole city. He couldn't do anything.

They continued through the city where the plundered goods were stacked up in heaps and women's shrill shrieks were heard out through the windows. They came out through the city gates, made long steps over the tunnels, and hastened to Ahmed Pascha's tent.

He was also unwilling to do anything. They had to threaten to go to the Sultan even if they would be cut to pieces on the way. Then the Pascha wrote an order to the Agha and sent it back with urgency. Some patrols were sent out under a practiced old tschaush, one of the sturdy under-officers with cudgeling weapons.

The lords exhaled. Suleiman also wanted the treaty to be respected. Out of politeness they talked for an hour with the Pascha. He apologized. It wasn't his people who had done all the mischief. It was Ferhad Pascha's. They had come the day after the capitulation, fifteen-thousand men. Essentially, they had been on the march in the east (he did not say against Sofi in Persia), but his emperor's majesty had found it best to call them back and ship them over to Rhodes. Just in case . . .

On the way home someone said:

"What bad luck that the rabble came now. It is as if we are pursued by misfortune."

"Don't say that we are being persecuted by God's divinity," said Passim. "Had they come two days earlier, the Sultan would not have allowed us to leave. You should thank God that he has not regretted it."

Down in the harbor, Gianantonio Bonaldi stood on the deck of his beloved boat and watched over the loading. His left leg was still in a splint.

One of the first days in December, he received a saber cut to the knee on the Spanish Barbican and Brother Gierolamo had dared to loosen the bandage. So he toddled around as if he had a wooden leg.

Some Turkish marauders had been by and nosed about the boats, but he had his sturdy Cretes to help him and that was enough to keep them away. But within the city on the other side of the walls, it was going badly. There the refugees came through the little Catharine gate. They ran out on the pier. One of them had been bludgeoned and was holding his head; another stumbled forward, hanging between two men who supported him. His long hair fell down his forehead and his eyes teared up in pain. It was the judge Fonteyn.

Bonaldi greeted him and bid him on board. The good doctor sank down on a chest and recovered himself enough to talk. He was plundered. Everything was stolen from him; then he was beaten, abused and almost murdered.

Bonaldi examined his wounds. He had black and blue marks, red swelling around some cudgels, but neither leg was broken and all his members functioned. That could not be said of Kastrofiliaka, his good friend who was innocently suspected of letter changing with the enemy and whom Fonteyn had long interrogated under torture.

"The Doctor can thank God," he said. "Many have looked worse who were tortured during the deepest of peace."

But the Doctor continued to vent. O *crudelissimi barbari*! They had made him a pauper! They had taken everything he had accumulated on this island! Scraped bare and plundered, he traveled home.

"Shame on the Doctor," said Bonaldi. "I think I travel home quite rich."

"Yes, you merchants, you *mercatores sagacissimi*, you always know to get along!"

"That was not what I meant. All that I had with me I have given away. To pay, feed, and give wooden legs to my people. And in the boat I have debt. But I have learned how valuable it is to have a good conscience and to be able to help the weaker. I believe I will never again be so bad off as to be dependent on money."

"Like the Doctor," he thought to apply, but the poor Fonteyn looked so disturbed that he did not have the heart for it.

"Look," yelled one of the men. He pointed to Tour Nailla on the other side of the inlet. On the crown of the proud slender tower waved a Janissary's flag. A drum roll echoed off the walls, followed by the shrill pipes and flutes, those which one heard so often from the other side of the moat. And finally was heard the muezzin with it: *La ilah ill Allah.*

No god but Allah. No Christ. It was time for Vespers and it was Christmas but no bells rang.

It was the end of the plundering. A portion of stolen goods was left. But the small thefts continued. No one was sure when the commander turned his back. A hollow angst brooded over the city. New people continuously streamed onto the wharf with their sacks. Over four thousand were now on the list.

The second day of Christmas, the Grand Master rode his horse for the first time since May. By his side was Bidoulx and Passim, four of the Grand Crosses followed, and in the rear was Antoine Golan with two packhorses.

It was a heavy gray-weather day with rain clouds and a cold cutting wind. Stiff legged and clumsily, they scampered over the tunnels and dikes. When the saltpeter mills finished milling, they were barely able to move.

They passed by the Turkish watch command and continued among the endless rows of tents, through the blockades and new posts. Just a bit closer, they came to the high quarters; then the order became stricter. Broad-shouldered, clean-shaven officers with long mustaches divvied their orders in a low voice. The Janissaries stood motionless with their arms crossed over their chest, their gaze lowered and their high white pointed caps bent forward.

They came to an open place lined with magnificent tents. The tents were open and servants carried in trays. There was music playing. They were asked to enter.

The wind blew hard and sharp. It was cold sitting in the saddles. The first half hour they looked around, exchanged a few words here and there, and continued to sit.

After another half hour, it began to rain harder. Their caps were soaked. When they moved, the water ran down from their berets into their faces and in under the neckpieces. The horses hung their heads.

Golart sat and looked at his Grand Master and wondered how long he would last. But the old man looked undisturbed and began to talk with

Bidoulx. Golart understood. Here the Religion's honor was on the line. They were besieged, but they could bear their defeat.

"This is an insult," said Bidoulx. "A well-calculated insult."

"I am not so sure," said the Grand Master. "It is Friday. They have their great feast day, their first after the victory. He most certainly has a great reception, and they are crowding in there to kiss his hand."

The second hour came to an end. Big wet snowflakes began to fall. It looked like ermine scarves on the horses' manes and over their own shoulders. They shook and the snow fell heavy and wet to the ground. It was getting dark.

"Here the darkness comes," said Passim. "To Rhodes I mean. Now he moves the candlestick as so often before."

"Strange," said Bidoulx. "That God even allows it to happen. Over there is Ephesus and Miletus and all that they call the apostles' own cities. I wonder if there is even one Christian soul there any longer . . . "

"Is it so strange?" asked the Grand Master. "It has gone just as he said. It is just as He said of the lamp stand in Ephesus. It will leave them if they do not repent. And now He has moved it. He is not conquered, just us Christians by the world and our own flesh."

It was quiet again.

Golart looked at the snow that fell on his packhorses. They were loaded with heavy transport baskets scantily covered with sail material. The snow lay wet and heavy over them. Luckily, it was mostly metal under there, gold and silver, bowls, pots and dishes, gifts to the Sultan and his paschas. They would not be insulted.

A quarter into the third hour, a gold embroidered lord with a swelling turban walked out of the greatest tent and bid the lords to sit. Golart threw his stiff legs over the saddle as fast as he could and ran forward to help the Grand Master. But His Eminence already stood on the ground and shook the snow out of the coat pleats. They carried the baskets into the tent.

In the evening, Golart met Father Giovanni, who curiously asked:

"So how was he, Suleiman?"

"I never did get to see him. But the Grand Master was magnificent. Not a shred of complaint."

The priest nodded.

"Yes, though he still lacks the ability to cry with those who cry. But it is enough."

On the third day of Christmas, the Turkish patrols kept order in the city. But they did something else too. They stood in particular spots, purposefully and without having to search. They walked around and asked after particular named people. Soon one realized who they were after: all baptized Turks and all freed prisoners who had become Christians. A warning was sent to some. The Turks went all over the city in time. No one escaped. They carried away the families, even if the spouse had always been Christian. All protests were futile. The Sultan took back what belonged to him. The treaty he entered did not apply to such.

Only one made it through the net. It was Amuratte, Suleiman's own cousin. He had gone underground in time and disguised himself as a French merchant. In the evening darkness, he snuck down to the harbor to get on board. Some idle workers looked for him diligently. One of them bent over with a little lantern. The Turkish patrol in the tower on the pier saw it, came running, and went straight way on board.

So, the last one was caught. No one doubted that Suleiman's eyes watched and that his hand reached as far as he determined.

André Barel was standing again. He still could not lift, nor could he wear battle dress. So he was commandeered as Aide de Camp to the Grand Master. He received people, answered their questions, and kept record of all the rules and directions the Grand Master drew up time after time. He had a good memory. People began to turn to him when they needed information.

On the fifth day of Christmas, the machinery began to function. The palace was emptied; people no longer ran around perplexed and puzzled. By the afternoon the halls were empty.

Then something unexpected happened. Horse hooves clip clopped in the garden, the Turkish watch called out, a trumpet sounded.

When André looked towards the gate, they had already begun walking, three noble Turks, the first a young man with brown hair, expensively dressed with magnificent heron feathers in his turban. Not until the Turkish scribe threw himself prostrate with his forehead on the ground did André understand who it was.

Luckily, he also had orders for this: "All Turkish banners and dignitaries are given the same honor as correspond to our own." Also: "One knee on the ground and deepest possible bow with the hat off."

He heard the interpreter ask for the Grand Master. Completely giddy, he looked up the stairs.

The Grand Master was dignified when he met his unexpected guest. The Sultan had gone up the stairs in the first hall. He had only two attendants with him.

The Grand Master winked at André to stand by the door. Passim came groaning, called there by the watch. But even he was standing in the threshold.

The conversation was in Greek. Suleiman used the elder of the attendants as an interpreter.

Ahmed Pascha whispered to Passim.

The Sultan talked long, and André had good time to study him. He was a young man, marked by work and responsibility. His face was pale though his hair was brown, an inheritance of a Tartar mother. His neck was long and slender, a little high like a bird's. The slender face had the stamp of a nose, an enormous hawk nose. The eyes were clever, melancholy, with a notion of tiredness.

"He says that we have nothing to fear . . . We may extend the time of departure if we want," whispered Passim.

The Grand Master bowed thankfully. That much André could understand. He had good reason for it. None of them wanted to remain on this island after Suleiman left. And all knew that he thought to leave as soon as the before-spoken twelve days were over.

The Sultan bid farewell. Passim was called foreword and followed through the gate.

"Do you know what he said?" he asked when he came back. "I heard it on the stairs. 'It will bring me bad luck to chase the old man out of his house.' As if that would be our Grand Master's greatest worry!"

Father Dominique came to meet them half running.

"Did you see the Tyrant?"

"Yes, but he didn't really look like a tyrant," answered André. "Is he not our hope and protection right now?"

Father Dominique did not think to answer.

"Possibly . . . But it is fearful enough to live under such conditions. Without weapons, dependent on another's good will."

"So live most here in this world," said André. "Our French peasants for example. Maybe God want us all to see how it feels."

Father Dominique made a grimace and went on his way with difficult gestures.

Passim, who went in the foray, came out of the chancellery again.

"Our friend Amuratte is dead. He was strangled in the morning. The Turks in the garden told me."

They looked at each other. Tyrant or no?

The new year's first day started with chaos on the harbor pier.

The message went out in the morning: Today we sail. The crowd became insufferable in the city gates and on the wharf. Over four thousand men wanted to board. The families wanted to bid farewell. Everyone kissed and cried, went on board and hopped off again to embrace a beloved cousin. Some had trouble finding their boat; they screamed after children that were leaving; men fell in the water between the boats; all rushed to the railing, putting the overloaded brigantines in danger of capsizing. The poor wanted to take their only goat with them and the bourgeois yet another chest. The people quarreled and shoved. The watches struck with the flats of their swords to keep people from piling up deck cargo unreasonably, which would have sunk the slim boats.

All asked for the Grand Master. But he had ridden over to the Sultan for a departure visit so that in the very last hour, properly and formerly dressed, he could carry on a relaxed and honorable conversation as is expected of the people's princes.

Even Passim knew his duty. When he was one of the last men left in the palace that evening, he met a Turkish patrol on the loggia. The commander spoke Greek and bid him to climb up in San Giovanni one last time. Courtesy forbade a no, and he followed. He did it unwillingly. Three days earlier he had looked in but waited at the door. The floor had been bestrewn with busted up pictures. The Grand Masters' graves had been broken up by marauding treasure seekers. Now the mess had been cleaned up. The saints were left with their faces trampled like armless and blind invalids. The stones had been laid in their places again. They were covered with mats.

"Here we have our mihrab. And there is our kursi," the Turk said. "His Imperial Majesty will come in the morning to attend Friday's prayer here."

"Will you do the same to all the churches in the city?" asked Passim.

"Of course, it is the only practical thing to do. All the Christians will flee outside the walls for security's sake."

Ah yes, thought Passim. So he keeps his promise. But then he thought about the Jews who had to flee from the island twenty years ago for security's sake. Why should the state, which had God's commission to protect men, always first think to protect itself?

He bid farewell.

"Say," said the Turk, "is it really necessary that we should be enemies? If we fought together we would conquer the world."

"That isn't quite as important to us," Passim, said cautiously.

"But think about it. In the end we believe in the same God. Only you Christians say that it is this Christ."

"God has done that, not us. And it is the most important thing He has done. Without it we do not know who He is and neither do we learn of Him."

"We shall see. On the other side, we meet—before the Judge."

"Yes, before Christ. We meet."

They looked each other in the eye for a long time without blinking. They saluted each other from both sides of the abyss that separated them, but not without respect.

At the first twilight the Grand Master came with the last of his knights and boarded the flagship, the galley Santa Maria. As the first, she led the rest out from the quay in front of Tour Naillac. Every other oar was unmanned. The unpracticed rowers successfully turned her, and she glided out over the chain. Luckily, a good east wind blew out in front of Saint Nicolas, and they hoisted sails. She rounded the point and glided down in lee behind the mount by Triana to wait for the others.

The mountain was covered with snow clouds, heavy and dark as lead. The night seemed to be thrown down out of them and swept land and sea in their darkness. Under the captain's stern tent, the Grand Master sat on a chest. Behind him stood William Weston, the commander with his mutilated hand under his jacket. He had had a finger shot off the day he saved the English boulevard, the day Richard Craig fell with the others. The others sat round about on the poopdeck, on the corsian and the arrumbada, engulfed in their black capes, silent and still, Bidoulx and Passim, Chalant, Golart, Barel, and the hundred and eighty others that remained of their six hundred.

Slowly, the other boats came around the point. When the Grand Carrack passed Saint Nicolas, they heard the trumpets blow La Ritirata, the signal for retreat, that which was blown only on bad days when one had to leave fallen brothers on defeated battlefields. They understood the meaning. The Order of St. John the Baptist said farewell to their dead and gave them their last greeting.

There were people gathered on the beach. They came streaming out of the city to wave farewell. All because the boats gathered out there, lit with light from the shore slope. It was like a graveyard on All Souls' Day. The Greeks in the nearest brigantine sang the old soldiers' song.

> My Rhodes, will I ever see you again?
> To Frankish lands I go,
> Somewhere waits on a foreign shore
> A castle I have not seen.
> The sea surges dark,
> Long are the refugee's days.
> My heart will be so bold,
> But it cries when it is not seen.
> My Rhodes, will I ever see you again?

Then something happened that the order's brothers would remember for a longtime. The Grand Master cried. Cried for everyone to see, openly and without shame.

Epilogue

THE STORIES IN THIS book really happened. Simultaneously, the sources say—often detailed and dramatically—of de l'Isle Adam and d' Amaral, of Pomerolx and John Buck, of le Loup, Martinengo, Bidoulx, Fournon, Passim, Weston and other knights, but also about Anasthasia and her twins, of Blas Diez, of the Jew Apella, and Gianantonio Bonaldi, of Antonio Bosio and his wine business on Crete, of the dragon head over Porte d' Amoise, about provisions master Iaxi, of the judge Fonteyn and his Moorish servant.

Those who want to see their world with their own eyes can still walk along Grand Rue (now called the Knights street) or on the Auvergne wall, climb down the boulevard and continue along the curtain by all the towers and outworks for which they fought so hard. The Turks built them up immediately after their victory, just as they had been, and so they have stood undisturbed to this day.

It was these walls that so many years ago woke my desire to know more about the drama that played out there. Now I have sought to retell it without making any conscious deviation from the historical course so far as we know it (and we know it fairly well, often down to minor details). I have tried to fill out the white flecks by listening also to the voices that reach us with distant echoes from the walls, or read what was written between the lines in the council's minutes and what the eyewitnesses said. Some characters like Brother Francois, Fra Giovanni, Brother Geirolamo, and Father Gennaios have grown out of this. Such names as Barel, Chalant, and Golart are found in the records, but only as empty names. I have changed surnames out of respect for the integrity of the descendants. The world in which they lived is therefore drawn according to the reality of the documents, also in details such as the stretched drum skins with bells, anesthesia, dysentery, the sharp shooters against the drag lines, and much else.

Certainly many may wonder if the men of the time were so like us as they are described here. I can only answer that I became more and more convinced of the matter the longer I studied them. A wooden translation of the speech would certainly sound ancient in our ears, so I have tried to form it as it must have sounded in their own.

After a hard sail, the refugees came to Crete. They saw with bitterness the flotilla of sixty galleys that the Venetians had drawn together to protect their possessions. It was many more than was needed to save Rhodes. Such pettiness was discovered also in the truth of the relief that never came. Frans the First had, despite the war with the emperor, promised to send ships to their disposal, but the landgrave of Provençe sabotaged his order, so it was in vain. Over all, the Religion's men were met by the same passive resistance. It was war. But one dared not risk. Even the Pope sent the infantry he had gathered to Lombardia instead of Rhodes. The knights were forced to handle it by themselves.

They chartered ships and went to sea, all because they were finished. But now it was Fall. Scared shippers put their ships on ground rather than sail in the Turkish sea. The storms took their toll. One ship sank off the coast of Monaco; another wrecked on the Sardinian coast. Some lost their way in the storm and night with one and all, no one knew where. One reached the Greek isles but harbored in the midst of a Turkish squadron, fought bravely, and was turned back worse for the wear.

For eight years the Knights of St. John lived as refugees. The Grand Master was responsible for the fact that they didn't disperse for the heaven's winds. He was able to lead them to a new home in Malta where they began from the beginning again. There again in the year 1565, they were able to stand in a last unforgettable trial of strength against Suleiman, who in the autumn of his years wanted to crown his life of conquering by laying Malta under his control and therefore create the key base he needed to launch a great invasion of Italy that would fulfill Islam's victory and secure the Crescent Moon on the Basilica of St. Peter's cupola, as Mehmed the Conqueror had done to the Hagia Sofia. But this time, luckily, his generals were not able break open the lock to Europe, and we can all be thankful for that. Suleiman himself sat at home in Constantinople. When the great armada—one of the greatest the world had seen—turned back defeated, the old man said, "My sword only sees victory when I swing it myself." A year later, he was dead.

Martinengo, Bonaldi, and Antonio Bosio were liberally rewarded for what they had done for the Religion in its extreme need. The great man, Bosio, came back to Rhodes as a conspirator, smuggled in weapons, and prepared a riot. But he gave up the attempt and instead tended the contacts with Emperor Carl, which led to Malta becoming the knights' new home.

Philippe Villiers de l'Isle Adam died in 1534 after years of hard work and many misfortunes, just as a new day dawned.

On his grave the order's brothers wrote *Victrix Fortunae Virtus*. It means, there is a faith that overcomes destiny. The end is not determined by luck or chance, but by Him, who, despite all our sin and mistakes, can use those who are placed in His service.

Printed in Great Britain
by Amazon